FIT BODY 4 LIFE

How to Unlock The Power of Your Cells to Reverse Aging & Disease, Shed Belly Fat and Transform Your Body from The Inside Out

Adi Crnalic

Exterior designed by **TRENDD** Development Solutions

Manufactured in the United States of America

ISBN: 978-0-578-76037-7
ASIN: B087L5LK3L

2015077379 EDITION 1

Published by Bio-Health

TABLE OF CONTENTS

Introduction

If you could, by making a few simple changes to your lifestyle, dramatically improve your health, add quality years to your life, lose fat from your most stubborn problem areas, have all the energy you could ever want, and live to be a vibrant and healthy one-hundred-year-old, would you follow the advice recommended in this book? I believe you would be foolish not to.

While I can't promise that by reading and applying the contents of this book you'll live to see your one hundredth birthday, I *can* guarantee that if you implement just a few nutrition, mindset, and lifestyle methods you're about to learn, you will add quality years to your life, improve your energy levels, have a brighter and more positive mood, develop a better mindset with less fear and procrastination, prevent and reverse disease, and look and feel several years younger—all while dropping excess body fat and falling in love with your bathroom scale and mirror.

My motivation for writing this book comes from witnessing far too many people from all walks of life suffer from the consequences of bad lifestyle choices while neglecting their health, both physical and mental. Low energy levels, excess belly fat, heart disease, diabetes, elevated blood pressure, brain fog, depression, anxiety, and even cancer are all *one hundred percent* preventable conditions. Most medical doctors are quick to prescribe all kinds of medications for any and every condition that ails modern man. However, modern medicine has failed us on a massive scale. With healthcare costs rising higher every year, traditional medical approaches are no longer an option for the average American. In the

United States, the average cancer drug now costs around $10,000 a month, with some therapies costing around $30,000 per month.

That's a staggering amount of money for treating a condition that is, as you'll discover in this book, very preventable. Heart disease and stroke cost Americans nearly a billion dollars a day in medical costs through lost productivity. By 2030, the annual direct medical costs associated with cardiovascular diseases are estimated to rise to more than $818 billion, while lost productivity costs could be more than $275 billion annually. Today more than thirty million Americans suffer from diabetes, with costs having risen to $327 billion in 2017 from $245 billion in 2012, a dramatic twenty-six percent increase in just five years.

My aim is to show you how simple it is to overcome and prevent the deadliest health conditions and reverse years—even decades—of neglecting your health and fitness by changing the way your body functions at the *cellular* level. Simply put, you'll discover how to drastically improve your health, fitness level, mindset, happiness, mental state, and other elements essential for living a full, vibrant, happy, long, and energetic life free from disease and illness.

When you are healthy and have a body that you are proud to show off at the beach or pool in summer, just about everything else in your life will become so much easier. When you apply the easy-to-follow nutrition tips and lifestyle changes that you'll learn in this book, your energy levels will rise, and you'll effortlessly lose body fat from your most stubborn areas. You will feel like you can overcome any challenge life throws at you and you will enjoy an overall increased awareness of wellbeing. In a sense, you will become a happier, leaner, fitter, and more productive version of yourself. And the best part is, the nutrition secrets you'll discover require no uncomfortable starvation, no super low-calorie dieting or other extreme measures that are difficult to stick to.

The truth is, reversing many years of bad food choices, an inactive lifestyle, and changing the shape of your body is not the easiest undertaking, and I would be misleading you if I said otherwise. I am well-aware of the challenges that come along with transformation. As a kid and teen, I had struggles with my weight, body image, and health.

I won't promise you that your journey will be easy and effortless; if it were, everyone would be fit, happy with their looks and energetic. What I can promise you is transforming your body and wellbeing is nowhere near as difficult or labor-intensive as it may appear to be initially. All you have to do is act by implementing the simple steps and methods you're going to discover within the pages of this book. Very soon, you too will have the know-how and skills to breeze through any obstacles or challenges that are holding you back from attaining the body, health, and energy you want and need.

You see, I know just how frustrating it can be when you feel like you have no control over your weight and health. As a child, I was healthy and happy until I reached my late teens and early twenties, and then, something started happening to my body; I started gaining weight. And it was not the good kind of weight—it was fat in places where even a small amount of extra weight does not look attractive at all—around the waist and midsection or belly area.

In my late teens, I bought into all sorts of misinformation that was out there at the time on how to gain muscle and lose fat. When I began my competitive bodybuilding career, I went on high-calorie diets to bulk up, which led me to pack on extra pounds of body fat that took months to get rid of.

Before my bodybuilding days as a young kid, I was considered frail, weak, and unhealthy due to terrible eating habits and an insatiable sweet tooth. I remember back in high school physical ED class, we used to play different sports each week, ranging from football to soccer and many other sports in between. What weighed on me the most in high school was that I was almost always one of the last kids to be chosen to play for the team. After all, no one wanted a skinny, underweight weakling on the team who could compromise a win and give victory to the other team.

Later on in high school, as I became interested in learning more about nutrition and exercise, I became aware of how the foods I was eating were affecting my looks, my mood, energy levels, and most importantly, my overall health and happiness. As a freshman in high school, I signed up for a basics-of-weight-training class, hoping that doing so would empower me to take my physique from frail, thin and weak to muscular, strong, and confident.

Pretty quickly, I started excelling in the weight room. Back in my high school days we had block classes with each class lasting about ninety minutes. I remember most kids being finished with weight training in less than forty-five minutes or so, while I lifted weights for the entire ninety-minute duration of the class. I just loved the way the weights felt in my hands— the feeling of watching my muscles work and seeing them expand before my eyes. It was unlike anything that I had felt before at the time. It was an energizing, empowering feeling.

Through consistent weight training, the guidance of my weight lifting class coach and reading fitness and bodybuilding magazines in my spare time, I put on more than fifteen pounds of lean muscle and shed several inches of body fat in a single semester.

I am not sharing my transformation story with you in order to impress you or to boast about my past accomplishments and achievements. There aren't many people I despise more than braggers and show-offs. You see, I don't consider myself gifted, nor as having any special physical skills, talents or abilities. A strong work ethic is not something that came naturally to me, nor is it something I was born with.

Rather, I am telling you about my past achievements to demonstrate to you that if a weak, frail, unhealthy-turned-overweight kid like me was able to completely transform his body and health in just a few months, you too can do it with the correct blueprint.

This book will provide you with plenty of insider information, most of which is largely unknown to the public. I hate to use the word "secrets" as there are very few actual secrets remaining in the world on any given subject, but your knowledge about what to put into your body and the connection between your physical and mental health will increase tremendously by the time you're finished reading. You will put yourself into the top five percent of the population that understands the connection between food, the environment and disease, and its causes and prevention. You will get simple directions on which foods and supplements to take that will change the way you look and feel in the shortest time. There is a saying that goes *knowledge is power*. I think that's a lie.

Knowledge is not power—knowledge *applied* is. After all, if the only thing you do is read this book or just skim through its pages and then apply very little (or nothing) that you learn, you will remain in the same spot that you are in today in a year from now, two years from now, possibly five years from now—and even for the rest of your life. The only difference is that you will be older.

I urge you to read several pages of this book in one sitting, then start implementing what you have learned immediately. I want you to live by the motto that when it comes to taking action, there is no later—there is only now. Do not wait to start until tomorrow, your health is far too important. Your health and wellness must become your top priority, because without it you have nothing. After all, you will be no good to anyone if you are constantly ill or lying in a hospital bed. No amount of money, wealth or possessions can make up for the misery and unhappiness brought on by preventable illness and disease. Possessing a rock-solid immune system is vital in today's chaotic, ever-changing modern world. A fit body & immune system allows you to experience life as you were meant to, and it *all* starts at the cellular level. When your cells are strong and full of integrity, your body is capable of fending off the deadliest illnesses, from viral diseases such as coronavirus and SARS, to cancer and heart disease, to the common flu and annoying seasonal colds. To those with strong and resilient immune systems, a longer and happier life is virtually guaranteed. Read this book every day and take action every day by executing what you are learning. Believe in yourself, surround yourself with others who will encourage you, and you will be light-years ahead of people who only talk about making a change in their lives, but never take the necessary action.

I'm looking forward to hearing and reading your success story.

Let's begin...

CHAPTER 1: READY, FIRE, AIM

Before You Get Started

There is only one thing you will need to do before you start and that is to take the word "perfect" out of your vocabulary. From now on, try not to say the word perfect in conversations, and don't think about making your life, your choices, or anything that you do "perfect."

By doing this your chances of success will increase tremendously. You see, the reality is that when you strive for perfection, you immediately set yourself up to fail. This is because you are striving for something that exists only in your mind, something that is not real. After all, how can anything be perfect?

The truth is, everyone has a different definition on what perfection is. It's sort of in the eye of the beholder, —and it only exists there. As a fitness & health coach I've witnessed far too many people not only fail to achieve their fitness transformation goals, but also their career and life goals because they strived for perfection. I am not talking about just clients, but everyone from close friends to family members.

Instead of just getting started, perfectionists wait until everything in their life is perfect before acting towards their goals. If you are a perfectionist, you know exactly what I am referring to. For example, here are some common "waiting-until-everything-is-perfect" excuses people tell themselves: "I'll start exercising consistently once the kids are off to college". . . . "I'll do it once I've moved to a new city or town" . . . "Once I get that promotion at work, a new job, etc., etc."

Understand: When you have something important you want to achieve or accomplish in life, such as transforming your looks, regaining your health, and looking and feeling a few years younger, don't wait until all the stars align or all the lights are green—that day will never arrive. In other words, do not wait for perfection.

Waiting until things are perfect to get started is an illusion; it's a lie we tell ourselves—sort of a scapegoat for inaction. You picked up this book for a reason, an important reason. You want to change the shape of your body and have enough energy to do the things you love while adding quality years and possibly decades to your life. You want to improve your confidence and receive compliments from friends, family, and co-workers on your improved, more attractive body. You want to fit back into that dress or that pair of jeans that have been in the closet for too long. You want to smile when you look in the mirror and be proud of the shape you're in. You want to learn the secrets to living longer and preventing the terrible diseases and conditions that are afflicting, financially draining, and wiping out far too many people in America and other developed nations.

Maybe someone in your family has had a major health scare or has died from a preventable condition such as heart disease or cancer, or maybe you yourself are suffering from a condition that your lifestyle brought on, and now you are ready to start making changes to regain your health and wellness. And for that I salute you. Sadly, most people only think and talk about changing, without ever actually taking the first and most important step.

Setting Your Goals
(30, 60, 90 Days, and Beyond)

Now that we've got procrastination and perfectionism out of the way, it's time to set your goals and achieve clarity on where you are headed and what the end of your transformation will look like. I will keep this part very simple because setting goals and defining your desired outcome should be anything but complicated. First, you must clearly define and write down your goals. After you have done this, it's time to grab a pen and a calendar. Mark today "Day 1" and then write down your goals for the next 30, 60, and 90 days.

For example, if your goal is to lose thirty pounds, get off cholesterol medication, and regain the energy you had ten or fifteen years ago so you can look and feel great during your next trip to the beach, then that is what you would write down as your ultimate or final goal.

It goes without saying but your goals must be realistic and *attainable*. An example of a realistic goal would be wanting to lose twenty pounds of body fat in three months, gain a few pounds of lean muscle, and improve your energy levels.

Never set goals that aren't realistic to achieve in 30, 60 and 90 day increments. You will instantly set yourself up for failure when you set a goal that is unattainable in such a relatively short amount of time. For example, a goal to lose fifteen pounds of pure body fat in 2 weeks, while possible in rare or extreme circumstances, is certainly not realistic.

You must understand. Transforming your body (and your health), as with any goal worth striving for, is a gradual process. It's more of a marathon and less of a sprint. What you're after is making small lifestyle changes that will become permanent. These are changes that you'll be able to maintain for the rest of your life. It never fails to amaze me how easily most people are duped into believing, even and especially in this day and age, that they can achieve amazing, head-turning results in only two or three weeks by following the newest fad diet advertised in a magazine, or by purchasing a late-night infomercial workout gizmo.

The late-night infomercial promise is not what this book is about. This book is about learning the value of hard work, persistence, and failing forward. At the end of the day, having some simple patience and discipline will carry you through to your 30, 60 and 90-day goals. Now that you are aware that there no quick fixes when it comes to changing your health and body, it's time to define your reason why.

What's Your Why?

By knowing and having a clearly defined why, you are far less likely to throw in the towel when things get difficult and challenging during your transformation. Your "why" is the reason you picked up this book, your reason for wanting to change. Be honest with yourself and ask and answer the following questions. Be sure that you answer each question before moving on to the next one. It's *very* important that you don't move on to the next question until you've answered and clearly defined each one first.

Why do I want a transformation?

What exactly do I want the end of my transformation to look like? (i.e. number of pounds lighter, inches lost, look and feel better, energy at a higher level).

Why am I seeking help/starting now, as opposed to six months ago, one year ago, or two years ago?

Once you have answered these three questions, you'll be ready to further refine your reason why. Next, ask yourself the following:

In relation to my body and health, where will I be in six months from today if I do not take action today towards achieving my goals?

How will I know when I have finally achieved my goal?

And finally, . . .

How will my life be different once I have transformed my body and health, and what will I be able to do and have that I'm not able to do or have now?

By answering these questions, you will have a very clear picture in your mind of exactly why you are embarking on your transformation journey. By knowing your reason why and by clearly defining your reasons, you will be far ahead of most people who start on a self-improvement journey, yet don't ask and answer these vital questions before getting started.

To share a story with you, several years ago I had a client who wanted me to train her for a figure competition. It was her first show and she seemed ready to commit herself to the twelve to fourteen weeks that it was going to take to be ready for it. One of the first questions I asked her during her initial consultation was why she wanted to get in the best shape of her life and compete.

Her answer was that she wanted to get a show-ready physique because she wanted to make her ex-boyfriend jealous. Her ex-boyfriend was going to be attending the show to support another competitor.

I then asked her if this was her primary reason why she wanted to compete, and she said; "Yes, nothing would make me happier than to see the look on my ex's face when he sees the new me onstage; I want to make him so jealous that he will regret breaking up with me."

After listening to her talk for several more minutes, I got straight to the point and told her she should not bother dedicating the time to prepare for this competitive physique show, if her only reason for doing it was to get back at her ex. She was a bit surprised by my response.

Understand: People are indifferent as to whether you succeed or fail at your goals. More specifically, people who have no vested interest in the outcome of your career, life events, or your fitness/health goals—or anything that may be important to you personally—are mostly indifferent as to whether you end up succeeding or failing.

This is because everyone, from your mother to your siblings, to your friends and co-workers all have their own challenges and obstacles to deal with. It is simply human nature for us to care about ourselves first before caring for someone or something else. If your reason for wanting to achieve a transformation is because you are trying to impress someone, get back at someone, make someone jealous, make someone envious of you, or any reason *other* than wanting to do it for yourself because you have a strong, inner emotional drive for wanting to prove to yourself that you are capable of changing the way you look and feel, then you are doomed before your journey even begins. This I can assure you.

If you are known as the "heavy set" or "chubby" girl or guy amongst your circle of friends and your family, you will be surprised, even disappointed at how few (if any) of your friends will be genuinely happy for you once you've lost weight and you look somewhat—or even a lot—different than you do now. The harsh reality is that most people don't like to see others do or achieve things that they themselves want to accomplish, but can't for whatever reason—be it a lack knowledge, resources, or just plain laziness.

If you come from an overweight and unhealthy family, and you are close to your family, your family will not like the fact that you are the one who stood up and decided to do something about your unhappiness with your body and health. Once you've transformed yourself, the people you hang around most often will, in a way, miss the old you and want the old you back. When you undergo a body transformation and improve your health and fitness, you'll in many ways become a better version of yourself and notice improvements in many other areas of your life. Your friends and family will not be used or accustomed to the new you.

Be ready to accept this reality and it will not come as a surprise when people do not support you or start treating you differently once you have a new body. You may even lose some friends during your transformation journey, but this is a small price to pay for a more attractive, energetic, healthy body and a longer life.

Like a skilled artist painting a masterpiece or a veteran music composer creating his next tune, you must possess a deep *desire* for wanting a transformation. You must see yourself succeeding in your transformation before you start. You must visualize yourself as a better version of yourself once you've finally attained your goal. Realize that once you have gone from body A (the way you look and feel now) to body B (how you'd like to look and feel), many things in your life will change, including the people you hang around and surround yourself with.

YOU BECOME LIKE THE TOP FIVE PEOPLE YOU HANG AROUND THE MOST. CHOOSE WISELY.

CHAPTER 2: FOOD, CALORIES AND DIETS

Why Low-Fat Diets Fail

Unfortunately, we have been made to believe that fat is bad. Dietary-fat has been vilified and bastardized since the middle of the twentieth century and is still believed to be the main cause of heart disease and obesity. We have been taught that foods such as cereal, rice, bread, and other "whole grains" are good for us and anything that is high in fat should be avoided. We have been taught that fat causes heart disease, obesity, and heart attacks and that it's the biggest evil since communism.

These lies have been fed to us repeatedly by some of America's largest and well-established health institutions—such as The American Heart Association and The National Institute of Health. These two major health institutions have been vilifying fat and touting the benefits of low-fat diets for decades . . . all for one reason—corporate interests.

You see, the diet-heart hypothesis, which states that eating foods high in fat and cholesterol raises your blood cholesterol levels and causes heart disease, is *the* main reason why low-fat diets are recommended by health authorities, even though low-fat diets have failed and continue to fail millions of people worldwide. We've been taught to believe that fat and saturated fat is bad and that foods like potatoes, rice, cereal, bread, pasta, and other "whole-grain" foods are better for you because they contain very little, if any, fat. The problem with the diet-heart hypothesis is that there have been more than a dozen new studies that have been done since the diet-heart hypothesis came out (about one hundred years ago) which have refuted the hypothesis over and over again.

The newest studies on high-fat diets have shown us that high-fat foods do not cause obesity and heart disease and that dietary fat, from the right sources, is as important to your health and well-being as are air and sunshine. In the United States and other developed countries, carrying excess body fat accounts for about forty percent of heart-disease cases as well as several different types of cancers such as breast, kidney, and colon. Carrying excess body fat also accounts for the majority of diabetes cases in the United States and throughout the world.

In trials lasting for about one year, people who ate between twenty and forty percent of their total daily calories from fat were shown to have no increase in their fat mass and bodyweight.

People have been encouraged to eat less fat and fewer calories from fat, yet this has led to a massive increase in obesity over the past few decades. Simply put, the fat that you are eating in your diet will not lead to weight gain, bad cholesterol, cancer, a heart attack, or cause you to become obese. Eating low-fat foods and keeping your calories from fat minimal has no health benefits whatsoever. What's worse, a low fat-diet can lead to weight gain and cause your health to deteriorate in the short and long-term.

That said, there is a big difference between eating fat from processed foods and eating fat from natural, whole foods that are unprocessed. Fat that occurs in nature is not only okay to eat, but has many health benefits—from helping you lose weight, to lowering you chances of developing heart disease, and by speeding up your metabolism. Before we dive into which fats you need to be eating and which fats to avoid, let us first look at why low-fat diets are still popular and are continuing to ruin the health of millions of Americans.

Enter the Sugar Industry

Recently uncovered documents have revealed that about fifty years ago, the sugar industry gave secret support to well-known Harvard researchers to write a convincing set of articles in the *New England Journal of Medicine* that downplayed the negative health effects of sugar. The article shifted the blame from sugar to fat as the "dietary culprit" behind heart disease and weight gain. The food industry goes to great lengths to hide the fact that they are sponsoring nutritional studies by disclosing statements with studies which state that the funder is not involved in the role of the publication, its conduct, writing, or design of a study. Unless there is some evidence or proof that a study was not funded, designed, or manipulated in any shape or form by a food industry sponsor, then these disclosures are accepted as fact with extraordinarily little doubt.

However, new evidence which shows that a sugar trade association not only paid for, but also started influential research to dismiss sugar as a major risk factor for heart disease and obesity has come to light. Even though fifty years ago, there were studies which have shown a direct relationship between high-sugar diets and heart disease and weight gain, the sugar association preferred policy makers and scientists to focus on the role of dietary fat and cholesterol. The sugar association paid tens of thousands of dollars to three nutrition professors at Harvard to publish a research review that would deny the evidence that linked sugar to heart disease and weight gain.

This sugar association-sponsored review appeared in the *New England Journal of Medicine* in 1967, where its authors admitted support from the food-industry-funded Nutrition Foundation. Despite having previously published studies where they linked sugar to heart disease, their review gave far more acceptance for studies which showed saturated fat as the main cause of heart disease compared to the studies that implicated sugar. While it may seem like this incident is a thing of the past as it happened more than fifty years ago, it is very relevant to what is happening today with the obesity epidemic. We now know without question that food companies purposely manipulate research in their favor.

In 2015, the acquired emails exposing Coco-Cola's comfortable relationship with sponsored researchers who were carrying out studies directed at minimizing the effects of sugary drinks on obesity and weight gain. The Associated Press has recently obtained emails that showed how a candy-trade association had an effect on and funded studies to show that kids who eat sweets have healthier and lower bodyweights than kids who do not.

As you see, the food industry in the United States has been funding nutrition research for many, many decades. Just like the tobacco, chemical, and pharmaceutical industries in America, the food industry is a multi-billion-dollar a year industry that puts its own profits over the health of the population by funding studies that produce results which confirm the benefits or lack of harm of the sponsors' products, even when independent (non-food industry) research comes to different or opposite conclusions.

Low-fat diets fail to satisfy you because when you eliminate fat from your diet, you end up eating foods that are higher in carbohydrates to make up for the void. You see, dietary fat is very filling, meaning that it promotes satiety after you eat it. Without enough fat in your diet and in each meal, you will almost certainly be hungry well before it's time to eat again. This will lead you to either eat more carbohydrates and sugar at the next meal, or it will lead you to snack between meals, most likely on foods high in carbohydrates and sugar. The problem with replacing fat with carbohydrates, as you'll discover, is that a higher carbohydrate diet is the primary cause of obesity and weight gain. This is the paradox of low-fat diets.

You will learn why you shouldn't fear fat. You will learn why you need fat in your diet, not only to lose weight but also to improve your cholesterol levels and many other health markers. So long as you are eating fat from the right foods, you are golden. Dietary fat is essential for many functions in your body and helps you lose weight by providing satiety, maintaining your metabolism, and keeping you healthy at the cellular level. By eliminating most of the fat from your diet, you will have to eat something else in place of fat to feel full and satisfied. And, as no one enjoys the feeling of hunger, you will end up compensating for the lack of fat in your diet by eating more carbohydrate foods to feel full.

Why Low-Calorie Diets Fail

In the same manner that you need fat in your diet to lose weight and improve and maintain your health, you also need ample calories. Over and over, we have been taught that eating a low-calorie diet is necessary for weight loss. While there is some truth to that belief (because losing weight does require a caloric deficit, or eating fewer calories than your body burns), eating fewer calories to lose weight and improve your health will eventually work against your fat-loss efforts. You see, calories are the fuel that your body needs to function properly. Without enough calories in your diet, your metabolism starts to slow down to compensate for the lack of energy (calories) coming in.

When your metabolism starts slowing down, so do several other important processes in your body. If you've ever been on a low-calorie diet and you got stuck in a plateau with your weight, you know exactly how frustrating and difficult it can be to break through the plateau and start losing weight again.

You see, your body is a highly specialized organism that's designed to do one important thing—to keep you alive. Through hundreds of thousands of years of evolution, the human body has developed itself into a survival machine capable of adapting to many different environments and stressors. When you go on a low-calorie diet, you activate your body's highly-evolved survival mechanisms, which in turn causes your body to trigger something called adaptive thermogenesis, a response where your body holds on to (secures) its fat stores for survival purposes. Your body does this because it perceives a lack of food with something like a famine, where it tries to compensate for the lack of food (energy) by reducing its energy (calorie) burning. Your body burns fewer calories and fat during a perceived famine mainly because it believes there won't be enough food to keep it alive, so hording body fat is your body's only option for staying alive. Like it or not, this is how your body works when it comes to body fat regulation. Therefore, it's ludicrous to try and "starve" the fat away because your body will never allow for it.

Getting rid of body fat as fast as possible requires a healthy and elevated RMR (resting metabolic rate). The number of calories you burn when you are not active or not exercising is considered your RMR. A high RMR is critical for losing excess body fat and has a big influence on the amount of fat and calories you burn by the end of the day. Low-calorie diets ultimately fail in the long run as they reduce your RMR, essentially crippling your ability to lose additional fat and get lean. When you burn fewer calories, you burn less fat; when you burn less fat, you lose less weight. Simple equation.

What you must understand is that when weight loss is your goal, you only want to get rid of a specific type of weight, not just all weight indiscriminately.

The only weight you need to concern yourself with getting rid of is body fat, also known as adipose tissue, which is the soft stuff that covers the muscle definition on your belly, arms, legs, thighs, butt, and other areas throughout your body. Humans and most other mammals have five different types of weight on their bodies: lean skeletal muscle, body fat/adipose tissue, organ, bone, and water. A low-calorie diet in most cases will cause a loss of lean muscle tissue, the primary driver of your RMR. When you have less lean muscle on your body, your RMR slows down, which again, makes losing fat more difficult.

Now, having said all of that, the following will sound contradictory to what I just explained above, but bear with me as I ensure it all will make total sense as you keep reading; losing weight (body fat) requires you to eat fewer calories, aka calorie restriction. *However,* maintaining a low-calorie intake for more than a few days is not necessary in order to lose body fat. In other words, you can eat more of a moderate-, but not high-calorie diet without starving yourself as you would with a low-calorie diet.

You see, the *type* of food you eat is more important than how much food you eat. To give you an example, one large egg contains about as many calories as seven or eight gummy bears, but the calories form the egg are completely *different* from the calories in the gummy bears. The gummy bears are loaded with carbohydrates (sugar), which your body likes to deposit into your fat stores (sugar is rapidly converted to body fat). However, an egg is made up of protein and fats, which are least likely to be stored as body fat, unless you are eating handfuls of eggs a day.

So, in turn you can eat a pretty decent number of calories every single day and still lose large amounts of body fat at the same time, without feeling deprived, moody, or very low on energy—like you would on a low-calorie diet. We will go over the ideal fat-burning diet, where most of your calories need to come from, and which foods to eat in the nutrients and calories section. Understand: when you eat nutrient-dense whole foods each day, it will be almost *impossible* to overeat and gain weight as whole foods are very filling. Try eating three sweet potatoes or four apples in one sitting and you will find it very difficult to finish eating.

Viewing Food as Fuel

"Eat to live, don't live to eat" is a quote to keep in mind while you're undergoing your health and body transformation. Over the next few weeks and months, I want you to think of the food that you eat as a fuel that you put into your body so you can do the things you love with as much energy, excitement, and enthusiasm as possible. With the Fit Body 4 Life 21-Day Meal Plan, you will be eating mainly to optimize cellular performance and re-set your metabolism; you will not be eating for pleasure, at least most of the time. That's not to say the foods that you'll be eating will be bland and tasteless—quite the opposite. The way you are going to eat in the coming weeks will completely change the way you look at food and what it can do for your appearance, health, mood, and energy levels.

You see, food is the most underutilized and most powerful drug. You can either use food to replenish your body and optimize your health so you can live a longer and more energetic life, or you can use food to damage your health by inducing disease which shortens your lifespan (whether you're doing it knowingly or unknowingly). When you feed your body in a manner that is consistent with its design, you become healthy and happy, and dropping extra pounds becomes almost effortless. Sadly, kids are never taught the importance of nutrition and how to eat properly when they are in grade school. School should be the very place where kids need to learn what to put into their bodies from an early age to minimize the chance of disease, obesity, and common preventable conditions caused by poor nutrition and being overweight. Unfortunately, nutrition classes are virtually non-existent in elementary, middle, and high schools in the United States—and it's a shame.

When you fully understand the importance of feeding your body the way it's meant to be fed, you will become lean and healthy at the cellular level. When you understand that nutrition literally is *everything* when it comes to losing weight and looking and feeling great, your entire outlook on food will change. It will change from eating to comfort yourself or due to an emotional reaction or stress, to eating only at times when your body needs fuel and nutrients to sustain itself so you can be at your best.

Controlling Hunger

When losing weight is your most important and primary goal, being hungry at different times throughout the day is expectable. Whether it's eight pounds or fifty pounds you want to lose, you will experience some hunger at various times throughout the day and night. The great news is that you can reduce your hunger by lowering the hunger hormone known as ghrelin.

Ghrelin plays an important role in regulating your hunger as well as several other hormones that signal your brain to eat. Unfortunately, ghrelin levels tend to increase when you limit your food intake, which makes it more difficult to control your hunger and lose fat. Since this hormone's main function is to increase your appetite, you will naturally want to eat more food when you initially start eating less food. A study done on humans has shown that ghrelin levels increased by twenty-four percent on a six-month, reduced-calorie diet—a significant amount.

Knowing this, it's vital that you keep your ghrelin levels as low as possible throughout your transformation. Ghrelin cannot be kept low by taking drugs, supplements, or with any diet. Therefore, you'll need to keep this hormone nice and low by implementing the following:

Increase your protein intake: A higher protein intake has been shown to reduce hunger and increase satiety by directly influencing your ghrelin levels.

Get enough sleep: Sleep is as vital to your weight loss and wellbeing as water is. If you are serious about transforming your body, you absolutely must make getting adequate sleep on most nights a priority.

Gain lean muscle: Studies have shown that folks with a higher percentage of lean muscle—aka fat-free mass—have lower levels of ghrelin. Incorporate weight training into your routine at least three times a week.

Maintain a stable weight and cycle your calories: Do this by avoiding diets that restrict too many food groups and excessive calories (crash diets).

The final word on ghrelin is that it's a very important hunger hormone that can literally make or break your fat loss. It plays a huge role in your hunger, your appetite, and your food intake. As you will be enjoying a sustainable nutrition plan and avoiding yo-yo dieting that causes large fluctuations in your weight and negatively affects your hormones, your ghrelin levels will remain nice and low throughout your transformation, which will have a huge impact on your progress.

Intermittent Fasting (IF)

By waiting a little while to eat something when you wake up in the morning, you will in a way re-program your body to use its own fat stores for fuel more efficiently. You see, the moment that you put food in your mouth, regardless of the type of food, you pretty much *stop* burning fat. Over the next few weeks and months, you will be teaching your body to function efficiently without any food for the first few hours in your day. In the mornings, your fat-burning potential is at its highest and you will be taking full advantage of this fat-burning window by either limiting or restricting your food intake until later in the day. Intermittent fasting is a way of eating where you fast for a certain number of hours each day and eat only during the remaining hours.

If done right, intermittent fasting can be the most effective way to lose stubborn body fat and restore your health quickly and safely. If the word "fasting" conjures up images of starvation and misery, realize that's far from the case when you do intermittent fasting correctly.

Quite simply, intermittent fasting will dramatically improve your health and enhance your body's ability to burn fat and it's nowhere near as difficult or painful as it sounds. In addition to helping you lose a lot of body fat in a short amount of time, intermittent fasting also normalizes your ghrelin (hunger hormone) levels.

IF also lowers your triglyceride levels and boosts your body's production of HGH (human growth hormone). HGH is known as the "youth hormone" because it plays an important function in the longevity process and your overall health and vitality. HGH also helps you burn fat because it's one of the fat-burning hormones.

In a nutshell, intermittent fasting involves:

1. Restricting your food intake to a specific time window (six to eight hours is ideal).
2. Skipping breakfast and eating most your food and

calories in the afternoon and evening.

3. Fasting for at least fifteen to sixteen hours, four to five days a week.

We will go into further detail about each of the three aspects above so that you can decide if intermittent fasting is right for you and your specific goals. Let's start with number one: Restricting your calories to a specific time window. Recent studies on participants who restricted their food intake each day to a six-to-eight-hour period demonstrated dramatic reductions in fasting blood sugar and insulin levels.

Low-fasting blood sugar and low-insulin levels play a huge role in the fat burning process. Insulin is a fat-storing hormone, so reducing your insulin levels is critical to losing body fat. Reducing your blood sugar levels is also very important for burning fat. By lowering your insulin levels, you will burn a lot more body fat throughout the day and during your workouts. Low insulin means your body's fat stores are being used as the primary energy source. This is exactly what you want when fat loss is your goal.

Number two: skipping breakfast and eating most of your calories later in the day. You've probably heard it many times before from so-called health "experts": "Breakfast is the most important meal of the day. Eat breakfast to kick start your metabolism. Never skip breakfast etc." Intermittent fasting breaks the "golden rule" of fat loss because it does not involve eating the traditional "breakfast." The word "breakfast" simply means to *break* your fast. You certainly do not have to break your overnight fast as soon as you get up in the morning and can choose to break it at any time of the day.

Eating breakfast foods—such as bagels, toast, orange juice, jam, and muffins—stops fat-burning dead in its tracks as these foods raise your insulin and blood-sugar levels, which means no fat will be burned.

A very low- or no-carbohydrate breakfast will also increase your insulin levels (but not your blood sugar) as protein foods such as bacon, eggs, sausage, and cheese increase your insulin (although not as much as carbohydrate foods). With intermittent fasting, you delay eating until about twelve p.m. or lunch time. At twelve p.m., the six-to-eight-hour eating window begins and you can choose to have as many meals or snacks as you would like during this time.

That said, to lose fat quickly you must still limit your calorie intake while doing intermittent fasting, especially if you have a lot of body fat to lose. Once you've reached your weight-loss goal, you can increase your calorie intake while continuing to do intermittent fasting and you will have no problems maintaining a healthy weight as long as you choose the right foods.

Ideally, you want to work out in a fasted state before you put any food into your system (around ten or eleven a.m.). However, if you cannot work out before your first meal or not until the evening, you can still reap all the benefits of IF. If you cannot work out until the evening, eat one light meal consisting of either fish or chicken breast with mixed steamed veggies and, if desired, a small piece of fruit. Small meals like this are digested quickly and will not interfere with fat burning during your workouts.

A word of caution, intermittent fasting is not to be done if you are diabetic, pregnant, or breastfeeding. You should also avoid intermittent fasting if you are very stress-reactive and live an overly stressful lifestyle. In addition, if you are suffering or have suffered from eating disorders, you should not do intermittent fasting.

Always be sure to pay attention to your energy levels and how you feel both physically and mentally while doing intermittent fasting. It's normal for your energy levels to dip when you are just starting out intermittent fasting as your brain is searching for fuel. As you continue to fast, your energy levels will stabilize as your body adjusts to the fast and you will have more energy in the mornings once your body has adjusted to fasting.

Here are some more important points to consider before you try intermittent fasting:

• When you are just starting IF (the first week or two), you can ease your body into fasting by starting off with a ten-to-twelve-hour fast and working your way up to sixteen hours of fasting. This is especially helpful if you are currently eating several meals and snacks every few hours throughout the day.

• Intermittent fasting is not a form of severe calorie restriction or starvation. You should consume ample calories from the right foods to provide your body with enough nutrients and energy to function optimally.

• Zero calorie beverages are OK to consume during your fasting period—although you should avoid diet sodas and drinks with artificial sweeteners. Coffee without sugar or creamer is fine if you're a coffee drinker.

• You do not have to do intermittent fasting every day. As long as the fat is coming off consistently, you can eat breakfast foods and other foods off the menu once or twice a week.

Intermittent fasting improves your health by affecting your cells and hormones in several important ways. It's your hormones, which are influenced by your cellular health, that are responsible for lowering your body fat percentage and helping you burn more fat throughout the day. Here are some changes that will happen in your body at the cellular and hormonal level when you fast:

Decrease in the fat storing hormone insulin: Fasting improves your insulin sensitivity. Your insulin levels will drop dramatically which will lead to rapid fat loss.

Increase in Human Growth Hormone (HGH): Your growth hormone levels will increase significantly, to as much as five-fold. HGH plays a large role in increasing your lean muscle and burning fat.

Better gene expression: The genes in your body that are responsibly for longevity and protection against disease will express themselves and function better.

Better cellular repair: When you are in a fasted state, your cells repair and rebuild themselves through a process known as autophagy. Your cells will be more efficient at removing and cleaning out old and non-usable proteins in your body.

The bottom line on intermittent fasting is that it is a proven way of restoring your health quickly and safely while doubling and even tripling your energy levels. To lose body-fat successfully, you must be healthy. Period. Look at losing weight as a side effect of having a healthy body that functions properly at the cellular level. If your health is not ideal, you will not achieve your goals no matter how often you exercise or how strict you are with your diet by avoiding certain foods. Your body is the equivalent to that of a highly-tuned, exotic, and expensive automobile. Only high-quality fuel will keep it functioning and prevent it from breaking down.

The one exception to intermittent fasting is that if your daily schedule does not permit you to fast for whatever reason, or if fasting is interfering significantly with your work or your family obligations, you can still burn fat rapidly and restore your cellular health by eating a small meal every few hours, including breakfast. Once you're getting most of your calories from the right foods, your health and wellbeing will improve significantly, no matter if you're fasting or if you're eating every few hours.

Nutrients and Calories

Instead of analyzing the calorie and nutrient content of everything you eat every day, which can be a tiring, laborious process, you will be focusing on eating real, whole foods that are dense in nutrients and provide your body with the protein, fats, fiber, and carbohydrates it needs to perform optimally and energize your workouts and days. The first thing you need to focus on is eating more fat. Now that you know that fat is not bad for you and the reason why fat has been demonized by the medical establishment, it's time to let go of your fear of fat for once and for all. No matter how large or small your weight loss goal is, taking fat out of your diet is the *worst* thing you can do for your health, metabolism, fitness, and longevity.

When you remove fat from your diet, what you are left with is carbs and protein. Neither of these two macronutrients can provide you with the satiety and feeling of fullness like fat can. In 1992, the US government released its food guide pyramid. At the base of the pyramid were carbs, and we were told to eat six to eleven servings of pasta, cereal, bread and rice per day. At the very top of the pyramid were the fats and oils, which we were advised to eat very little of. Almost immediately, the food industry hopped on the government's low-fat bandwagon, creating everything from low-fat and fat-free cookies, to low-fat salad dressings and fat-free ice cream and yogurt.

Since these so-called foods were low in fat, which people falsely believed to be good for their health, thanks to the good old USDA, entire boxes and cartons of low-fat processed foods were consumed. As most people listened to the government like all good citizens should, sugar consumption has increased to a whopping 152 pounds per year, and flour consumption has skyrocketed to 146 pounds per year. Despite the evidence pointing to sugar as the primary cause of not only obesity, but also diabetes, cancer, and heart disease, most Americans consume almost twenty percent of their daily calories from foods that are loaded with sugar and made almost exclusively of sugar. Sugar is the hidden culprit behind modern-day disease. Sugar, especially from liquids such as soda, sports drinks, and fruit juice is highly addictive, causing you to crave more sugar, creating a vicious cycle which causes you to eat more calories than you would from solid food and food without added sugar.

You see, unlike fat, of which there are good and bad sources, sugar is pretty much sugar. All sugar breaks down into glucose (blood sugar) almost immediately after it hits your tongue. All sugars have the same negative consequences on your waistline and on your health. There are many different names for sugar, but do not be misled, no matter what kind of sugar you eat—honey, agave nectar, cane syrup or any of the hundreds of other names for sugar—sugar is sugar at the end of the day.

It's the exact opposite when it comes to fat, as there are different fats in the foods you eat. Fat comes in many different forms. There are monounsaturated fats, saturated fats, polyunsaturated fats and hydrogenated, or trans fats. Man-made trans fats and fats from vegetable oils (including margarine) are the only fats that you need to avoid.

A final word to help you let go of your fear of fat: there are no studies that have ever shown that fat—whether saturated, monounsaturated, or polyunsaturated—causes heart disease and obesity. Eating the right fats is essential to your health, weight loss, and longevity. Recent studies have demonstrated that higher-fat diets are better for weight loss compared to low-fat diets and for reversing dangerous conditions like hypertension, high cholesterol, heart disease, and chronic inflammation.

If you get rid of the fat in your diet, you will create a large void of essential nutrients that your body needs to function well. The nutrients you are left with for filling the void are protein and carbohydrates. Carbohydrate foods cannot fill this void because they empty out of your digestive tract at a faster rate compared to fat, which leaves you feeling hungry sooner after eating. Protein cannot fill this void either, as protein foods are quick to digest as well. This makes it especially important to eat enough fat with each meal. Since fat is so important, let's begin with foods that contain ample good fats. These foods need to make up the base of your diet.

The Best Healthy Fat Foods
Olive Oil

Olive oil is the natural oil extracted from olives. It's rich in monounsaturated fat called oleic acid, which is a good fat that's very beneficial to your arteries. It has been shown in studies to help reduce inflammation and activate several anti-cancer genes. Because monounsaturated oil is very resistant to heat, olive oil is one of the best healthy choices for cooking. Olive oil is a great source of antioxidants such as vitamin E and vitamin K, which fight disease and keep your immune system strong. Because olive oil fights inflammation (the leading cause of heart disease), it's very beneficial to consume every day, even multiple times a day, unlike most other vegetable cooking oils (canola, sunflower, corn oil, and rapeseed oil) which are terrible for your health as they contribute to inflammation and heart disease. I will go into more details about vegetable oils and what makes them bad for your health in the foods-to-avoid section.

In addition to its powerful anti-inflammatory effects, olive oil also reduces your chances of suffering a stroke. The link between olive oil and a lower risk of stroke has been studied extensively. In a large review study that included over 841,000 subjects, researchers found that olive oil was the only source of monounsaturated fat associated with lower risks of both heart disease and stroke. This is a very significant finding, as stroke is one of the leading causes of death in the United States and throughout the world.

Olive oil pairs very well with any type of vinegar in salads and is excellent for sautéing and marinating meats. When you are purchasing olive oil, make sure that you are getting the highest quality oil. Go with extra virgin and organic if possible.

Unfortunately, the olive oil industry is not tightly regulated, and some manufacturers use cheap fillers like highly inflammatory soybean oil and other oils to cut production costs. Real olive oil has a very deep, rich, distinctive, and intense flavor and aroma. According to the International Olive Council and the USDA, olive oil should have zero defects and greater than zero fruitiness. However, neither organization enforces these standards, which means manufacturers don't have to honor them.

In September 2102, *Consumer Reports* released its results from testing more than twenty-three olive oils from Spain, France and California. Out of the twenty-three that were tested, only nine passed the tests as being genuine olive oil as stated on the label. Among brands that failed were Bertoli and Goya. Some passing oils were Trader Joes, California Estate, and McEvoy Ranch. There have been other instances where brands failed to pass the authenticity test. In the same year (2012), Consumer Reports tested twenty-one olive oil samples from vendors who supply restaurants. Over half the samples tested (sixty percent) failed to pass the authenticity test. When they analyzed these oils in the lab, it was found that two of the olive oil samples were part canola oil, a highly inflammatory oil that is much cheaper to produce and had none of the benefits of authentic olive oil.

In 2010 and 2011, several of the most popular brands sold in the grocery-store-brand samples were tested and a whopping sixty-nine percent of imported olive oil and ten percent of the California oils failed the tests. A few of the brands that failed were Filippo Berio, Pompeian, Bertolli, Colavita, Star, Rachael Ray, and Newman's Own Organic. The brands that passed with perfect scores were McEvoy Ranch

Organic, Kirkland Organic, California Olive Ranch, Lucero, Cobram Estate, and Corto Olive.

To ensure that you're getting the full benefits of olive oil, only purchase the brands I've outlined above. According to the tests, these brands are reliable and contain only what's stated on their label. Real, authentic olive oil has a very rich scent and aroma and has a deep flavor.

Wild Caught Salmon

Wild-caught salmon is one of the healthiest foods on the planet. It's is very high in omega 3 fatty acids and other essential nutrients. A four-ounce serving contains about 3500 mg of essential omega 3 fatty acids, which is very high compared to other fish. Studies have shown that people who eat fatty fish—like salmon—on a regular basis have a lower risk of suffering from depression, heart disease, and dementia. In addition to its high omega-3 content, wild-caught salmon is very nutrient dense. It's packed with protein, B-vitamins, potassium, selenium, and magnesium.

Now the bad news about salmon: Unless it's otherwise noted, salmon served in restaurants and most frozen and pre-packaged salmon found in the grocery store comes from the farmed variety. Compared to wild salmon, farmed salmon is *not* good for you and can damage your health instead of improving it. Unlike wild salmon, which is caught in the wild where it eats food that it's meant to eat and roams its natural environment, farmed salmon is bred in fish farms, known as aquaculture, where it's treated with antibiotics, sprayed with pesticides and fed a high fat, unnatural diet which includes genetically modified ingredients (GMOs).

Farmed salmon has almost twice the fat and calories per serving compared to wild salmon. Farmed salmon also contains far more omega-6 fatty acids per serving compared to wild salmon. Omega-6 fats can contribute to inflammation if overconsumed. But the worst part about farmed salmon is the high amounts of harmful contaminants that it contains. Fish, both wild and farmed, tend to accumulate contaminants from the environment which are found in the water they swim in and the foods they eat.

Some of these contaminants include polychlorinated biphenyls dioxins, (PCBs) and several other unappetizing, chlorinated pesticides. Without a doubt, the most dangerous pollutant found in salmon is the PCBs, which have been shown to cause cancer and many other health problems

One study investigated over 700 salmon samples from around the world and found that on average, the PCB concentrations in farmed salmon were eight times higher than in wild salmon. The bottom line on salmon is that the farmed variety should not be part of your diet and you need to avoid eating it. Stick with wild salmon for all the health benefits of this delicious fish.

Avocados

Avocados come from the avocado tree, called Persa Americana. Avocados are a fruit, not a vegetable. Most fruit is high in carbohydrates due to its natural sugar content, but avocados have almost no sugar and are mostly made up of healthy fats. Multiple studies have shown that this unique fruit has amazing health benefits when eaten on a regular basis.

To begin with, avocados are high in potassium, vitamin K, vitamin E, folate, and fiber. One 3.5 ounce serving of avocado has about 160 calories, 7 grams of fiber, 15 grams of healthy fats, and only 9 grams of carbohydrates, with 7 of those grams coming from fiber. The fats in an avocado come from monounsaturated fatty acids, the same type of fat that's found in olive oil which reduces deadly inflammation and lowers your chances of getting cancer.

What's more, studies have shown that avocados reduce your chances of getting heart disease by lowering LDL (bad) cholesterol and increasing good (HDL) cholesterol. Avocados have a powerful, positive effect on your cholesterol levels as regular consumption reduces your total triglyceride levels and boosts your heart health.

Due to their high fiber and healthy fat content, avocados are very filling, which means they are an excellent weight loss food to eat often. Avocados can be eaten several different ways. You can slice half an avocado into your salad, or eat it as a side item along with lean meats. Avocados can also be mixed into green smoothies for added antioxidants and a healthy fat boost.

Walnuts

Walnuts are very high in an essential fatty acid known as ALA, which is different than DHA and EPA found in salmon. ALA is an omega-3 precursor fat that your body converts into usable essential fat when you consume it, unlike EPA and DHA from fish and fish oil, which do not need to be converted by your body. Walnuts are also high in antioxidants, which makes them a potent food for preventing cancer and heart disease. Most of the calories in walnuts come from fat, which makes them a high-calorie food ideal for substituting in place of high-carbohydrate foods. Even though walnuts are high in fat, (the good kind) and high in calories, studies have shown that they do not increase the risk of obesity if they are eaten in place of other high calorie and high fat foods.

The ALA fats in walnuts reduce inflammation, improve your heart health, and your blood fat composition. In addition to being high in the precursor omega-3 ALA, walnuts are also an excellent source of several vitamins and minerals including Vitamin E, Vitamin B6, Folic acid, phosphorus, copper, and manganese.

Snack on a small handful of walnuts once or twice a day between meals by themselves or with a piece of fruit. To boost your omega-3 intake and curb bad-food cravings, eat them often. As walnuts are high in fat, they make a great appetite suppressant and are perfect to eat between and before meals.

Eggs

There has been a lot of debate and controversy over the past few years in the medical and health community about egg consumption and an increased risk of elevated cholesterol levels. The main reason why eggs are considered unhealthy by some experts is because they are high in cholesterol. Cholesterol is a waxy-type substance found in food and it's also produced by your body. Several decades ago, a number of large-scale studies linked high blood cholesterol levels to heart disease. Because of these findings, the American Heart Association, among many international health organizations, recommended limiting dietary cholesterol intake.

This led to a significant reduction in egg consumption all over the world. Egg whites were touted as being healthier as all the fat and cholesterol in eggs are found in the yellow part, or yolk. While it is true that whole eggs are a very rich source of cholesterol, eating foods high in cholesterol does not lead to a significant increase in blood cholesterol levels, as recent studies have shown. You see, your liver produces large amounts of cholesterol every single day and when you eat eggs, the liver slows down its production of cholesterol to even out the body's levels of cholesterol.

It's worth stating that cholesterol elevation from egg consumption varies from person to person, meaning that your neighbor may not see any increase in his or her cholesterol levels after eating several eggs, but a member of your family may see their cholesterol levels go up after eating one egg. In about seventy percent of people, eggs don't increase cholesterol levels, with the other thirty percent—known as "hyper responders"—can see a slight increase in blood cholesterol levels.

There is one exception to this 70/30 split. People who have a genetic disorder known as familial hypercholesterolemia are better off avoiding or minimizing their egg consumption. Unless you have this genetic disorder, eating a few eggs each day is perfectly fine and recommended. Egg yolks are high in essential fats and contain numerous important vitamins and minerals such as Choline, Vitamins B5, B12 and B2, Folate, Selenium, and several others. One egg has just 75-80 calories along with 6 grams of protein and 5 grams of healthy fats. No other foods can match the nutrient, protein, and healthy-fat punch of eggs, which makes them a true superfood.

It's important to understand that eggs raise your HDL good cholesterol, which as studies have shown, directly lowers your risk of developing heart disease, stroke, and other deadly disorders. If you don't get enough cholesterol in your diet, your VLDL cholesterol levels can increase. VLDL, known as very low-density lipoproteins, are the *most* dangerous type of blood cholesterol and significantly increase your risk of suffering heart disease and stroke. Eating eggs and other cholesterol-containing foods often will keep your body—more specifically, your liver—from producing too much of its own cholesterol, mainly the LDL or bad type.

An important note on eggs: whenever possible, buy pasture-raised and organic eggs as they are higher in omega-3 fatty acids and are higher in vitamins compared to non-organic, non-pasture-raised eggs. Avoid frying eggs in oil as doing so will add unnecessary calories and fat. Instead, use a high-quality cooking spray made from olive oil, avocado oil, or coconut oil if you prefer to fry your eggs. Boiling or baking works best when you are reducing calories. Finally, be sure that you are eating whole eggs, not just the white. Tossing out the yolk means you are tossing out all the amazing health benefits of eggs. The egg white only contains protein, whereas the yolk contains the omega 3s, vitamins, and minerals.

Nuts and Seeds

Nuts and seeds (Brazil nuts, almonds, peanuts, pistachios, macadamia nuts, pecans, pumpkin seeds, sesame seeds, flaxseeds, chia seeds)

Nuts and seeds are excellent sources of various vitamins, minerals, fiber, protein, and good fats. We've already gone over the benefits and nutrients of walnuts, which are at the top of the list of nuts as they are loaded with omega-3s, vitamins, and fiber that aren't found in such high amounts in other nuts. Other than peanuts, which are a legume and not a nut, nuts are excellent to eat in place of a meal or between meals as a snack. One downside of nuts is that they are high in a plant nutrient called phytic acid. Phytic acid blocks the absorption of important nutrients such as iron, calcium and zinc. Phytic acid is known as an anti-nutrient for this very reason. Phytic acid interferes with your body's absorption of nutrients while you are eating a meal but does not interfere with absorption for the rest of the day, unless you keep eating nuts and seeds throughout the day.

The good news is that there are ways to reduce the phytic acid content of nuts and seeds and make them easier for your stomach to digest. One highly effective way of reducing phytic acid is by sprouting, fermenting, or soaking nuts before eating them. You can buy sprouted nuts at health food stores or you can sprout them at home. You can also soak nuts in water overnight to reduce their phytic acid content.

Unless you have a nut allergy, eat a variety of nuts and seeds a few times a week to increase your omega-3 intake. Nuts are perfect as a quick snack or mixed in with oatmeal, yogurt, and other recipes. When shopping for nuts, choose raw or lightly/dry roasted. Roasted nuts contain less healthy fats as the roasting process removes some of the healthy fats. Also, be aware of additional ingredients on the label of mixed nuts. The only other ingredients that should be on the label of mixed nuts is salt. Additional ingredients such as oil indicates that the nuts have been roasted and contain fewer beneficial nutrients and fats.

Nut Butters

Almond butter, hazelnut butter and other nut butters are very nutritious and filling, just like the nuts that they're made from. Apart from conventional peanut butter, nut butters contain ample amounts of good fats which help keep your heart and arteries functioning smoothly. They are also a good source of fiber, which helps to keep you full and satisfied between meals. Nut butters are an excellent substitute for butter and can be used as a spread, in smoothies, and in various recipes. Choose almond butter, hazelnut butter, and cashew butter as they are higher in heart-healthy fats compared to peanut butter. Peanut butter is the most popular nut butter and it's on the favored list by both health-conscious folks and kids, but it's not the best nut butter in the grocery store in terms of health benefits.

When shopping for peanut butter, always go with the natural version that does not contain any added sugar, excess salt, or hydrogenated oils, also known as trans-fats. Even better, choose organic peanut butter as it's very low in aflatoxin, a type of natural mold that is considered a carcinogen. The only ingredients that should be on the label of your peanut butter is peanuts and salt. Some natural peanut butters also contain palm oil, which is a healthy fat that binds the peanut paste and peanut oil together in the natural variety to keep the oil and paste from separating. Peanut butter is a good source of protein and several vitamins and minerals, such as manganese, iron, and niacin. At about 200 calories per two tablespoons serving, peanut butter and other nut butters are not low-calorie foods, so you must watch your intake if fat loss is your goal. Nut butters are excellent to use in smoothies and shakes and can be eaten on their own as a-between-meal snack. Unlike raw nuts, most people find nut butters easier to digest as the grinding down process turns the nuts into a pre-digested form, which is easier for your stomach acid to break down and digest.

The Role of Carbohydrates

Unlike the foods that I have outlined above that are rich in essential fats, foods that are rich in carbohydrates are *not* essential for your health and well-being. This is because your body can make plenty of carbohydrates out of the protein and fat that you eat through a process known as gluconeogenesis. For example, let's say that you're waking up from a nice eight-hour sleep. You haven't eaten anything throughout the night, so there is no (or very little) available blood sugar (glucose) left in your body. Yet, your body still needs to have energy to move around and get you out of bed. One of the ways your body can produce the energy (glucose) you need, is to convert non-carbohydrate sources (like amino acids from protein foods) in your liver into glucose. Your body then takes that glucose and uses it to maintain your blood sugar at an even, healthy level.

This is a natural process that occurs in your body when you eat minimal carbohydrates, such as in a low-carbohydrate diet. There are countless nutrition experts that preach the benefits of a low-carbohydrate diet and how it's the optimal diet for humans while others believe low-carb diets are a potentially-harmful fad. The fact is, a low-carb diet can be very beneficial and healthy *if* it's followed correctly and if you're eating nutrient-rich foods that keep you feeling satisfied. As wonderful as a low-carb diet can be for your health and weight loss, it can leave you feeling deprived even if you are eating a decent number of calories throughout the day. This is because carbohydrate foods, as mentioned earlier, empty out of your digestive tract relatively quickly, which makes you crave food again soon after you eat them.

This makes it essential to eat more fat while going low-carb. If you are skeptical about going low carb, know that low-carb diets are supported by over twenty high-quality studies in humans, which show that they are the most effective way to lose weight rapidly. However, going low carb does not mean that you can eat limitless amounts of fat and protein to make up for the carbohydrates that you are avoiding, as some experts would have you believe.

You will adopt a more flexible and sustainable eating plan by eating carbohydrates on a regular basis. By including the right carbohydrates at the right times, not only will it feel like you're not depriving yourself, but you will think about food less and less throughout the day, which will allow you to lose pounds and inches rapidly and maintain your results over the long-term. Diets that severely restrict carbohydrates, such as the popular Atkins and Ketogenic diets, work well for most people; however, they are *not* sustainable and come with a weight gain rebound once they are discontinued.

If your primary goal is weight loss, follow the Three Phase Macronutrient Revamp, where you will reduce your carbohydrate intake initially and then start eating more carbohydrates as you continue the plan. The Fit Body 4 Life 21-Day Meal Plan is mostly void of any starchy carbohydrates as it is designed to program your body to use fat for energy, instead of carbohydrates.

Understand: If you are eating too many carbohydrates, all you are doing is burning off glycogen (stored carbohydrates in your muscles and liver) when you exercise. You will not burn body-fat. After you have completed the 21-day meal plan, you can be a little bit more flexible and allow yourself to enjoy more carbohydrates while continuing to eat more plant-based and healthy fat foods to maintain an optimal metabolism that keeps the weight off.

The 3 Phase Macro Nutrient Revamp

Phase 1: Reduce your carbohydrate intake so that you are eating no more than 80 grams per day if you are a woman. If you are a man, you can eat up to 120 grams of carbohydrates in this phase. Be sure that you eat this minimum number or as close as possible each day during phase one. Going slightly over these numbers is fine. The only carbs allowed for most days are the ones that are outlined in the below section.

Phase 2: Once you lower your carbohydrates to the amounts outlined in phase one, slowly increase your intake of healthy fat foods until you are eating at least fifty grams of fat per day if you are a woman, and up to seventy grams per day of you are a man. It's *crucial* that at least ninety percent of your total fat intake comes from healthy fat foods. Avoid bad fats (except for cheat meals if you desire something higher in fat— more on cheat meals later on).

Phase 3: Once you reach your goal weight, you can start eating more carbohydrates and more healthy fats. By the time you've reached this phase, your metabolism will be finely tuned, allowing you to burn a lot more fat and calories when you are at rest and when you exercise. Your insulin and blood sugar levels will be nice and stable, and your body will be able to handle the additional carbohydrates and fat that you will be eating. You will not have to worry about gaining back the weight you've lost as your cravings for sweets and high-fat junk foods will be non-existent by the time you reach phase 3.

The Best Carbohydrate Foods

These foods are made up of mostly carbohydrates and need to be restricted. Even though they are very nutritious and good for you, eating too many carbohydrate-rich foods will stop fat-burning dead in its tracks. Carbohydrate foods raise the fat-storing hormone insulin as well as your blood sugar levels, both of which need to remain low for fat burning to occur. Eat the following foods in small amounts up to the limits outlined in the 3 Phase Macronutrient Adjustment Phase above.

Sweet Potatoes

Ounce for ounce, sweet potatoes are more nutrient and fiber dense than any other carbohydrate food. A medium-sized sweet potato, baked or boiled has about 30 grams of carbohydrates and 120 calories. Most of the carbs come from starch, with the remining carbs coming from sugars. There are several varieties of sweet potatoes that you can buy, with the most common type being an orange color on the inside and light brown color on the outside. Sweet potatoes are high in the antioxidant beta-carotene, which raises your blood levels of Vitamin A. In the United States, sweet potatoes are commonly called yams, which is not correct as yams are a different species with a different nutrient profile. Sweet potatoes are somewhat related to regular potatoes, containing many more nutrients and fiber, making them a superior choice for weight loss and maintenance. Sweet potatoes are a great source of Vitamin A, Vitamin E, Vitamins B6 and B5, Vitamin C, potassium, and manganese.

Sweet potatoes are an excellent side item to lean meats and fish and pair well with greens such as kale, spinach, collard greens and mustard greens.

Quinoa

Quinoa (pronounced KEEN-wah) is a popular health food in many countries. Compared to other grains such as rice, quinoa is much higher in fiber and essential nutrients as well as protein. In fact, quinoa is the only grain that has all nine essential amino acids. Quinoa has been eaten for thousands of years in South America, only recently becoming popular in North America. It is considered a superfood. Quinoa comes in three different varieties: red, black, and yellow. All varieties share the same nutrient profile with one cup of cooked quinoa containing eight grams of protein, four grams of fat, five grams of fiber and about 220 calories. Quinoa is a good source of manganese, magnesium, folate, copper, iron, phosphorous, and zinc. It also has small amounts of omega-3 fatty acids, calcium, vitamin E, and vitamin B3. Quinoa is usually grown organic and it's non-GMO and gluten free. Put quinoa into your salad, or pair it as a side item with chicken, lean red meat, or fish.

Oats

Oats are an incredibly filling food high in essential fiber and a few important minerals. Oats are gluten free and are processed in several different forms to make oatmeal. Oatmeal comes in steel cut, rolled, crushed and instant. Oats are also included in foods such as granola bars, muffins and cookies. However, eating oatmeal is the best way to get the full health benefits of oats as they are in the least processed form and do not include any additional flour, sugar, additives or preservatives, which are usually included in muffins, cookies and other baked goods that contain oats. One cup of cooked oatmeal has about 300 calories, 50 grams of carbohydrates, 13 grams of protein, 5 grams of fat, and 8 grams of fiber. One of the things that make oats such a powerful health food is that they are rich in antioxidants known as Avenanthramides.

Avenanthramides have been shown to help lower blood pressure by increasing the production of nitric oxide. Nitric oxide is a gas inside the body that dilates your blood vessels and is responsible for enhancing blood flow. Avenanthramides have also been shown to be anti-inflammatory and have anti-itching effects, along with lowering your LDL and total cholesterol levels. Oats can be prepared several different ways—the most common and quickest way being cooked in water or milk. Steel cut and rolled oats are higher in fiber compared to quick cooking oats. Also, quick cooking oats that are neatly packaged in little pouches sometimes have added sugar and artificial flavorings, so be sure to read the ingredient label if you are purchasing quick-cooking oats. The only ingredients that should be on the ingredients' list of your oatmeal is oats. You can easily add your own ingredients such as cinnamon, nuts, seeds and small amounts of honey to further boost the antioxidant content of your oatmeal.

Buckwheat

Buckwheat is part of a group of grains known as pseudo cereals, which are seeds that are consumed in the same way as cereal grains. The main difference is that buckwheat does not grow on grass like other cereal grains. Although its name contains the word wheat, buckwheat is not related to wheat, so it is a gluten-free grain. Buckwheat has become a popular health food in several different countries as it's very high in dietary fiber, has several important nutrients and minerals, and it's very filling along with being an excellent controller of blood sugar. Buckwheat is most commonly processed into noodles and flour and it's often combined with other flours such as rice and corn in gluten-free flour products.

A cup of buckwheat has about 580 calories, 22 grams of protein and 120 grams of carbs along with 17 grams of fiber and 6 grams of fat. Buckwheat is a very starch-dense food and is made up of almost purely carbohydrates. It's a very slow digesting carbohydrate thanks to the fiber and complex carbohydrates it contains.

Apples

Unlike the carbohydrates that I've already outlined, apples are not a starchy carbohydrate food. Instead, they are made up of mostly fructose (a natural fruit sugar), which is broken down and metabolized by your liver. Unfortunately, your liver can only process small amounts of fructose at one time, so eating too many fruits while you're trying to lose weight is a big no-no if weight loss is your goal. That being said, it's very difficult to gain weight from eating too much fruit such as apples, thus eating fruit freely once you've already reached your target weight is completely fine. Apples are a powerful antioxidant food as they contain plant compounds called phytophenols. The skin of an apple contains most of the nutrients and fiber while the flesh is mostly sugar. When choosing apples, go with smaller to medium sized versions as they contain less natural sugar. Additionally, choose organic apples whenever possible as regular apples are high in harmful pesticides.

Apples have been shown to reduce your risk of heart disease, improve your blood sugar and reduce your risk of developing cancer. Apples pair well with nut butters and are a perfect healthy dessert after a meal.

The Best Protein Foods

For weight loss and adding lean muscle, protein is absolutely essential. You can't transform your physique without the essential building blocks that make up your entire body (muscles, bones, organs etc.) and are used for every metabolic process in your body. More specifically, these building blocks are called amino acids, which can only be obtained by eating foods that contain protein. In total, there are twenty amino acids that your body uses to build proteins and they are separated as essential and non-essential.

Non-essential amino acids are produced by your body and don't need to be consumed, while essential amino acids cannot be produced by your body and need to be obtained through foods that are high in quality protein. For general health, weight loss, and muscle building, you need all essential amino acids in the right amounts every day. Animal sources of essential amino acids are the best and highest quality you can consume, followed by plant sources.

Animal proteins are considered complete proteins as they contain all essential amino acids your body needs to build new lean muscle tissue, speed up recovery from exercise and keep you healthy. Following this paragraph, you will discover the best animal protein foods that, when eaten daily, will put you on the fast track to losing weight and building a lean, fit body that turns heads. While foods such as nuts, soybeans, beans, and lentils contain a decent amount of protein, they do not make our list of best protein foods as they don't contain essential amino acids; thus, their protein quality is considered low when compared to the foods rich in essential amino acids such as the following:

Egg Whites

Egg whites are rich in essential amino acids that your body converts to lean muscle tissue. One large egg contains about six grams of protein, with about two grams coming from the yolk and four from the white. Since egg yolks are a rich source of essential fats and many vital vitamins, I do not suggest that you throw away the yolk and only eat the white for protein. Instead, add an additional two to three egg whites to whatever egg dish you are eating. For example, if you are preparing an egg omelet with two or three whole eggs, simply add an additional two or three egg whites into the mix for a potent meal high in essential amino acids.

Chicken

Ounce for ounce, chicken contains more essential amino acids than any other meat in the grocery store. Chicken is rich in essential amino acids and contains all the building blocks your body needs to develop new lean muscle tissue, speed up your metabolism, and help speed up recovery from your workouts. If possible, always choose organic and free-range chicken instead of conventional or non-organic chicken. You'll find that organic chicken is better and fresher tasting as organic chicken hens are not fed a diet of GMO grains or any animal by-products. Organic chicken hens usually have plenty of outdoor access, so they are healthier overall compared to non-organic chicken hens, which makes for a higher quality meat that tastes better and fresher.

When weight loss is your goal, the white meat part of the chicken is best. White meat, or chicken breast has almost no fat and contains the highest amount of protein and the least number of calories compared to the rest of a chicken. In addition, be sure to trim the skin and any visible fat off the chicken before cooking. Although it's a natural animal fat, chicken skin is high in fat and calories, which can interfere with your fat-loss progress.

Always go with baked or oven-roasted chicken—never fried. Frying adds unnecessary fat and calories, which you obviously don't need when you're working hard to transform your body.

Lean Red Meat

The leanest red meat comes in at a close second after chicken when it comes to high quality amino acids. Many people, including myself, tend to have a difficult time digesting red meat. If this tends to be the case for you, you will know it almost immediately after eating red meat. Eating any food should never make you feel sluggish, lethargic or ill-at-ease. Only the highest quality fuel should be put in your mouth at each meal. This means if a food does not sit well with you, then you certainly do not have to eat it, no matter how great of a nutrient profile it contains.

Based on my personal experience and research, it is my belief that game meat such as venison, buffalo, and elk tend to be easier to digest and process as compared to cattle or beef. This is because our hunter-gatherer ancestors thousands of years ago hunted and ate these game meats which were part of their habitat. As our early human ancestors ate wild game meat, this allowed our digestive systems to adapt and get used to digesting these meats throughout thousands of years.

Modern cows or cattle, on the other hand, were not farmed for beef on any large scale until just a few hundred years ago. What this means is that our digestive systems have not yet had the time to adapt to processing cow meat or beef, leading to sluggishness and an overall less-than-ideal feeling after it. If you love beef, I highly suggest that you start eating different game meats and stop eating or strictly limit your consumption of beef. You may find that game meat digests better and does not make you feel heavy or sluggish after eating.

In addition to being easier to digest, game meats are leaner than beef, another reason to choose it over beef. Bison, elk, and venison meat is not easy to find, so visit your local butcher or look for companies that sell game meat on the internet by doing a Google search.

Cheese & Yogurt

If you can tolerate dairy, eat yogurt and cheese several times a week. Yogurt and cheese are animal-derived, which means they're full of quality protein that is rich in essential amino acids your body needs. Along with being a good source of essential amino acids, dairy products are also a great source of calcium which is essential for strong bones.

With that said, not all dairy products are created the same. Many health experts will argue that dairy products are not natural for humans to consume, and that is certainly true. As humans, by nature, we are only supposed to consume mother's milk as babies to aid in growth and development. Any dairy consumption after the growth period, especially from another animal, is not natural to humans. However, people in some parts of the world have been eating dairy for thousands of years, which has allowed them to develop digestive systems that can process large amounts of dairy without any problems.

About three quarters of the world's population is lactose intolerant. Lactose is the main carbohydrate in dairy and is also known as "milk sugar." As infants, our bodies produce a digestive enzyme called lactase, which breaks down lactose from mother's milk. As adults, many people lose the ability to produce lactase. This is known as lactose intolerance and it affects about seventy-five percent of the world's population. Lactose intolerance has symptoms such as nausea, vomiting, diarrhea, and other symptoms.

Some lactose-intolerant individuals can consume fermented dairy products such as yogurt and high-fat dairy products like butter. Many lactose-intolerant individuals can also eat cheese without any problems, while some people have a difficult time digesting any form of dairy.

If you can tolerate dairy, always choose grass fed and organic dairy products such as cheese, milk, yogurt, and butter. Cows that are pasture-raised have many more essential omega-3 fatty acids and another essential fat called CLA (Conjugated Linoleic Acid). Grass-fed cows also produce milk that is much higher in several very important fat-soluble vitamins, especially vitamin K, which is a critical vitamin for heart and bone health.

By choosing organic dairy products, you will avoid the pesticides and other harmful by-products that find their way into your food. As I've already covered in the first few protein foods listed, organic and free-range animal products are always the best option when it comes to your health and the environment.

Pasture-raised cows are far healthier animals than their feedlot-raised counterparts, which means their meat is more nutritious and healthier to eat on a regular basis compared to conventional agriculture products. As the fat in cow's milk is made up mostly of healthy fats (CLA, DHA & EPA), always go with full-fat dairy products, whether weight loss is your goal or not. Choose fermented dairy products like yogurt and kefir, as they are a rich source of beneficial fatty acids and health-boosting vitamins.

Most low-fat dairy products tend to have added sugars, which is a big reason to avoid them. The reason for this is that sugar makes up for the fat that is removed, and fat is what makes food taste rich and hearty. Always read the ingredients' list of the yogurt and other dairy products that you plan to purchase to ensure they do not contain added sugars. As all dairy has lactose (the natural milk sugar), it is normal to see a few grams of sugar listed on the nutrition facts' label. However, if you see words such as "cane sugar," "cane syrup," "corn syrup," or "high-fructose corn syrup" on the ingredients' list, avoid buying as these are all known as added sugars.

Turkey

Like chicken, turkey is very high in protein and contains all of the essential amino acids your body needs. Four ounces of skinned turkey breast will provide you with thirty to thirty-five grams of protein and less than one gram of total fat. Recent studies have shown that turkey, when eaten daily in small to moderate amounts, is associated with a decreased risk of pancreatic cancer when eaten skinless. Like chicken, eating organic turkey is the best way to go. Choosing organic turkey ensures that the meat you are eating does not contain any pesticides or animal by-products found in non-organic turkey.

Like chicken, turkey is a lean meat and should be purchased fresh. Harmful additives like MSG, sodium erythorbate and others are not allowed in fresh turkey, unlike frozen and processed turkey, which always contains additives. You should go even further and choose only free-range turkey, also known as pasture-raised. Pasture-raised and organic turkey is the healthiest turkey you can buy. Turkeys fed an organic diet and raised in a free-roaming environment contain the leanest and healthiest meat and the most amount of lean protein pound for pound.

Fish & Seafood

Most fish are excellent sources of lean protein along with essential omega 3 fatty acids. Unfortunately, most Americans eat very little fish in their diets. According to a 2002 report by the U.S. Environmental Protection Agency, U.S. adults average less than one ounce of fish per week. A long-term, recent study involving over 40,000 U.S. adults took a very close look at fish consumption and found that at least one serving of fish per week helps men lower their risk of heart disease.

Researchers at Harvard University and at the University of Kuopio in Finland compared men who very rarely ate fish to men who ate fish at least two to three times per week. Men who consumed more fish had a fifteen percent lower risk of cardiovascular disease compared to men who only ate fish occasionally, or about once a month. This connection between once-per-week fish intake and lowered risk of cardiovascular disease remained despite other negative factors, such as smoking or positive factors like exercising, that were considered. As for the specifics of the study, the researchers did not include shellfish in their analysis, but they did include all other types of fish, including fatty fish such as salmon and non-fatty fish such as cod.

Unfortunately, due to the pollution of lakes, oceans, and rivers, and due to the still-pending implementation of organic seafood recommendations adopted by the U.S. Department of Agriculture, fish remains a controversial food with respect to health. That said, when it comes to eating fish, if you choose high-quality wild fish and stay away from the farm-raised variety, your cellular health and fitness will only benefit.

As previously discussed, wild-caught fish such as salmon is one of the healthiest and most nutrient dense foods on earth. Salmon is packed with lean protein, omega 3 healthy fats, vitamin A, vitamin B6, folate, vitamin B12, selenium, potassium, and phosphorus. If salmon is not your type of fish, there are plenty of other seafood species to choose from. Unlike meat from land animals (chicken, turkey, beef), fish flesh is easier and quicker to digest, which makes it convenient to eat shortly before workouts and at other times when you're on the go and need a quick boost of protein.

Apart from salmon, the most protein- and nutrient-packed fish are wild-caught trout, Atlantic mackerel, Pacific sardines, and white shrimp. Large game fish such as swordfish and tuna are also excellent sources of protein and nutrients. Unfortunately, swordfish and tuna fish are high in mercury, which is a neurotoxin that can cause serious negative health effects if consumed in high amounts—especially in young children and the elderly.

Fish is healthiest when it is eaten baked or steamed. Avoid frying fish and eating fish that is breaded as these cooking methods add additional fat and empty calories, which cancels out the health benefits of fish. Any type of seafood goes well with green vegetables or a mixed salad. Fish pairs well with green beans, spinach, and other nutrient-rich greens.

Nut Butters

As outlined in the best heathy fat-foods section, nut butters are full of nutrition and appetite-suppressing dietary fiber and protein. While the protein quality of nuts is not of the same quality as the animal-based protein foods already outlined, eating nut butters is a tasty way to boost your overall protein intake. Almond butter, cashew butter, and peanut butter contain energy-boosting healthy fats along with quality amino acids from protein to keep you going.

CHAPTER 3: MINDSET MASTERY

Your Subconscious Feedback Loop

Now that you realize the importance of eating the right foods in the right amounts at the right times—as well as which foods to choose and which to avoid—it's time to get an understanding of how your mind works and how it is the ultimate determining factor to your success and happiness.

To put it simply, having a better understanding of *how* your mind works is the key to overcoming any obstacle or challenge that stands between you and your goals.

You see, everything that goes into or enters your mind— from TV, to radio and music, or to the voice of your boss or co-worker speaking to you—is considered your input. You must think of this input in the same manner as you think about food. By allowing only positive input to enter your mind, you will be light-years ahead of people who allow anything and everything to enter their minds (i.e. gossip, TV news, pop culture television etc.)

To give you a great example, allowing negative input to enter your mind is the equivalent of eating a box of doughnuts a few times a week and expecting to be a few pounds lighter and inches smaller by the end of the week. No matter how hard you exercise or how healthy you eat to try and make up for your doughnut binges, weigh loss just will not happen.

This is where being aware of your subconscious feedback loop comes into play. You see, your subconscious feedback loop is basically the "system" that governs your thoughts, ideas, feelings, actions, and expectations of yourself and others. It's like a software program that's always running in the background and influencing your every action; the only difference is that this software can be reprogrammed by your environment and by other people to make you do things without even realizing it.

Your subconscious feedback loop is very powerful because it works on the mind at a deeper level, a level that you are not even aware of. A recent article published in the *New York Times* explains how easy it is to alter a person's perception or judgement. Here's a small part of the article:

> "In a recent experiment, psychologists at Yale altered people's judgements of a stranger by handing them a cup of coffee. The study participants, college students, had no idea that their social instincts were being deliberately manipulated.

> On the way to the laboratory, they had bumped into a laboratory assistant, who was holding textbooks, a clipboard, papers, and a cup of hot or iced coffee—and asked for a hand with the cup.

> That was all it took. The students who held a cup of iced coffee rated the person they bumped into as being much colder, less social, and more

selfish than did their fellow students who had momentarily held a cup of hot java."

Here is what this all has to do with your health and transformation: Outside factors influence your thoughts, decisions, actions, and, ultimately, your ability and desire to attain your goals.

Ultimately, your success in anything is influenced by two major factors:

The people you associate with.

and

The thoughts that occupy your mind.

Several years ago, a friend of mine, Frank, told me about a trip he and his family took to Alaska where they were sightseeing the glaciers. It was an interesting story to hear as I had never visited Alaska. One of the ports that my friends' ship stopped at was a town where they did a lot of fishing for crabs.

Frank said...

"As we were walking along the water checking out the scenery, I saw a man who was fishing off the rocks for crabs and he had a five-gallon bucket next to him and inside of it were a bunch of crabs, each about the size of your hand. As we stood there watching the fisherman do his thing, I noticed that one ambitious crab was climbing on top of the other ones and was getting ready to reach up for

the rim of the bucket and boost himself up to freedom.

This little crab was going to make a run for it!

Just as the little crab started reaching for the rim of the bucket, all the other crabs in the bucket reached up, grabbed him by the legs and pulled him right down. The crab fisherman explained to me that crabs do that instinctively and so he never needs to put a lid on the bucket."

It's at this point that I said, "Wow!" I realized that we all have people like this in our lives. These are people who drag you down, keep you down and want you to be in the same boat (or bucket) that they are in. For lack of a better word, we will call these people crabs.

To be successful in the long run, you absolutely *must* avoid crabs in your life. If you know who these people are in your life—family or relatives—and cannot eliminate them completely, then the least you can do is reduce the amount of time you spend around them.

Next is number two:

The thoughts that occupy your mind.

These are the things that influence your feedback loop because they control, alter, and manage your subconscious mind, and your subconscious mind controls your conscious mind, which is what makes you do the things you do, minute by minute.

It goes like this:

Let us say your goal is to lose thirty pounds and look amazing at an upcoming class reunion. For you to *lose* weight you must *do* something (exercise and diet). For you to exercise and diet, you need to take an *action* to go to the gym and to buy healthy foods that help you burn fat. For you to take this action you need to make a *decision* to do something.

But your decisions are controlled by your *thoughts* and your thoughts are formed by the *input* that goes into your conscious and subconscious mind.

Lose 30 Pounds >> Diet & Exercise >> Action >> Decision >> Thoughts >> Input

Your input is what you get from the things you watch, listen to, read, and the people whom you surround yourself with. A perfect example would be if you watch the news, then all you hear about is danger.

And if you listen to gossip, then you believe that people are bad, and when you read the papers all you see is unemployment, bad economy, and scarcity. I don't know about you, but as a health coach and an entrepreneur, if the thoughts that are floating around in my mind are danger, people are bad, the economy, unemployment, and scarcity, then the actions I take are not going to result in my accomplishing or creating anything significant that positively impacts and changes people's lives.

To accomplish your goals and continue succeeding, you need to relentlessly manage the input that's coming into your mind because your subconscious feedback loop is always running in the background and influencing your thoughts, decisions, actions, and, ultimately, your success and happiness. To give you an example, I stopped watching TV (especially the news) years ago, because mostly all I heard on the news was bad stuff happening, from unemployment to kidnappings, to house fires to murders, and on and on.

Second, you need to eliminate the crabs in your life. It may not be easy to eliminate people in your life who are around you the most (friends, family, etc.), but you'll be amazed at what you can accomplish when you get rid of folks who are negative and do nothing but drag you down.

If you cannot get rid of the crabs in your life completely, at the very least significantly reduce the amount of time you spend with them. Your fitness, health, and happiness depend on it.

Why You Must Fail to Succeed

Failure can be viewed and thought of in several different ways. Unfortunately, when we fail to accomplish a significant goal, whether it be climbing a mountain, losing any number of pounds and inches, or any other goal small or large, we tend to respond with negative self-talk that goes something like the following, both of which are self-defeating and ultimately lead to a cycle of repeat failure.

"I failed to achieve XXX goal after trying my best, which means I am a failure and will never accomplish XXX. I should just give up before I fail again or embarrass myself"

"I did not accomplish XXX, and I don't think I can because I've tried my best and things just aren't working out my way. I was not meant for this. It's too difficult etc.

I don't know about you, but if any of those thoughts went through my head after not attaining a goal or reaching for something important in my life, I would have never even considered writing this book.

Sadly, most of us let temporary failures and setbacks get in the way of accomplishment, whether it be short- or long-term accomplishment. Failing to achieve a goal or task does not mean that *you* are a failure. Rather, it simply means that the there is another way of accomplishing what you set out to achieve. In other words, failure teaches you what does and does not work, and it's up to you to make a change and keep trying to figure out something that does work. It took the inventor Thomas Edison 1,000 unsuccessful attempts to invent the lightbulb. When a reporter asked him how it felt to fail 1,000 times, Edison replied, "I didn't fail 1,000 times; the lightbulb was an invention with 1,000 steps."

Thomas Edison figured out 999 ways a lightbulb could not be created, and one way that it could. His success at creating the lightbulb was due to his many failures. Simply put, without failure, success and accomplishment would not be possible, nor would it feel so good when you have attained a goal you've strived and struggled for. Failure teaches you persistence, patience, and perseverance. Failure teaches you the importance of consistency, discipline, and good habits. Everyone fails, but not everyone lets failure stop him or her from eventually succeeding. This is the attitude and determination that you must possess in order to achieve any breakthrough in your life. Transforming your body and health is one of the most satisfying feelings you will ever experience. Seeing your body morph and change into the shape and size you've envisioned is thrilling and exciting. Getting complimented on your new look and having tons of energy—

along with feeling a couple of years younger—is an intoxicating, amazing feeling.

To get the body want, you *must* view failure as just another steppingstone to success. Each time you fail, you are one more step closer to achievement. You must also view failure as something that makes you stronger and wiser, something that is required to get to where you want to be—to achieve the outcome you want. The bottom line on failure is that it teaches us a lesson; it teaches us to try again, to try something different, and to keep trying until we succeed.

Rejecting and Overcoming Fear & Doubt

Since the beginning of human civilization, fear has been a basic, simple emotion for people to deal with. When we confront something overwhelming, especially the threat of dying in the form of disease, plagues, wars, and natural disasters, we feel the emotion of fear. Fear allows us to take note of a danger or threat and retreat in time. Unlike wild animals, for human beings, fear serves as an additional positive purpose in that of remembering threats in order to protect ourselves better next time. Our civilization depends on this ability to forestall and foresee dangers from the environment. Fear is the strongest and oldest emotion known to us, something deeply etched in our subconscious mind.

However, as time passed and we moved away from our primitive ways and early civilization, something strange started to happen. The terrors and fearful situations that we came upon began to lessen in frequency and intensity, as we gained an increased understanding and control over our environment. But instead of our fears lessening as well, they began to multiply in number. We started to worry about whether people liked us or not, how we fit into the group, and our status in society. We developed anxiety for our health, our children, the future of our families, our livelihoods, getting older, and many other things. Back in our primitive days and the earliest years of civilization, the fear we felt in nature was real—intense and powerful. It was something simple and physical, such as escaping a predator or taking cover in a snow or rainstorm.

The fear we feel now days is more of a generalized anxiety and not an intense, real fear such as our ancestors had to deal with. As modern humans, we must find something at which to direct our anxiety, no matter how improbable or insignificant. In the nineteenth century, an evolution of fear began to happen when people in the journalism and advertising field discovered that if they framed their stories with a basis of fear, our attention could be captured much quicker and easier.

Since fear is an emotion we find hard to resist and control, the advertising and journalism industry directed our focus and attention to new possible sources of anxiety: a new crime wave, environmental hazards, the latest health scare, and other sources of potential constant threats to our safety and our ways of living. You see, the media is a highly sophisticated organization that can give off the feeling, through striking imagery and video, that we are frail creatures in an environment full of danger, even though we live in a world many times safer and more predictable than anything our early human ancestors knew. Thanks to the modern media, our anxieties have significantly increased.

As outlined in the previous section about your subconscious feedback loop, you absolutely must limit your exposure to negative outside input, especially the news, as it does not serve your subconscious mind in a positive way. The best way to do this is to stop watching the news or at least severely restrict the amount of time you spend watching the news. If something important or possibly threatening or life-changing has happened or is about to happen to you, you will find out about it. Fear is not designed to be felt as we feel it in the modern world. Fear is designed to stimulate powerful physical responses, allowing us to retreat in time. After a fearful event, the anxiety and fear are supposed to go away. If you cannot let go of your fears, you will find it difficult to eat, sleep, or do many other basic things necessary to your health and survival.

As dominant as we are on this planet, human beings are the only animal that cannot get rid of its fears, especially the fears that lie inside us and color the way we view the world. When you shift from feeling fear due to some threat, to having a fearful attitude towards life itself, you come to see every event and situation in your life in terms of a risk. We tend to exaggerate the dangers to our vulnerability and tend to focus on the adversity that may arise. When times are prosperous, we tend to fret over things, even small, banal things that have no bearing on our health or lifestyle.

Understand: fear creates its own self-fulfilling dynamic. If you give into fear, you tend to lose energy and momentum, which makes you lose confidence. A lack of confidence translates into inaction that lowers confidence levels even further, and the process cycles on and on. As President Franklin Delano Roosevelt said while he confronted The Great Depression when he took office in 1933, "The only thing we have to fear is fear itself—nameless, unreasoning, unjustified terror, which paralyzes needed efforts to convert retreat into advance."

In the same speech President Roosevelt gave in 1933, he emphasized that your attitude—which has the power to help shape your reality—is what separates failure from success in life. If you view current and future life events through the lens of fear, you will tend to stay in retreat mode. What you must do is view each problem or crises in your life as a challenge and opportunity to prove something to yourself, a chance to strengthen and toughen yourself, and a call to action. By looking at things as mere challenges, you will convert something negative into something positive, simply by a mental process that will lead to positive action as well.

Now days, we do not face anything near as bad as the devastation of the 1930s and the years of war that followed. The reality of modern life in the twenty-first century is far different. We live in times where our physical environment is safer and more secure than it's ever been in history. If you reside in the United States of America, you live in the most developed and prosperous nation in the world, and you have access to technology and resources that our grandparents and great grandparents could not imagine a century ago. Although we don't face the same problems that our parents and grandparents faced, we do face challenges as well. The world has become more competitive, and the economy is as vulnerable as it's ever been in certain areas. However, as with any situation, the determining factor will be the attitude with which you choose to look at the reality around you. Giving into fear means giving excessive attention to the negative, which conjures up the adverse circumstances that we dread. If you go the opposite way by developing a fearless approach to life, attacking every challenge with boldness and energy, then you will create a far different dynamic. What you must understand is that we as humans are all afraid. We are afraid of taking bold action, standing out from the crowd, stirring up conflict, and offending people.

Through thousands of years of evolution, our relationship to fear has evolved from a primitive fear of nature to a type of generalized anxiety which is connected to the fearful attitude that now dominates us. To achieve something great—to go beyond that which you have already succeeded or mastered—you must overcome this downward trend and evolve beyond your fears.

As with fear, doubt is a self-limiting emotion that restricts and limits your actions. When you doubt your abilities, you create the same self-fulfilling cycle that fear creates. You see, doubting yourself and your abilities is the quickest way to guarantee failure. When you let go of doubt, you will at the same time alleviate the fear that caused you to doubt yourself in the first place. To succeed, you must let go of your doubts and confront your fears, and you must do this over and over— each time you face a new challenge. Do not seek to avoid the situations that cause you anxiety; that will only cause you to doubt yourself more and further amplify your fear. Understand that you cannot opt for everything to be safe and comfortable in your life and expect to achieve any type of breakthrough. You will find it extremely difficult to accomplish something as significant as permanently transforming the way you look and feel, while adding years to your life, if you always seek comfort. The reality is that lifting weights is painful, running on the treadmill or at the park is challenging, and shopping for fresh food and then preparing almost everything you eat from scratch is time consuming and requires planning.

Life in the twenty-first century affords us a relatively comfortable way of living. There is a restaurant and grocery store within a short driving distance from our homes. We do not have to climb mountains or pass over rough terrain to obtain food. We simply get in a car and arrive at our destination. No energy expended, no predators to watch out for, no terrain to overcome. Our environment is not pressing on us with obvious dangers, violence, or limitations to our movement and mobility. In such an environment, our main goal then becomes to maintain the security and comfort we have, which makes us become more sensitive to even the slightest risk or threat to the status quo. However, when you find it easier to tolerate feelings of fear, you will live outside this passive mode that limits and restricts most people.

Once you accept fear as a normal element of your existence, and not something to escape from or avoid feeling, you will find an inner strength that will surprise you. Facing a natural disaster, a death of a relative or someone else close to us, or losing something you value will not be so bad as you had feared. Like our ancient ancestors who faced their fears daily, whether it was escaping predators or dealing with the elements and other dangers of their immediate environment, you must also confront your fears repeatedly if you want to succeed.

By accepting fear as just another part of accomplishment, you will desensitize yourself to the emotion of fear. Succeeding does not mean becoming fearless, which is not possible as fear will always be present in some shape or form. Rather, succeeding means that you have learned how to channel your inner doubts and fears by moving away from the negative and toward the positive.

Understand: No one is born without fear. It is not natural or normal to not feel fear. It's a process that requires tests and challenges. What separates people who go under from those who rise above their current circumstance is their willpower and their hunger for achievement. Eventually, when you put yourself in an offensive position to overcome your fears, as opposed to staying in a defensive position, you develop a fearless attitude. You learn the value of being unafraid and attacking every situation with a sense of urgency and boldness. You will see the great power this type of attitude brings and it will become your dominant mindset. When we think of fearless types in history, we think of men like Napoleon Bonaparte. Napoleon represented the classic fearless type.

Beginning his career in the military just as the French Revolution began, Napoleon faced constant challenges and dangers on the battlefield as a new type of warfare was emerging. One wrong move would have led him to the executioner's axe. He emerged from the war with a fearless spirit by welcoming the chaos of the times and the vast changes happening in the art of war. In the spring of 1800, Napoleon was preparing to lead an army into Italy, but his field generals warned him to wait as the Alps were not passable at that time of year. Napoleon knew that waiting would ruin the chances of success, so the general replied to them, "For Napoleon's Army, there should be no Alps." Napoleon proceeded to personally lead his troops through rough terrain and past numerous obstacles. It was the force of his will that brought his army through the Alps, catching the enemy by surprise and defeating them. There are no Alps and no obstacles that can stand in the way of a person without fears.

The Importance of Positivity

In the same manner that giving in to fear generates a vicious cycle of lowered self-confidence and self-doubt, a negative attitude will squash your chances of succeeding. When you are aware of your subconscious feedback loop and the importance of controlling and managing your input, you will automatically develop a more positive attitude and outlook as you will be avoiding the people and things that are sources of negative input. Furthermore, being positive is also a choice, in the same manner as choosing what shoes to wear to work, or what radio station to listen to when you are in your car. Feeding your body nutritious whole foods and reducing your intake of junk and processed foods will certainly have a positive impact on your attitude and mental outlook. Fresh, unprocessed foods, especially organic vegetables and fruits contain powerful plant nutrients that alkalize your blood, detoxify your body, and promote a positive attitude and mental state.

"Garbage in, garbage out." It is a term used to describe that what goes into your body also comes out. Garbage is junk food and processed food, and mental garbage is anything that induces unnecessary and unwanted doubt, anxiety, and fear. A prime example of mental garbage would be the TV news. As you are already aware, the significance of avoiding and minimizing your exposure to television news is vital to reducing negative input through your subconscious feedback loop.

CHAPTER 4: BODY REJUVENATION

Restoring Your Cellular Health

Cells make up every unit and part of our bodies. Cells are the fundamental units of life from which all our organs and tissues are made. Cells are the tiniest organisms living in your body and are constantly communicating with each other. If your cells are not operating efficiently, the functioning of your tissues and organs becomes weakened or compromised—resulting in a decline in physical and mental capability which then opens the path to disease and numerous adverse health conditions. Ensuring that your cells are properly nourished will ensure a lower risk of disease and other health conditions. The most important role your cells play is keeping your DNA safe from damage and supplying energy for everything you do throughout the day and while you are sleeping.

You see, DNA is stored within your cells in the nucleus, and your cell ensures that your DNA stays safe as long as you are supplying your body with the right nutrients. Research has shown that a poor diet low in nutrients and antioxidants—as well as excessive exposure to toxins such as pesticides—causes your DNA to become damaged. This DNA damage is known as mutation, and it affects the ability of your cells to function properly by reducing the integrity and energy production of the cell. In other words, excessive DNA damage leads to cell death, and cell death leads to disease and illness. Inflammation is the most common effect of cell death and can show up as cancer many years later. By eating nutritious, antioxidant-filled foods, and a wholesome diet as outlined in the Fit Body 4 Life 21-Day Meal Plan, you will naturally optimize the integrity and health of your cells, which will lead to rapid fat loss and higher energy levels.

Our bodies are made up of trillions of cells (about 37 trillion) and every day, thousands of new cells are created from old cells. When you feed your body with the right nutrients, you also feed your cells with the raw materials needed for the creation of new cells. "You are what you eat" is a phrase that I like to use when speaking to new clients about the importance of diet, and it's one hundred percent accurate. Feed your body in a manner that is consistent with its design—meaning plenty of unprocessed whole foods rich in vitamins, minerals, essential fats, protein, and fiber—and you become healthy, energized, strong, and ready to tackle any challenge life throws at you. On the other hand, feed your body with nutrient-void foods and empty calories that contain simple carbohydrates, sugar, omega 6 fats, pesticides, artificial food additives, preservatives, and other man-made ingredients, and your health and energy levels plummet. Achieving long-term, sustainable fat loss results is dependent on a diet that is consistently rich in nutrients that support weight loss along with health-boosting antioxidants and vitamins.

While each cell in your body varies in size and shape, all cells contain similar components that carry out specific functions. At the microscopic level, three components are involved in the function of your cells. They are:

- **The cellular membrane**
- **The nucleus**
- **The mitochondria**

Understanding how nutrition affects and influences the function and structure of these three cell components will allow you to better appreciate how the food that you are eating helps to promote the integrity of your cells, and ultimately your overall health, longevity, and well-being.

Cellular Nutrition

Overall, there are about fifty food-based nutrients needed for optimal cell health. Eating the foods outlined in the nutrition plan and choosing foods from the best protein, healthy fats, and carbohydrate foods section in this book will ensure that you get adequate amounts of these nutrients day in and day out.

Water-Soluble Vitamins:

Biotin

Vitamin C

Folic Acid

Vitamin B1 (thiamin)

Vitamin B2 (riboflavin)

Vitamin B3 (niacin)

Vitamin B5 (pantothenic acid)

Vitamin B6 (pyridoxine)

Vitamin B12 (cyanocobalamin)

Fat-Soluble Vitamins:

Vitamin A (Retinol)

Vitamin D

Vitamin E

Vitamin K

Minerals:

Magnesium

Sodium

Potassium

Chlorine

Phosphorus

Calcium

Trace Minerals:

Arsenic

Cobalt

Copper

Chromium

Fluoride

Manganese

Leucine

Histidine

Isoleucine

Methionine

Lysine

Phenylalanine

Threonine

Valine

Essential Fatty Acids:

Linoleic Acid

Alpha-linoleic Acid

Arachidonic Acid

Essential Amino Acids:

Arginine

Leucine

Histidine

Isoleucine

Methionine

Lysine

Phenylalanine

Threonine

Tryptophan

Valine

The best way to ensure that your cells are getting ample amounts of the above nutrients, amino acids, and minerals is to eat a diet rich in whole foods. While dietary supplements can certainly help with boosting your intake of these essential nutrients and they will be discussed later, they are *not* to be used as a sole or primary source of nutrition. Your cells require a full spectrum of vitamins from food, especially B-Vitamins, to support energy production and to keep free radical levels to a minimum. In addition to needing ample B-Vitamins, your cells also need ample amino acids from protein and omega 3 fatty acids. Finally, your cells need high amounts of antioxidants such as vitamins C, E, and D to protect your DNA against free radical damage which leads to mutation. There are other plant nutrients, known as phytonutrients, which help protect your DNA against free radical damage. These include compounds known as anthocyanidins and catechins found in grape skins, grapes, and green tea.

Not eating a wide variety of vegetables, protein, and healthy fats will make your cells more susceptible to developing holes, known as leaky cells. Leaky cells are not able to function properly and protect you from DNA damage, which can lead to cancerous cells. Damage to your cells' energy-producing machinery leads to an increase in free radical production, which destroys your cells' ability to function properly.

The outer envelope that encloses a cell is known as the cellular membrane. The cell membrane is the structural boundary that encloses every one of your cells and keeps their internal workings safe. The cell membrane also serves as a type of filter where nutrients can enter and waste by-products can exit. Finally, the cell membrane allows your cells to communicate with each other, which is what allows you to carry out normal, everyday functions.

Next up is the cell nucleus, which is responsible for gene expression and the coronation of genes, specifically protein synthesis and cell growth. The nucleus is also responsible for regulating the integrity of the cell and it contains all the genetic material that makes up the cell, which would be your DNA, your chromosomes, and other genetic material. Last, but not least, the cell mitochondria are responsible for producing ATP (adenosine triphosphate). ATP is the main energy molecule used by the cell and is often referred to as the "cell powerhouse." Optimal ATP production is necessary in order to perform everyday tasks, especially exercise and other strenuous activities. Your cell mitochondria produce ATP through a process known as cellular respiration or aerobic respiration, which uses oxygen through a process known as the citric or Krebs cycle.

Understand: the more functional mitochondria that you have in your cells, the greater your durability, longevity, and overall health will ultimately be. A growing number of biologists support the theory that the number of mitochondria you produce—and their function—determine human longevity. Unfortunately, as we get older, our mitochondria degrade and become dysfunctional, and dysfunctional mitochondria is what leads to aging, looking and feeling old, and ultimately, death. With the right combination of simple lifestyle modifications and the avoidance of toxic elements that lead to mitochondria destruction, you can dramatically improve your quality of life, energy levels, and your lifespan by way of boosting your body's mitochondria production, known as mitochondrial biogenesis.

A compound called pyrroloquinoline quinone, or PQQ, is emerging as a powerful nutrient that boosts your mitochondria production. Plant foods such as kiwi, papaya, green peppers, parsley, tofu, and other plant foods are excellent sources of PQQ. PQQ can also be obtained through dietary supplements, which can further boost mitochondrial biogenesis. Refer to the supplements section for more on PQQ and optimal supplementation dosage.

Apart from consuming an antioxidant-rich diet high in plant foods and exercising consistently, you can boost your mitochondria production even further by calorie restriction. Do not mistake calorie restriction for starvation. Calorie restriction does *not* mean eliminating the foods that you need to lose body fat and the foods that speed up your metabolism and keep you healthy. Rather, calorie restriction is a way of eating where you eliminate foods and drinks that *interfere* with or suppress fat burning. More specifically, foods that interfere with fat burning are generally high in unnatural (man-made) fats and empty calories (sugar, refined white flour, etc.). I cannot overstress the importance of staying away from empty calorie foods *most* of the time while on your transformation journey. You can certainly indulge in your favorite sweet treats or salty carbohydrate and fat-rich dishes occasionally, about once or twice a week depending on your goal and how fast you're making progress, but you absolutely must *limit* your consumption of empty calorie foods at all other times if you are serious about transforming your body and health and maintaining it for life. If you are having a difficult time eliminating empty calorie foods from your diet, refer to the section on intermittent fasting.

Realize that once you've attained your desired weight, health and looks, you can gradually re-incorporate some of the foods you've been avoiding while on the Fit Body 4 Life 21-Day Meal Plan or if you are following your own low carb-high healthy fats whole-food meal plan. What you'll find by the end of your transformation is that your cravings for sweets and other foods will diminish significantly. Remember, sugar is *eight times* more addictive than the drug cocaine. The more refined sugar (the crystalized white stuff added to almost every processed food) you eat, the more sugar you will crave. While on the Fit Body 4 Life 21-Day Meal Plan, you will be eliminating added sugar from your diet and your cravings for sweets will vanish, while portion control will become much, much easier.

Optimizing Your Hormones

As with our mitochondria, our hormones gradually decline with age. Maintaining optimal hormone levels and boosting your body's production of fat-burning and muscle-building hormones is an essential step toward looking and feeling younger, losing stubborn belly fat and slowing down the aging process. Your endocrine system consists of a group of glands that regulate numerous bodily functions by secreting and producing hormones. In essence, hormones serve as messengers which coordinate and control bodily functions and activities. When it reaches a targeted site, a hormone binds to a receptor, much like a key fits into a lock. Once the hormone binds onto its receptor, it transmits a message that causes the targeted site to take a specific action. A hormone receptor may be located within the nucleolus or on the surface of a cell.

Ultimately, hormones control the function of entire organs in your body, affecting various processes such as growth and development as well as sexual characteristics and reproduction. Hormones also influence the way your body uses and stores the calories you consume and control the volume of fluid and the levels of salts and sugar or glucose in your blood. Simply put, very small amounts of hormones can trigger very large and dramatic responses in your body.

Although hormones circulate throughout the body, each type of hormone influences only certain organs and tissues. Some hormones affect only one or two organs, while others have influence throughout your entire body. For example, the thyroid-stimulating hormone produced in the pituitary gland affects only the thyroid gland. In contrast, the thyroid hormone produced in the thyroid gland affects cells throughout the body and is involved in important functions such as regulating the growth of cells, controlling heart rate, and affecting the speed at which calories are burned. Insulin, secreted by the islet cells of the pancreas, affects the processing or metabolism of glucose, protein, and fat throughout the body.

Most hormones are derived from proteins. Others are steroids, which are fatty substances derived from cholesterol that your body produces. The most important hormone for age reversal and the maintenance of a youthful appearance is human growth hormone, known as HGH. Unfortunately, HGH is associated with cheating and steroid use in sports and gets a bad reputation for this association.

You see, growth hormone is a vital hormone that has some important benefits when it comes to your health and fitness. It's responsible for raising your body's natural testosterone levels and speeding up the rate at which your body burns off fat, especially belly fat. When it comes to burning stubborn belly fat and building a lean, attractive body that gets noticed, growth hormone is *the* hormone you want coursing through your blood in ample amounts.

Unlike natural growth hormone which your body produces on its own in the pituitary gland, synthetic growth hormone, known as HGH, must be administered externally through injection and can be very expensive to use on a regular basis. The great news is that unless you have a growth hormone deficiency—which is very rare—you do not have to supplement with expensive HGH to see and feel the benefits of this powerful hormone when it's optimized. Unfortunately, your growth hormone levels naturally decline as you age, starting at around twenty-five and accelerating once you reach thirty-five, at which point you enter a state called somatopause. In general, most men lose about fourteen percent of their GH production each decade and others by up to fifty percent every seven years. According to a study in the *Indian Journal of Endocrinology and Metabolism*, by the time a man reaches sixty-five, he generally secretes less than one-third the amount of GH compared to when he was thirty-five.

In adolescence, GH is responsible for helping kids grow taller. As an adult, maintaining healthy growth hormone levels keeps you healthy physiologically by providing you with an overall sense of well-being and keeping you engaged and happy. Physically, growth hormone keeps your heart healthy, your cholesterol levels stable, and your bones solid, along with controlling inflammation and boosting your body's ability to heal faster from injuries. When it comes to body transformation, growth hormone is potent at shedding belly fat, increasing lean muscle tissue and strength, metabolizing fat and protein, and synthesizing amino acids.

You see, growth hormone stimulates the release of IGF-1, which is the primary driver of tissue growth. Together, IGF-1 and GH help you burn more fat and build more lean muscle. You can maintain optimal growth hormone levels as you age by maintaining a primarily whole-foods based diet, keeping your stress levels low and under control, and avoiding excessive alcohol.

Here are some additional ways to increase your growth hormone levels and maintain them as you age:

Get at Least Seven Hours of Sleep Every Night

When you sleep, your pituitary gland makes GH and secretes it into six to twelve bursts per twenty-four-hour cycle. While this production is influenced by various factors, sleep is one of the biggest requirements for GH secretion. During sleep, your body's growth hormone levels are higher than any other time of day or night and tend to peak between eleven p.m. to two a.m. Not getting enough sleep consistently and interrupted sleep interferes with your body's ability to secrete GH. Improve the quality of your sleep by avoiding caffeine at least four to five hours before bedtime, turning off the TV and computer at least an hour before going to sleep, and avoiding heavy meals at least three hours before going to bed.

Supplement with Arginine

The amino acid Arginine, known as L-Arginine, has been shown to stimulate the release of GH when taken in high doses. While you will get plenty of arginine in your diet by eating protein-rich foods, supplementing with L-Arginine will ensure that you are providing your body with sufficient amounts of this GH stimulating amino acid. Interestingly, one study found that individuals who combined Arginine along with exercise did not get a boost in growth hormone, while another study found that Arginine supplementation without exercise caused a significant increase in growth hormone production. To benefit from Arginine supplementation, take it only on days when you do not exercise, and take at least three to four grams at one time, with at least one serving thirty to sixty minutes before bed.

Exercise

The absolute best way to boost your body's natural GH levels is to work out. While weight training is important to building lean muscle and maintaining a fast metabolism, high intensity interval (HIT) exercise has been shown to provide a superior boost of growth hormone compared to any other forms of exercise. Repeated sessions of aerobic or cardio sessions in a twenty-four-hour period have been shown to provide the highest boost in GH levels. Due to its demand on your metabolism and increase in lactic acid, high-intensity exercise increases HGH the most. You can perform interval training, sprints, weight training, or circuit training to spike your natural growth hormone levels and maximize your fat burning.

Do Intermittent Fasting

As outlined in the chapter on Intermittent Fasting, the benefits of fasting are numerous and go beyond just weight loss. Not only will you burn a lot of fat in a short amount of time while re-setting your metabolism when intermittent fasting, your growth hormone levels will get a nice boost when you avoid eating until lunch time or later. One study found that three days into a fast, growth hormone levels increased by over 300%. After one week of fasting, they had increased by an astounding 1,250%. Other studies found similar effects, with double and triple growth hormone levels after just two to three days of fasting. If you aren't doing intermittent fasting, delaying your first meal for a few hours after you wake up will elevate your growth hormone levels just as effectively. Go at least ten hours without eating from the night before until you wake up the next day. Shorter fasts have also been shown to benefit growth hormone production.

Avoid Added Sugar & Refined Flour Foods

Added sugar in the form of cane sugar, corn syrup, high fructose corn syrup, evaporated cane sugar, and other added sugars increases your insulin levels, and insulin lowers growth hormone production. Refined flour products also raise your insulin levels, and therefore need to be avoided most of the time as they are just like added sugar, adding empty calories to your diet which leads to dangerous insulin spikes and less growth hormone production. Refined flour foods are products that are made up of enriched and bleached white flour such as white bread, toast, muffins, bagels, cupcakes, cakes, and other pastry foods. One study found that healthy non-diabetic individuals had three to four times higher HGH levels than diabetics, who have impaired carb tolerance and insulin function. Of course, the occasional sweet treat containing added sugar or made up of white refined flour will not inhibit your growth hormone production if you avoid eating them on most days.

In addition to supplementing with Arginine on non-workout days, try Glutamine, Creatine and Melatonin to further increase growth hormone levels.

Glutamine:

Studies have shown that a single two-gram dose of the amino acid Glutamine can boost your growth hormone levels in the short term. Glutamine can be taken at any time of the day but is best taken after a workout, as it can assist with workout recovery by speeding up the removal of lactic acid from your bloodstream.

Creatine:

Creatine is a safe, natural supplement that not only increases muscle mass and strength but has also been shown to protect your brain against neurological disease, in addition to boosting your body's growth hormone production temporarily. Supplementing with twenty grams of creatine per day has been shown to significantly increase growth hormone levels for up to six hours. A serving of creatine is about five grams, and anything over this amount taken at one time can cause an upset stomach.

To benefit from creatine's growth hormone boosting effects without upsetting your stomach, start with a smaller dose and gradually build up to until you're taking twenty grams of creatine per day. If you've never taken creatine before, start with a five-gram dose once a day thirty to sixty minutes before a workout. After about a week, take another five-gram serving immediately after your workouts. During week three, take one serving of creatine first thing in the morning, either before or after your first meal, and double the serving size of your pre-workout creatine to ten grams until you're taking a total of twenty grams of creatine per day.

Melatonin:

Melatonin is a hormone that your brain produces naturally. It plays an important role in sleep and blood pressure regulation and it's safe to consume in small amounts in supplement form. Supplementing with melatonin can increase both the quality and duration of your sleep along with boosting your growth hormone levels. To benefit from melatonin's sleep-improving and growth-hormone-boosting effects, take a single serving of melatonin (one to five milligrams) around thirty minutes before bed. Start with a lower dose first to assess your tolerance, then increase the dose if needed. While melatonin is a safe and non-toxic supplement, it may alter brain function in some users. See a qualified doctor or natural health practitioner before supplementing with melatonin.

The Importance of Testosterone

When it comes to hormones, testosterone is considered the king hormone. In males, testosterone is produced mainly in the testicles. In women, testosterone is produced in the ovaries, although in much smaller amounts. Testosterone production in the body begins significantly increasing in the late teens and starts to decline after the age of thirty. Testosterone is the primary sex hormone, and it has a huge effect on your muscle mass and bone density, body fat levels, mood, and red-blood cell production.

Low testosterone levels in men can cause a wide variety of symptoms including weight gain, low sex drive, low energy, depression, and low self-esteem. While testosterone levels naturally decline as you age, there are multiple ways you can boost your testosterone levels to maintain optimal levels of this critical hormone. If you think you may be suffering from low testosterone levels, I highly suggest a simple blood test to measure your levels. The normal range for men is between 250 and 1100ng/dL for adults, and between 8 and 60 ng/dL for females. Low levels of testosterone could be a sign of pituitary gland issues. The pituitary gland sends a signaling hormone to the testicles to produce more testosterone. Low testosterone levels could be an indicator that your pituitary gland is not working properly. If you are a male over thirty and you have been experiencing symptoms of low-T for an extended period, I recommend going to see your doctor for a blood test. While testosterone levels start to decline after the age of thirty in men, be aware that there are symptoms, conditions, and certain medical treatments that have a negative impact on your testosterone levels. Cancer treatments, chronic stress, AIDS, kidney disease, and alcoholism all have a negative effect on testosterone levels. Unusually high testosterone levels could be a sign of adrenal gland disorder or testicular cancer.

If your testosterone levels fall above 1100ng/dL, ask your doctor for an adrenal gland test and a testicular cancer test.

As with increasing your growth hormone levels, boosting your natural testosterone levels and maintaining adequate levels comes down to a diet made up of mostly whole foods, while avoiding processed and refined foods. Regular exercise and adequate sleep also play an important role in maintaining normal to high testosterone levels. When it comes to boosting testosterone levels for men, there are many myths floating around and supposed "shortcuts" that promise a boost in testosterone. Apart from adhering to a consistent diet rich in nutrient-dense whole foods, regular exercise, and adequate sleep, the only substance that can significantly raise your T levels are androgens, also known as anabolic steroids. If you are a male over fifty-five, are exercising regularly, and are eating an adequate diet but are experiencing low T and the symptoms that come with low levels, such as depression, low self-confidence, low sex drive, fatigue, difficulty concentrating, less frequent erections, and difficulty sustaining erections, ask your doctor about testosterone replacement therapy after getting a blood test.

Total & Free Testosterone

If you get your testosterone levels tested, you will get a variety of different numbers. These are total testosterone, bioavailable, and free testosterone. Knowing what these numbers mean is important to optimizing your T levels, and then taking the appropriate steps to restoring your levels. Most of the time, testosterone binds to something called SHBG, short for sex hormone binding globulin. Less frequently, testosterone binds to something called albumin. Free testosterone is all on its own and does not bind to anything.

About sixty-five percent of the testosterone in your blood binds to SHBG, with most of the remaining binding to albumin and about two percent remains free. Total testosterone represents all the testosterone available in your body in any state. Only bioavailable testosterone, which is free testosterone, and albumin-bound testosterone are important when it comes to achieving optimal testosterone levels. If you are a female, low testosterone levels can lead to some of the same symptoms of low T that men experience, including a low sex drive, depressed mood, muscle weakness, and lethargy. There are many doctors who are researching low testosterone in women and treatments for low testosterone. However, new treatments are being studied that may provide help to women affected by low testosterone levels. As with men, a blood test for testosterone will measure a woman's testosterone levels.

According to the Boston University School of Medicine, if a woman's plasma total testosterone level is less than 25 ng/dL in women under fifty years old, it is considered low. Testosterone levels lower than 20 ng/dL in women aged fifty and older are considered low. Doctors may have difficulty detecting low testosterone levels in women because female hormone levels constantly fluctuate from day to day. Women still on their period should have their blood testosterone levels tested about eight to twenty days after the menstrual period starts.

Because the ovaries are a major producer of testosterone, the drop-in hormones produced by the ovaries associated with menopause means that some pre- and post-menopausal women may experience low testosterone levels. Normally, a decline in libido has been linked to post-menopausal drops in estrogen. However, researchers are identifying more and more links between decreased testosterone production and affected libido.

In many women, the ovaries continue to produce hormones like testosterone. Therefore, doctors suggest that some women with low testosterone may have something in their genetic makeup that affects their ability to produce the compounds DHEA and DHEA-S, which are the precursors to testosterone. Some women may also be deficient in enzymes that process DHEA and DHEA-S into testosterone. Treatments for low testosterone in women have not been studied on a large scale by medical experts. While doctors are aware of the effects of excess testosterone in women, the symptoms of inadequate testosterone are not as well known. As a result, doctors do not always have the same regimen for treatments related to low testosterone levels.

Speak with your doctor after getting a testosterone blood test to determine the best route of action if you are a female experiencing low T levels. You doctor can administer small amounts of testosterone injections or prescribe an over the counter DHEA supplement. In the body, DHEA is a precursor to testosterone and could increase the amount of testosterone a woman's body produces.

When to Consider a Testosterone Level Test

If you're experiencing the following symptoms on a consistent basis, meaning they're present daily, and you've been experiencing them for more than a few weeks despite adhering to a nutrient-rich diet high in antioxidants and low in processed foods and you are getting adequate sleep, go see your doctor for a testosterone level blood test.

Note: Certain medical conditions, medications, and some medical treatments can cause testosterone levels to drop. Opiates, barbiturates, androgen or estrogen therapies, and anti-convulsants can cause significant drops in testosterone. Apart from these medications, other causes of low T are cancer treatments, liver problems, being more than thirty to forty pounds overweight and excessive alcohol consumption.

Low Testosterone Symptoms (in Men)

Little interest in sex (low libido)

Unable to sustain or get an erection

Depression

Lethargy, weakness & overall low energy levels

Inability to concentrate

Low motivation

Unexpected weight gain

Hair loss

Decreased strength during exercise

Signs of gynecomastia (an abnormal increase in breast tissue size)

Low Testosterone Symptoms (in Women)

Fatigue

Depression

Declining muscle and bone mass

Difficulty concentrating

Weight gain

Painful intercourse

Your doctor will typically perform the blood test in the morning, as testosterone levels are highest in the a.m. The most common treatment for low testosterone for men over forty is TRT, or testosterone replacement therapy. Thanks to a loophole in FDA regulations, pharmaceutical company marketers can urge men to talk with their doctors if they have any possible signs of low T through direct to consumer advertising on TV, in magazines and on the internet. If your testosterone levels fall way below normal range, and not just slightly or a little below range, TRT is probably a viable and ideal option for you. However, if your T levels are only slightly below normal, and the only symptoms of a possible T deficiency you're experiencing are low energy levels and occasional low libido, I would not suggest undergoing TRT as these symptoms are normal in aging men and not a cause for concern.

In men, testosterone levels decline after the age of forty by about one percent every year. On the opposite side, having abnormally elevated testosterone levels can be an indicator of serious medical conditions. Abnormally high T levels can be a sign of ovarian cancer in women and testicular cancer in men.

If after getting your testosterone levels checked, you find that your T levels are in a normal range, or slightly below normal and you would like to boost your T levels without TRT, I recommend trying any of the following natural testosterone boosting methods. Note that the following methods and supplements will only be effective if you follow a whole-foods-based diet and adhere to a consistent exercise routine along with getting adequate rest and sleep.

How to Boost Your Testosterone Levels

Reduce Your Stress Levels:

In today's fast-paced, hurried society, reducing your stress levels can be easier said than done. We worry about our jobs and children and we stress over finances and relationships. Research has shown that being chronically stressed out increases your cortisol levels. Cortisol is a stress hormone that your body releases in small amounts during the day in response to different stimuli. However, chronically elevated cortisol levels can quickly cause your testosterone levels to plummet. Testosterone and cortisol levels tend to seesaw, when one goes up the other one comes down. When you are stressed out, you crave more food due to your cortisol levels being elevated, which in turn will cause you to gain weight. Weight gain from elevated cortisol causes abdominal fat accumulation known as visceral fat, which is the fat that surrounds your vital organs.

Visceral fat is the most dangerous fat to carry as it not only reduces your testosterone levels, but it significantly elevates your risk of developing heart disease and diabetes and raises your LDL, the bad cholesterol. Whenever possible, eliminate stressful situations and people from your life. If you cannot eliminate stress at work, ensure your diet is very low in refined carbohydrates and sugar. Empty carbs and sugar increase cortisol production (cortisol is a stress hormone). Following the Fit Body 4 Life 21-Day Meal Plan will ensure you are not consuming added sugar and getting ample vitamins and minerals that help reduce the effects of stress. If your job causes you lots of stress, I recommend you supplement with a high-quality B vitamin complex product. B vitamins can help reduce stress by balancing neurotransmitters in your brain. Vitamins B6, B12, B9, B3 and B1 are crucial to keeping your nervous system healthy.

Get Plenty of Sunshine (Vitamin D):

Vitamin D is known as the sunshine vitamin. Along with having numerous health benefits including helping with weight loss, it may also work as a natural testosterone booster according to a study done by German researchers. Ideally, you will want to get at least twenty minutes of sun exposure per day to optimize your body's Vitamin D levels. If you live in the far north in a climate without much regular direct sunshine and getting daily sun exposure is not realistic for you, I highly recommend that you supplement with a quality Vitamin D product.

Sadly, almost half of the US population is deficient in Vitamin D, and an even higher percentage of US adults lack sufficient levels of this critical vitamin. To ensure your blood vitamin D levels are where they need to be for testosterone boosting and health, supplement with at least 3,000 IU of Vitamin D per day.

Minimize Your Exposure to Estrogen-Like Compounds:

Estrogen is a hormone that reduces the amount of free testosterone available in your body. Being exposed to products that contain estrogen-like compounds has been shown to lower your testosterone levels. Estrogen-like compounds come from BPA, parabens, and other chemicals found mostly in plastic containers and packaging. These chemicals seep their way into your food and get absorbed directly into your bloodstream with food. To minimize your exposure to estrogen-like compounds, do not cook your food in plastic containers and don't re-use plastic water bottles and gallons. For example, if you are re-heating food that you stored in a plastic container, do not re-heat it inside a plastic lunch box or storage container.

Remove all food from the plastic lunch box or container and use a paper plate or china ware when using a microwave. I recommend avoiding microwaves altogether when cooking and re-heating food as there is strong evidence that shows eating microwaved food causes food molecules to mutate and become carcinogenic, which can lead to cancer. What's more, microwaving food has also been shown to dramatically reduce the nutrient content of vegetables and other foods.

Avoid Excessive Alcohol:

While small to moderate amounts of alcohol consumption has been shown to have a positive impact on your health and longevity, heavy alcohol consumption can suppress your body's natural testosterone levels. If you drink alcoholic beverages often, limit your alcohol consumption to one to two drinks per day. Even better, cut alcohol from your daily diet and only have it once or twice a week. Keep in mind that all alcoholic beverages have calories, so limiting your consumption will only accelerate fat loss.

Don't Shy Away from Meat, Eggs and Butter:

Meat, especially red meat, if it's one of the leaner varieties such as sirloin, top round, or London broil, is an excellent testosterone booster. This is because red meat is rich in cholesterol, and cholesterol is a direct precursor to testosterone in your body. As with any other food, it's important to choose only the highest quality meat you can find at the grocery store; this means grass fed is a must and organic if possible. Regular or conventional beef does not have the same health benefits as grass-fed beef due to the difference in feed between feed-lot cows and pasture or grass-fed cows. Just like lean red meat, eggs are an excellent source of saturated fat and cholesterol which help boost your natural testosterone levels. Go with grass-fed butter and organic cage-free eggs. The way you prepare beef and eggs will either contribute to their positive effects on your health or diminish their health benefits. Avoid frying eggs, even in olive oil as frying adds extra fat calories that you don't need. The same goes for grass-fed beef. Trim as much visible fat as possible before cooking, and grill, broil, or roast beef at a medium heat. Avoid adding any oils or high calorie sauces to the pan. Even the leanest beef will release some of its fat during cooking, which ends up at the bottom of the pan and gets re-absorbed into the meat.

Supplement with Fenugreek:

Fenugreek is a plant that's been used in alternative and Chinese medicine to treat various health conditions. Fenugreek is a plant that grows in the forest with pods that contain small brown-golden fenugreek seeds. It's commonly used as a spice and sometimes found in personal-care products such as shampoo and soap. Fenugreek is a good source of several important nutrients, but its beneficial effects are used primarily for testosterone- and libido-boosting purposes. In one study, researchers provided 500 mg of fenugreek per day to thirty college-aged men. The men combined fenugreek with an eight-week weight-lifting program and performed four training sessions per week, with half of them receiving the supplement. When researchers compared the fenugreek-supplement group to the non-supplement group, they noted a slight decline in testosterone in the non-supplement group and an increase in testosterone in the fenugreek group. The fenugreek-supplement group also experienced a two percent reduction in body fat.

In another study lasting six weeks, researchers provided thirty men with 600 mg of fenugreek per day to monitor changes in sexual function and libido. What they found is that most participants saw an increase in strength and improved sexual function. While more research is still needed on the effects of fenugreek supplementation and testosterone levels, the research that's already been performed looks very promising. When combined with a sound whole-foods diet along with the aforementioned testosterone-optimizing steps, fenugreek has a lot of potential to help further boost your testosterone levels. Take 500-700mg of fenugreek extract once a day before or with a meal. Although fenugreek is safe to take in small amounts in supplement form, you may experience side effects with higher doses. You can increase the dose to 900mg-1000mg once a day if you do not experience any side effects during the first two to three weeks of supplementation at 500mg to 700mg daily.

Supplement with D-Aspartic Acid (D-AA):

D-Aspartic Acid or D-AA, is an amino acid that research has demonstrated to have impressive testosterone-boosting effects. Studies have found that D-AA, in supplement form, increased testosterone and luteinizing hormone in just twelve days. Luteinizing hormone or LH, is a hormone that is responsible for controlling testosterone levels in men. A study from the University of Naples in Italy found that testosterone levels increased about forty percent in men given approximately three grams of D-AA for twelve days, compared to a placebo (fake D-AA). LH increased by twenty-five percent. What's interesting about these findings and what makes D-AA a promising testosterone booster is that the study participants were young males between the ages of twenty-six and thirty-seven, at the peak of testosterone production—not elderly men or men suffering from low testosterone. D-AA is a promising supplement for boosting testosterone; however, more research is needed before it gets a strong recommendation. Consider taking D-Aspartic Acid if your blood levels of testosterone measure below average and you are following all the testosterone-boosting steps already outlined.

Optimal dosing is three to five grams of D-Aspartic Acid per day with breakfast on non-workout days, and thirty to forty-five minutes before training on workout days. While D-Aspartic acid is considered safe to take in the short term, you should not take it for longer than ninety days as it lacks research on long-term safety. If you experience headaches or mood swings or a sudden onset of acne while taking D-AA, lower the dose to one to two grams per day and gradually, over the course of two to three weeks, increase your dose to 3g per day. Unfortunately, many sports and performance enhancement supplement manufacturers use fillers and chemicals to extend the shelf life of their products, and these additives can be responsible for side effects like headaches and even mood swings.

Carefully read the ingredients' list of D-AA supplements when shopping to ensure there are no chemicals or fillers in your D-AA supplement. D-AA capsules usually don't contain any fillers or additives and thus are the best option compared to D-AA powders.

Antioxidants

Antioxidants are truly amazing. They help your body combat everything from the flu to the common cold and cancer by fighting free radicals. Antioxidants are found in many different types of foods, especially vegetables and fruits. Antioxidants come in two different forms: water soluble and fat soluble. Water-soluble antioxidants perform their function in the fluid inside and outside of your cells, whereas fat-soluble antioxidants act primarily in cell membranes.

Here is a list of a few important antioxidants you get through your diet:

Vitamin C

One of the most important water-soluble antioxidants and an essential dietary nutrient, vitamin C is abundant in citrus and tropical fruits such as kiwi, oranges, mandarins, pineapple, apples, mangoes, and berries. Veggies also contain Vitamin C, though most vegetables don't contain as much vitamin C per serving as most fruits. Some veggies that are high in Vitamin C are bell peppers, kale, broccoli, and Brussel sprouts.

Vitamin E

Vitamin E is the main fat-soluble antioxidant that plays an essential role in protecting cell membranes against oxidative damage. Vitamin E is found in spinach, almonds, sunflower seeds, avocados, hazelnuts, peanut butter, and other nut butters.

Flavonoids

A large group of antioxidants are found in plant foods. Flavonoids have many beneficial health effects, including reducing your risk of developing CVD (cardiovascular disease). Eating a wide variety and ample amounts of veggies and fruits daily will ensure that you're providing your body with these essential antioxidants.

Antioxidant Supplements – Should You Take Them?

Again, eating a wide variety of whole, unprocessed foods will ensure that your body is getting all the essential antioxidants it needs to keep your immune system strong and healthy. Therefore, I do not recommend taking antioxidant supplements. The only exception to this would be if you have a genetic or acquired disorder that hinders your body from absorbing important vitamins & minerals. Otherwise, a proper whole foods-based diet will cover all the essentials your body needs to function optimally and burn fat efficiently.

You see, when it comes to antioxidants, more is *not* better. Taking in more antioxidants than your body needs is not only expensive, but it can increase your risk of death according to several research studies. Antioxidant supplements can be very helpful at times when you are not able to eat ample whole foods, and at times when you aren't able to eat much in general due to medical conditions such as being hospitalized or undergoing surgery.

Real foods, not supplements, contain thousands of different micronutrients that work together to keep your body strong and healthy. Taking just one or two isolated antioxidants through supplements will not keep you as healthy or provide the protection against free radicals as a real food diet containing a wide variety of foods.

Reducing Inflammation

Inflammation is not a bad thing. Through inflammation, your body fights off infections, illness, and injury. Inflammation is a natural process that happens in your body in response to stress. However, chronic inflammation that lasts for weeks, months, and even years is a very bad thing.

Chronic inflammation is the driver behind deadly conditions such as diabetes, obesity, heart disease, cancer, and fatty liver disease and must be eliminated in order to lose excess weight and extend your lifespan. Your lifestyle has a huge impact on your inflammation levels. Consuming large amounts of sugar, refined carbohydrates, and other simple carbohydrates, such as corn syrup and high fructose corn syrup, causes inflammation inside your cells.

Processed foods high in vegetable oils such as canola, soybean, safflower, and trans fats are the largest contributors to chronic inflammation and need to be minimized and avoided most of the time. These toxic fats lead to an imbalance in your omega 3 to omega 6 ratio, which promotes inflammation. In addition, eating processed meats and consuming alcohol in excess causes a spike in your body's inflammation levels.

Being inactive and leading a sedentary lifestyle is the biggest non-dietary contributor to inflammation. Moving around often and stretching every few hours is critical to controlling inflammation if your job involves a lot of sitting. After about one and a half to two hours, get up and perform some basic stretches along with walking to the bathroom. This will ensure that your blood circulation remains normal, preventing dangerous clotting.

The Best Anti-Inflammatory Foods:

Avocados

Avocados are packed with potassium, fiber, magnesium and healthy monounsaturated fats that fight inflammation. They also contain carotenoids and tocopherols, which have been shown to reduce your risk of developing cancer. In a recent study, people who ate a few slices of avocado along with a hamburger had lower levels of inflammatory markers in their blood compared to participants who ate the hamburger alone.

Berries

Strawberries, blueberries, raspberries and blackberries are packed with fiber and plant nutrients that fight inflammation and protect your cells from disease. Berries contain antioxidants called anthocyanins which have powerful anti-inflammatory effects that have been shown to reduce the risk of disease.

Extra Virgin Olive Oil

Extra virgin olive oil contains a high amount of heart-healthy monounsaturated fats, making it one of the healthiest foods you can consume. Olive oil's anti-inflammatory properties have been well analyzed in studies. Consuming olive oil often has been linked to a reduced risk of developing cancer and heart disease and other deadly conditions. Olive oil contains an antioxidant compound called oleocanthal, which has been shown to have the same anti-inflammatory effects of drugs like ibuprofen. Be sure to always choose extra virgin olive oil as the anti-inflammatory benefits are much greater compared to refined olive oil.

Dark Chocolate

Not only is dark chocolate delicious and fun to eat, but it has got some awesome health benefits. Unlike milk chocolate, dark chocolate is packed with anti-inflammatory antioxidants thanks to its high cocoa content. When selecting dark chocolate, go with a minimum of seventy percent cocoa content as the higher the cocoa content, the more antioxidants and the less sugar the chocolate will have. Based on an impressive study that analyzed the antioxidant content of more than 3100 foods, dark chocolate was found to have more antioxidants per three and a half ounces than the same serving size of other high antioxidant foods such as berries. What's more, dark chocolate has a powerful effect on lowering your blood pressure. Study participants who ate small to moderate amounts of dark chocolate every week saw their systolic blood pressure (the upper value) drop by an average of 4.5 mmHg and their diastolic blood pressure (the lower value) drop by an average of 2.5 mmHg. To experience the powerful anti-inflammatory and antioxidant health benefits of dark chocolate, eat two to three pieces of dark chocolate at least three to four times a week as part of dessert or a between-meal snack. You can further boost your body's ability to fight inflammation by combining several high-antioxidant foods together in one meal such as raspberries, blueberries, and/or strawberries along with dark chocolate.

Fatty Fish

(Salmon, Sardines, Mackerel): Most types of fish are high in healthy omega-3 fats (EPA and DHA), which fight and eliminate inflammation. EPA and DHA reduce the deadliest form of inflammation that has been linked to heart disease, metabolic syndrome, diabetes, and other serious conditions.

When choosing fish, go with wild salmon, sardines, or mackerel. These fish contain the highest omega 3 fatty acids per serving compared to other fish such as flounder, tuna and herring. Other fish that contain high amounts of anti-inflammatory EPA and DHA are swordfish and orange roughy. Choose wild fish over farmed whenever possible and eat fish at least three times a week to benefit from the inflammation fighting power of DHA and EPA. If you suffer from heart disease or diabetes, I highly suggest you supplement with a daily omega-3 EPA & DHA supplement in addition to eating fatty fish several times a week. This combo along with the other anti-inflammatory foods outlined will have a dramatic effect on improving and eventually reversing your condition.

Green Tea

Green tea ranks right up there with fatty fish and dark chocolate as one of the most antioxidant-packed, anti-inflammatory foods on the planet. Green tea is high in a group of antioxidants called EGCG. EGCG inhibits inflammation by reducing and removing waste by-products in your body. Drink a cup of green tea first thing in the morning before breakfast or your first meal and an additional cup in the afternoon. Avoid drinking green tea close to bedtime as it contains caffeine which will interfere with sleep. Finally, choose the highest-quality green tea you can find as some lower-quality green tea brands have been shown to be high in fluoride.

Artichokes

Artichokes are not a common vegetable but should be as they are high in disease-fighting antioxidants and they pair well with most any salad and other veggies. Artichokes have been used in ancient medicine to fight jaundice, which is a condition that causes deterioration of the liver and yellowing of the skin and eyes. Artichokes are especially rich in the antioxidant known as chlorogenic acid. Studies have shown that the antioxidant and anti-inflammatory benefits of chlorogenic acid may reduce the risk of certain cancers, type 2 diabetes, and heart disease. The antioxidant content of artichokes will vary depending on how they are prepared. Boiling artichokes may raise their antioxidant content by eight times, while steaming them may raise it by fifteen times. Frying artichokes has been shown to reduce their antioxidant content. To boost the antioxidant levels in your blood, toss a head of steamed or boiled artichokes into your salad or eat them as a side item with fish or chicken.

Kale

Kale is a cruciferous vegetable that is in the same family as broccoli and cauliflower. Cruciferous vegetables contain some of the most powerful disease- and cancer-fighting nutrients you can eat. Kale is high in vitamins A, K and C. Red kale is higher in antioxidants than green kale with both varieties being a good source of plant-based calcium, which is critical to bone health and many cellular functions. Add two to three cups of raw kale to your salad, or eat it lightly seasoned and steamed as a side dish to meals that contain meat.

Beets

Beets are a root vegetable known as beetroot. They have a mild, delicate taste and are a good source of potassium, iron, folate, and fiber. Beets are rich in a group of antioxidants called betalains. These give beets their reddish color and have been linked to numerous health benefits including a reduced risk of colon and stomach cancer.

Additionally, beets contain powerful compounds known to suppress inflammation. A study found that taking betalain capsules made from beetroot extract significantly relieved osteoarthritis pain and inflammation. Slice two to three cooked beets into your salad at least twice a week or eat them with other vegetables as part of a veggie platter.

When shopping for beets, unless you're buying raw beets which need to be cooked prior to eating, choose pre-cooked beets that do not have any additional sugar, flavorings, or preservatives added. Cooked beets have a naturally sweet and delicate taste and do not need any added ingredients to make them palatable.

Spinach

Spinach is a very nutrient-dense vegetable that's loaded with vitamins, minerals, and antioxidants that supercharge your immune system. Spinach is a great source of the antioxidants lutein and zeaxanthin, which protect your eyes from damaging UV light and other harmful light waves. These antioxidants help combat damage to the eyes that free radicals may cause over time and help maintain your vision as you age.

Red Cabbage

Also known as purple cabbage, red cabbage has an impressive nutrient profile. Red cabbage is rich in vitamins C, A, and K and has more than four times the number of antioxidants than regular cooked cabbage. This is due to red cabbage containing anthocyanins, a group of antioxidants that give red cabbage its color. Anthocyanins are also found in strawberries and raspberries and have been linked to several awesome health benefits including reduced inflammation and a lower risk of developing heart disease and several cancers.

Note that the way red cabbage is prepared will affect its antioxidant profile. Boiling and stir-frying red cabbage will boost its antioxidant profile, while steaming red cabbage may reduce its antioxidant content by almost thirty-five percent.

Red cabbage makes an excellent side dish to most foods and pairs well with boiled eggs, fish, eggplant, and sweet potatoes.

Goji Berries

Goji berries have been part of traditional Chinese medicine for over two thousand years. They are a dried fruit, part of two related plants called Lycium barbarum and Lycium chinense. Goji berries are considered a superfood as they are rich in several vitamins, minerals, and antioxidants. Based on a FRAP analysis, which measures the antioxidant content in foods, goji berries contain 4.3 mmol of antioxidants per 3.5 ounces or 100 grams.

In addition, goji berries contain unique antioxidants known as Lycium barbarum polysaccharides. These powerful antioxidants have been linked to a reduced risk of heart disease and cancer and may help slow skin aging. One interesting study found that when healthy elderly people drank a milk-based goji berry drink every day for ninety days, their blood antioxidant levels rose by fifty-seven percent.

While goji berries seem very promising when it comes to combating disease and boosting the immune system, more human-based research is needed on goji berries. To boost your blood antioxidant levels, add two to three tablespoons of Goji berries into oatmeal for an energizing pre-workout snack, or eat a handful of goji berries along with fresh fruit and mixed nuts as a between-meal snack.

CHAPTER 5: KEEPING THE FAT OFF

You now have a good understanding of what to eat to improve your cellular and metabolic health with a whole foods-based diet. By simply making the switch to eating whole foods and reducing or eliminating your intake of processed foods, you will re-program your body to burn fat around the clock and keep fat from accumulating. Your cells and metabolism will become supercharged and your body will have no difficulties burning fat. If you are new to exercise, the combination of whole foods and a workout routine will have a dramatic impact on the way you look and feel within just a matter of days. I strongly recommend an exercise routine that involves resistance training, walking at a fast pace or jogging, swimming, or riding a bicycle for just thirty minutes a day, two to three times a week. Exercise releases endorphins in your brain, which are a natural mood booster. Cardiovascular exercise (cardio) will only further enhance your fat burning and your energy levels plus mood when combined with a whole-foods diet.

You will have no problems keeping fat off when you restrict your carbohydrate intake on most days and eat more fat. Lower-carb, higher-fat diets are much easier to stick to because they reduce cravings and are more satisfying. This is because dietary fat gets digested slowly and is very filling, whereas carbs digest quickly and empty out of your system much faster. Not only will you lose weight and keep future weight gain at bay when you eat a lower-carbohydrate, higher-fat whole-foods diet, but you will also prevent and greatly reduce your chances of getting a heart attack, reduce your LDL (bad) cholesterol and boost your HDL (good) cholesterol levels.

Banishing Your Fear of Fat

Unfortunately, most Americans have grown up in an era that equated a low-fat diet with good health and a normal or low weight. Doctors, scientists, nutritionists, and the government have brainwashed us into believing that when you eat fat, it clogs your arteries and gets stored into fat on your body. The reality is that nothing could be further from the truth. These assumptions were based on flawed science which led to a generalized fear of fat, - leading to a big fat health mess. Fat, also known as adipose tissue, accumulates on your body not because you are eating too much fat in your diet, but rather because we've been led to believe that rice, cereal, pasta, potatoes, and bread are better and healthier than butter, meat, eggs, and cheese. When we replaced fat with sugar and carbs, overweight people and obesity skyrocketed. In 1992, the government published its Food Guide Pyramid. At the base of the pyramid were carbs, and we were advised to eat six to eleven servings of rice, bread, pasta, and cereal a day. At the very top of the pyramid were fats and oils, which we were told to consume sparingly.

The food industry jumped on the low-fat bandwagon and created hundreds of low-fat foods from low-fat yogurt to low-fat salad dressings to fat-free desserts. Since we were made to believe foods low in fat were healthy, people ate entire boxes of fat-free cookies and other "healthy" snacks. As we now know, "low-fat" means anything but healthy. The majority of pre-packaged low-fat foods are heavily processed and full of empty calories from sugar and white flour. Thanks to the government's advice in the early 90s, the average American now consumes 152 pounds of sugar and 146 pounds of flour per year. That is a staggering number of empty calories. Almost twenty percent of most people's daily calories come from sugar-laden beverages like soda, tea, juice, and sports drinks.

Liquid sugar is many times worse than other carbohydrates and gets deposited straight into the body's fat tissue. Sugar, especially liquid sugar is biologically addictive, which means it increases your craving for more sugar. This creates a continued, addictive cycle of sugar consumption and, since the body does not recognize liquid calories as food, you end up consuming many more total calories per day than you would from solid food. Sugar-sweetened drinks cause the most damage to your health. In a dramatic study in the journal *Circulation,* researchers attributed 184,000 deaths per year to the consumption of sugary drinks. We now know from research that sugar and refined carbohydrates are the true culprits behind heart disease and obesity—not fats, as we've been told. Only carbohydrates have such a dramatic, negative effect on the hormone insulin, which is responsible for storing and depositing nutrients (carbohydrates) into fat cells. When you simply switch from a high-carbohydrate, low-fat diet to a moderate, or even high-fat, low-carbohydrate diet, wonderful things start to happen. Eating liberal amounts of fatty fish, olive oil, butter, eggs, lean meats and cheese while simultaneously reducing carbs from all sources does wonders for your health and waistline. This is because our bodies were *meant* to function on fat.

You see, dietary fat is high-octane fuel for our bodies, while carbohydrates are low-grade, cheap fuel that does not provide us with the replenishment our bodies need to function at an optimal rate. Over the last few years, scientific evidence has been mounting that high-fat diets outperform low-fat diets for weight loss and for reversing every indicator of heart disease risk from hypertension to inflammation to high cholesterol and diabetes. Joslin Diabetes Center at Harvard, one of the top diabetes centers in the world, was named after Dr. Elliot P. Joslin. In the 1920s he recommended a diet of seventy-five percent fat, twenty percent protein, and five percent carbohydrates to treat diabetes. In the 1950s and 60s, fat became demonized and a low-fat, high-carbohydrate diet (fifty-five to sixty percent carbs) was recommended by scientists and doctors. At that time and for many decades, the American Diabetes Association (ADA) promoted this diet as the diabetes epidemic got worse year after year. Researchers at Joslin Diabetes Center are now once again recommending diets of up to seventy percent fat for treating type 2 diabetes.

Sadly, most Americans are still not getting the message about the importance of fat, and we still have a long way to go. The ADA (American Diabetes Association) is still promoting old and dangerous advice, recommending the avoidance of refined carbs (great advice) but still pushing the low-fat message. This is despite studies finding that people who ate fatty nuts have a lower risk of developing type 2 diabetes, and those who consume a liter of olive oil per week along with nuts daily have a significantly lower risk of suffering heart attacks and death from all causes. The original assumption that all fat, no matter which fatty foods you are eating, causes heart disease was replaced with the idea that only saturated fat is bad and that monounsaturated fats and polyunsaturated fats are good. But new research has revealed that that not all polyunsaturated fats (found in vegetable oils) are as good as they initially appeared to be, and that saturated fat deserves some vindication.

The Truth About Saturated Fats

A comprehensive review in 2014, led by Dr. Rajiv Chowdhury, looked at seventy-two of the best studies on fat and heart disease (more than 600,000 people from eighteen countries) and concluded that there was *no* link between total fat or saturated fat and heart disease. The study also did not support the heavily promoted policy and recommendations to increase polyunsaturated fats (from vegetable oils). However, the study did find that trans fats (hydrogenated oils) increased heart disease and omega 3-fats decreased heart disease. The researchers looked at three different types of studies. They analyzed thirty-two population studies with 512,420 people for dietary habits, seventeen studies with 25,721 people that measured blood levels of different fats, and twenty-seven randomized control trials including 105,085 people, assessing dietary supplements of omega-3 fatty acids.

This was a groundbreaking study that revealed what is truly going on in the fat and heart-disease story. The best part of this study was how it broke down all the different types of saturated fats and polyunsaturated fats and how they impact heart disease. Saturated fats are too often lumped together as one big evil type of fat, which is very incorrect. The truth is that saturated fat comes in many varieties, each having different effects.

There are odd- and even-chain saturated fats and different types of polyunsaturated fats. The fact that these were actually measured in the blood of real people and not just based on dietary recall records (who can remember what they ate for lunch a week ago?) makes these really important to pay attention to. What these blood levels of fatty acids tell us is very insightful. This is where all the nuggets of insight are that explain what's really going on at the root of the cholesterol, fat, saturated fat, and polyunsaturated fat story.

What they found out about saturated fats was truly eye-opening. It's important to know first that there are different types of saturated fats. There is palmitic acid, myristic acid, margaric acid, pentadecanoic acid, lauric acid, and stearic acid. They are classified as even- or odd-chain fatty acids. Some of them are produced in the liver while others come from diet. The types of fats circulating in the blood that were associated with heart disease were even-chain palmitic and stearic acid. You see, most palmitic and steric acids in the body are produced in your liver when you eat carbohydrates; they do not come from eating fat. Carbs and alcohol (a form of sugar)—not saturated fat—trigger high blood levels of palmitic and steric acid. Another interesting finding was that the odd-chain fats that come from butter called margaric acid, showed a reduction in heart-disease risk. Yes, you read that right, butter showed a reduction in heart-disease risk.

Additionally, the study showed no benefit from consuming omega-6 fats in vegetable oils; in fact, it showed that omega-6 fats lead to heart disease. What's more, the study showed that omega-3 fats from supplements and fish were most protective against heart disease, and that an omega-6 fat called arachidonic acid was the only omega-6 found to reduce the risk of heart disease.

Arachidonic acid is not found in vegetable oils, but rather is made by the body and is found in the highest amounts in poultry, beef, and eggs. One of the main authors of the study, Dariush Mozaffarian, from Tufts University, stated, "Current evidence does not clearly support cardiovascular guidelines that encourage high consumption of polyunsaturated fatty acids and low consumption of saturated fats."

To sum up:

- Omega-3 fats from fish are the most protective against heart disease.

- Omega-6 fats from vegetable oils show no health benefits and may increase risk of heart attacks.

- Saturated fats (palmitic acid and steric acid) in your blood that trigger heart attacks come from eating refined carbs and sugar, *not* from ingesting fat.

- Omega-6 fats from eggs, beef, and poultry (arachidonic acid) show to be protective against heart disease.

- Saturated fats (margaric acid) that come from dairy and butter show a reduced risk of heart disease.

In conclusion, most vegetable oils need to be avoided most of the time. Eat more fish, beef, eggs, chicken, and other meats. Just stay away from refined carbs and sugar, and your risk of suffering a heart attack will go down significantly. In addition to this eye-opening study, there have been several studies that unfortunately have been ignored by medical associations and policymakers. In a review of twenty-one studies done on almost 350,000 people over the course of twenty-three years, saturated fat was not shown to be associated with increased risk of heart attacks, stroke, or death. The lead author of this study review, Dr. Ronald Krauss, was formerly the head of the Dietary Guidelines Committee at the American Heart Association. He fought their fervent belief in the dangers of saturated fat and eventually left the association due to his difference of opinion. Dr. Robert

Hoenselaar from the Netherlands found that the "results and conclusions about saturated fat intake in relation to cardiovascular disease, from leading advisory committees, do not reflect the available scientific literature."

A wide range of leading scientists published a review in the journal *Open Heart,* where they went back and reviewed all the randomized controlled trials comparing high and low-fat diets done up to 1983, which is around the same time the government recommended that Americans cut the fat, cholesterol, and saturated fat from their diets. Not even one of these randomized trials showed that reducing saturated fat, cholesterol, and total fat in the diet led to a reduction in heart disease.

What about the link between high saturated fat intake and elevated cholesterol levels? In a review published in 2014, the authors noted that there was very little data showing that eating saturated fats caused high cholesterol. What they discovered was that only in the case of an omega-3 deficiency (which sadly affects more than 90 percent of Americans) do saturated fats cause elevated cholesterol and other health problems. Simply put, when you eat enough omega-3 fats, the effect of saturated fat on your cholesterol levels is either neutral or beneficial. An impressive study published in *Lipids* in 2010 confirmed this conclusion. It compared the effects of a very low-carb, high-fat diet with a high omega-6 or high saturated-fat diet. The researchers examined blood levels of cholesterol, fats and inflammation before and after different dietary changes. The study participants' diets were controlled (the researchers provided all the food). When they then measured blood levels of important markers of cardiovascular health such as cholesterol, saturated fat, and inflammation markers, they discovered that doubling the saturated fat intake had *zero* impact on these important markers. Again, eating twice as much saturated fat had absolutely no impact on blood levels of saturated fat. What's more, the group that ate double the saturated fat in the absence of sugar and refined carbohydrates had lower levels of inflammation overall.

Keep in mind that this study was not done on the population, but rather it was a comprehensive experiment where researchers supplied all the food and measured true and immediate responses of the body to various diets, thus making these results highly reliable and credible.

Inflammation & Saturated Fats

While there is evidence that suggests that inflammation is caused by saturated fats in humans and animals, and inflammation is the underlying cause of type 2 diabetes, obesity, heart disease, dementia, and cancer, there are some important caveats to keep in mind. You see, saturated fat causes inflammation *only* in people who eat very little omega-3 fats and too many carbohydrates. Eliminate high-carb foods and add omega-3 rich foods or supplements and saturated fat is not a problem. There is interesting evidence between omega-3 fats and how they interact with saturated fat. Unfortunately, thanks to very effective mass marketing by food corporations of processed and packaged foods that contain almost no nutritional value and are packed with sugar and omega-6 fats from vegetable oils, a staggering ninety percent of Americans have insufficient levels of omega-3 fats. When you don't get enough omega-3 fats in your diet and you eat saturated fat, the saturated fat triggers the production of arachidonic acid, which then turns into inflammatory compounds called eicosanoids. Understand: a lack of omega-3s and too much saturated fat equals *disaster* on your arteries, health, and waistline, and this disaster is even further compounded by eating too much sugar and carbohydrates.

Simply add some omega-3 into your diet and saturated fats will reduce inflammation by turning off genes that produce cytokines, which are inflammatory molecules and they promote the production of anti-inflammatory eicosanoids. When saturated fats are consumed along with omega 3s, saturated fat will lower your triglycerides and increase your HDL good cholesterol and promote the formation of less harmful, large LDL particles. In a study of overweight men and women, researchers found that even when on a high-fat diet of fifty-five percent total calories from fat and twenty-five percent total calories from saturated fat, there was no impact on inflammatory markers or oxidative stress, two factors that are known to cause heart disease and accelerate aging.

In other studies, saturated fat only seemed to promote inflammation in the presence of too little fiber and too many carbs, and sometimes there was no connection at all. In one study where the same participants were given either soybean oil or butter at different times, there was no increase in inflammatory markers. What was even more revealing was that only saturated fat was able to reverse liver damage in rats when they consumed sugar in the form of alcohol, where polyunsaturated fat had no effect at all. Nonalcoholic steatohepatitis (NASH), commonly known as non-alcoholic fatty liver disease, caused by eating too much sugar and carbohydrates, is now the most common type of liver disease and the number one cause of liver transplants. Reducing your overall sugar and carbohydrate intake and boosting your consumption of saturated fats will lower your chances of developing NASH. There is now very strong evidence to show that saturated fats lower inflammation when consumed with a low-carb, high-fiber, and omega-3 rich diet. And lowering inflammation levels is the *key* to weight loss and disease prevention.

To sum up:

- Saturated fats only cause problems when combined with a low-fiber, low omega-3, and high carb/sugar diet.

- Saturated fats actually *improve* your overall cholesterol profile when combined with a low-carb diet by lowering triglycerides, raising HDL, and decreasing the smaller, dangerous LDL particles.

- Blood levels of certain saturated fats are associated with heart disease, but it's carbohydrates that increase those blood levels of saturated fat and not the saturated fat that you eat.

- When compared to higher-carb, lower-fat diets, higher-fat and saturated-fat diets do better at improving every single risk factor for heart disease and weight loss.

- Despite billions of dollars spent on research and half a century, there is *no* link between saturated fat intake and heart disease

Cholesterol & Saturated Fats

Just as a high-carb diet causes inflammation when combined with low omega-3 intake and low saturated fats, it will also cause your LDL bad cholesterol levels to increase under the same circumstances. You see, the multibillion-dollar drug industry is behind the number one selling class of drugs currently on the market: statins. The main effect of statins is to reduce LDL (bad cholesterol), which turns out *not* to be the most important factor in preventing heart disease. One of the biggest myths in medicine today is the connection between cholesterol and heart disease. Meat and butter have been vilified due to the fact that saturated fat raises cholesterol. The belief was that since high blood cholesterol causes heart attacks and saturated fat raises cholesterol, then reducing saturated fat intake should reduce deaths from heart attack. However, an ever-growing body of evidence does not support this belief. In order to understand how dietary cholesterol is harmless, we first need to look at how cholesterol gets metabolized (processed) in your body.

What's important to know is that most of the cholesterol found in your blood is made in your liver. The liver gets signaled to produce cholesterol and fat when you eat sugar and carbohydrates. This process is called lipogenesis, and it's a basic science taught in biochemistry classes, but somehow has been ignored by most scientists and doctors who study cholesterol. High-carb diets increase the production of triglycerides and at the same time lower HDL—the good cholesterol—and increase the number of LDL particles. High carb diets also reduce the size of your small LDL cholesterol particles. LDL itself is not bad, but the small LDL is. This type of lipid profile is very dangerous as it causes atherosclerosis, or hardening of the arteries, which is at the root of strokes, heart disease, and, in most cases, dementia. Reducing your fat intake will certainly lower your LDL bad cholesterol, and may seem like the right thing to do, but it's in fact the worst thing for your health as changing your diet from higher fat to higher carbs shifts your cholesterol profile from the harmless light and fluffy large LDL particles to the smaller and dense, dangerous particles. A study comparing the effects of a low-fat diet to a higher-fat diet that had the exact number of calories, found that the low-fat diet (which was high in sugar and carbohydrates), led to significantly higher triglycerides in both normal weight and overweight people. Another analysis of more than sixty studies showed that increasing saturated fats raised both LDL (which is not harmful if it's in large particles) and HDL, while lowering triglycerides and increasing LDL particle size. These changes are beneficial to your health and not harmful. You see, it's not the typical LDL value that's attributed to heart disease, but rather, it's the LDL particle size and number. The LDL measured by your doctor is simply the weight of LDL in your blood (in milligrams per deciliter) and not the small, dangerous LDL particles.

Request your doctor to order an NMR (nuclear magnetic resonance) lipid test. This test is offered by LabCorp or the Cardio IQ test offered by Quest Diagnostics. These advanced technology tests put your cholesterol in a mini MRI machine to examine the size and number of the particles. Other cholesterol tests don't do this and, therefore, are not a true measure of your lipid health.

Understand: the primary factor that stimulates your liver to produce smaller, more dense cholesterol particles is *refined carbohydrates and sugar*. Cholesterol is simply a fatty substance produced by your liver that is necessary for thousands of bodily functions. Cholesterol is a key building block for hormone production such as testosterone, progesterone, estrogen, and cortisol. Cholesterol is so important that without enough of it you would die. In fact, people who have the lowest cholesterol as they age have the highest risk of death. Higher cholesterol levels can actually increase life span under certain circumstances. What's important to understand when it comes to cholesterol is that the *type* of fat you eat is more important than the *amount* of fat in your diet. Refined vegetable oils, (omega-6 PUFAs) and hydrogenated fats (trans fats) increase abnormal cholesterol, whereas omega-3 fats from fish and fish oil and monounsaturated fats found in olive oil, avocadoes, and nuts and seeds actually improve the amount and type of cholesterol your body produces.

The biggest culprit of abnormal cholesterol in your body comes from sugar. Simply put, the sugar you consume converts to fat in your body and the worst culprit of all is high fructose corn syrup. High fructose corn syrup is abundant in sodas, fruit juices, and processed foods and is the main nutritional cause of abnormal cholesterol levels. When fructose is consumed in high amounts without the presence of fiber found in whole fruit, it triggers cholesterol to be produced in your liver, a process known as lipogenesis. A study published in the *American Journal of Clinical Nutrition* analyzed the effects of sugar on cholesterol. Researchers performed a meta-analysis of thirty-nine randomized controlled trials on sugar intake. The study showed that people who ate higher amounts of sugar had significantly higher levels of triglycerides and total LDL cholesterol. Higher cholesterol levels occurred in people even when they did not gain weight, which means that high-sugar and high-carb diets—not weight gain—caused elevated cholesterol.

As most health-conscious people are now aware that total cholesterol or LDL levels are not as important as good (HDL) vs Bad (LDL) levels. Ideally, your HDL levels should be above 60 mg/dl) and your triglycerides levels should be less than 100mg/dl. Apart from keeping your levels in the above ranges, your main concern should be whether or not the cholesterol in your blood is oxidized or rancid. Your risk of developing arterial plaque is significant if it is. Oxidized or rancid cholesterol is a result of free radicals and oxidative stress, which trigger a vicious cycle of inflammation and plaque or fat deposits underneath the artery walls. When small LDL particles are oxidized, they become a hazard by contributing to the build-up of plaque (cholesterol) in your arteries. Eating foods that are high in cholesterol is perfectly fine if they're from the right type of fat as it will not have an impact on your blood cholesterol and heart-disease risk. Leading health authorities in Canada, New Zealand, Europe, Australia, India, and Korea have stated that there is no upper limit on the amount of cholesterol considered safe in the diet. Looks like America is finally catching up with the rest of the world. The 2013 American College of Cardiology/American Heart Association Task Force on Practice Guidelines did not recommend lowering total fat.

What's more, they completely gave up on decades of advice to reduce dietary cholesterol, which had everyone eating bland egg whites and avoiding lobster and shrimp. They noted that dietary cholesterol had zero effect on blood cholesterol and that, in about twenty-five percent of the population, dietary cholesterol raised bad LDL cholesterol levels but also increased HDL, resulting in a neutral effect on cholesterol levels.

Statins & Cholesterol

Contrary to what most people in the United States have been led to believe about statin drugs, they are far from being a miracle to humankind by lowering your risk of heart attack and death. You see, despite heavy mass-marketing via feel-good television commercials and magazine ads that portray cholesterol-lowering drugs as a savior of mankind, statins fall short of the hype. What the science on statin drugs proves is very different from what we've been brainwashed into believing by pharmaceutical companies. Most doctors are now aware that oxidative stress and inflammation are the biggest causes of heart disease, not cholesterol. A groundbreaking paper in the *New England Journal of Medicine* outlines the science of why inflammation, not cholesterol, is the center cause of atherosclerosis. It explains how white blood cells, known as macrophages, are driven into the walls of your arteries to protect you against rancid or oxidized cholesterol. White blood cells absorb the toxic or oxidized cholesterol and that is what causes plaque build-up which leads to heart attacks. As it turns out, the reason statins have any effect whatsoever is not because they lower your cholesterol, but because they lower inflammation and act as antioxidants. Statins do have some benefits, but there are many better ways of reducing your inflammation and getting antioxidants with far fewer side effects.

In 2011, a Swedish study led by a group of researchers looked at the relationship of statin-drug prescriptions and heart attacks in their country. They found that between 1998 and 2002, the rate of statin usage by men and women aged 40 to 79 tripled, yet this had no impact on the corresponding rate of mortality and heart-attack incidence. That's right, tripling statin use had zero impact on heart disease. So, if statins do not help to reduce heart attacks, who should be using these drugs? Some findings to consider when it comes to statins and cholesterol lowering:

- If you are over 69 years old and have high cholesterol, there is no proof that statins will reduce your risk of heart attack or death.

- If you reduce your bad cholesterol (LDL) but don't reduce inflammation (measured by a test called C-reactive protein), there is no health benefit to statins.

- Extensive cholesterol treatment with the drugs Zetia and Zocor lowered cholesterol much greater than only one drug alone, but it led to more plaque formation in the arteries and did not lower heart attacks.

- Countries with higher-than-average cholesterol levels than America such as Spain and Switzerland have less heart disease.

- Elderly patients with lower cholesterol have a higher risk of death than those with higher cholesterol

- Roughly twenty percent of people who take statins experience side-effects including pain and muscle damage, memory issues, neurological problems, and sexual disfunction.

- Evidence has shown that it's the ability of statins to lower inflammation that accounts for the benefits of statins, and not their ability to lower cholesterol.

- Statins have been linked to a significantly higher risk of diabetes. In one study of about 26,000 healthy people, those taking statins to prevent heart attacks were 87 percent more likely to develop type II diabetes.

A dramatic study published in 2009 in the *American Heart Journal* found that about seventy-five percent of patients who were admitted to hospitals with heart disease had normal cholesterol levels. The authors looked at 231,836 hospital admissions from 541 hospitals, accounting for fifty-nine percent of all heart-attack admissions in the U.S. from 2000 to 2006. Cholesterol levels were assessed within the first twenty-four hours of admission. What they found was a bit shocking. Almost seventy-five percent had normal LDL (bad cholesterol) levels under 130 mg/dl, and more than fifty percent had optimal LDL levels (under 100 mg/dl). For the argument that cholesterol benchmarks need to be lowered even further, the study also found that more than seventeen percent had LDL levels below 70 mg/dl. Data still remains that shows high LDL to be a problem, but only remains one of many other factors, and not the most important factor. None of this is to say that statins are not effective in saving lives of people who are prone to heart attacks. They work fairly well for most middle-aged men who have already had heart attacks, including men who have many risk factors for heart disease, diabetes, high blood pressure, and obesity. However, for most people for whom statins are prescribed—people who have never had a heart attack—they don't provide any real benefit and come with a slew of risks and side-effects.

Dangerous Fats to Avoid

As you know by now, the "eat-less-saturated-fat" message touted by some of America's largest institutions was based on the misguided belief that saturated fat was the cause of heart disease. We were made to believe that if we ate too much saturated fat, it would clog the arteries and choke our hearts to death. This message could not be more misleading as we now know. We understand that inflammation—not saturated fat— is the primary cause of most major life-threatening diseases. Saturated fat is harmless in the context of a low-sugar and low-carb diet. Cheese, butter, eggs, whole-milk, beef, yogurt, coconut oil, and other foods that are high in saturated fat do not increase your risk for heart disease when you avoid refined carbs and sugar and only consume slow-digesting carbohydrates in small to moderate amounts such as oats, quinoa, sweet potatoes, and other low-glycemic and gluten-free whole grains. The food industry happily complied with any fad or recommendation of the day by our largest health and medical institutions. With the low-fat craze in full swing, the food industry got busy creating a radical shift in their products. They replaced saturated fats with "healthy" vegetable oils like shortening and margarine that contained hydrogenated fat (trans fat), which has turned out to be one of the only fats proven by science to cause heart disease and metabolic syndrome. Products such as cookies, salad dressing, flavored yogurt, and other processed foods were marketed as top health foods with the labels "low-fat and "fat-free" front and center. The problem is that they replaced the fat in these foods with sugar and removing the fat from any food will make it tasteless and unappealing, unless, of course, sugar is added.

In the late 1970s, big agriculture companies such as Monsanto and Cargill, fueled by new agriculture subsidies that promoted astronomical increases in the production of soy and corn, poured high fructose corn syrup and hydrogenated fat into more than 600,000 processed foods. Eighty percent of these foods contained added sugar, which led to a massive spike in diabetes due to the highly addictive nature of sugar. And, as sugar is the main driver of the fat-storage hormone insulin, America's overweight and obesity rate skyrocketed. Eating low-fat foods became as common as showering every day, as the population plowed through pasta, bagels, bread, pastries, and muffins. When the low-fat craze began, not a single state in the US had an obesity rate over twenty percent. Most states now have obesity rates over twenty-five percent and some are as high as thirty-five percent. What's alarming is the fact that a full seventy percent of adult Americans and forty percent of kids are overweight.

Reversing these numbers is as simple as switching from a low-fat, high carbohydrate diet to a higher-fat, lower-carb-and-sugar diet. But not just any fat will do; while eating plenty of natural (unrefined and unprocessed) saturated fat is a big step, avoiding dangerous inflammation-causing fats is just as important. Most of our health problems arise when our omega-3 to omega-6 ratio is out of balance. The modern diet supplies us with far too many omega-6 fats from corn, canola and sunflower oils. These high inflammatory omega-6 fats are found in most processed foods and conventionally-raised meat.

When there are too many omega-6 fats and not enough omega-3 fats circulating in your blood, bad things start to happen. An imbalance has been found to depress the immune system, contribute to weight gain, interfere with fat burning, and cause inflammation. One of the world's leading researchers on omega-3 fats, Dr. Artemis Simopoulos, explains that "excessive amounts of omega-6 polyunsaturated fats (PUFA) and a very high omega-6/omega-3 ratio, as found in today's Western Diets, promote the pathogenesis of many diseases, including cardiovascular disease, cancer, and inflammatory and autoimmune diseases, whereas increased levels of omega-3 PUFA (a low omega-6/omega-3 ratio) have suppressive effects." In an article published in *Biomedicine and Pharmacotherapy*, Dr. Simopoulos does an in-depth review of the risks of going against our evolutionary balance of omega-3 and omega-6 fats. When you consume too many omega-6 fats, your body oxidizes your LDL (bad cholesterol), turning it rancid and making it more likely to cause heart disease. It also makes your blood stickier and more likely to clot and blocks the absorption of vital omega-3 fats into your cell membranes. Remember, the food you eat has a direct effect on the expression of your genes. Foods containing omega-3 fats reduce the expression of inflammatory genes in your body, while omega-6 fats promote the expression of inflammatory genes.

Avoid the following fats and oils as they contain high amounts of omega-6 fats, trans fats (see hydrogenated oils), and little, if any, beneficial omega-3 fats:

All Vegetable-Based Cooking Oils and Fats

(canola, soybean, cottonseed, safflower, corn, shortening, and margarine): The fat or oil from these foods are heavily processed and refined, which destroys most of the omega-3 fats found in them. The heavy processing and refinement of these foods turns the omega-6 fatty acids in these foods rancid, making them toxic to your health. Unfortunately, most restaurant foods are prepared with these processed fats as they are cheap to purchase in bulk (compared to higher quality oils such as olive and coconut) and they can withstand higher cooking temperatures compared to olive and coconut oil. The only exception to consuming these fats is when you're eating out on special occasions. Otherwise, never consume these fats by cooking your food with them. Go with grass-fed butter, sustainably-sourced palm oil, avocado oil, olive oil, and virgin coconut oil when cooking at home.

Hydrogenated Oils

Known as trans fats, put simply, hydrogenated oils are evil and nasty, and wreak havoc on your arteries and cholesterol. Their only purpose is to extend the shelf life of processed foods. In 1994, it was estimated that trans fats caused 30,000 deaths annually in the United States from heart disease. Trans fats have also been linked to cancer. A study done on trans fatty acids and cancer showed that postmenopausal women who had high levels of trans fat in their diet doubled their risk of getting colon cancer. In 2013, trans fats were ruled as "not safe to eat" by the FDA. Trans fats are found in processed foods like cookies, margarine, crackers, chips, frosting, coffee creamer, muffins, and fast food. If you are buying a processed food (to enjoy once a week in moderation), always read the nutrition labels before buying. If the words "partially hydrogenated oil" appear on the nutrition label, do not buy it, even if the Nutrition Facts label on the product says contains zero grams of trans-fat or if the words "No Trans Fat" appear on the front. Due to a loophole in product labeling laws, a product labeled "Trans-fat free" can still contain up to 0.5 grams of trans fat per serving. A serving size of most foods (especially processed foods) is usually very small, which means you can easily end up eating a gram or two of deadly trans-fats without realizing it! To be one hundred percent sure that you are not consuming this dangerous man-made fat, avoid processed foods altogether and stick with whole foods.

Eating plenty of natural fat from different sources such as eggs, grass-fed butter, cheese, meat, yogurt, avocado, olive oil, nuts and seeds, and other unrefined and unprocessed foods guarantees that dangerous fats won't make their way into your diet. As terrible as refined omega-6 vegetable oils and trans fats are for your health and waistline, occasionally consuming them in small amounts when you're eating out or enjoying a once-a-week treat won't sabotage your cholesterol and health. If you're eating ample healthy fats on most days, any harmful fats that you consume occasionally won't have a negative effect on your cholesterol levels and other health markers. Remember, the total fat in your diet does not affect your risk of heart disease, nor will it increase your risk for becoming overweight. It's the *type* and *quality* of fat that will impact your health markers along with the avoidance of added sugars and high-carbohydrate foods.

The Skinny on Healthy Fats

It's been found that populations who consume the highest amounts of olive oil and nuts have the lowest rates of heart disease in the world. That's not a surprise because nuts, seeds, and olive oil are pure fat foods containing some of the highest levels of heart healthy omega-3s and monounsaturated fats. Countries such as Greece and Italy have the lowest rates of heart disease in the world thanks to diets high in monounsaturated fat. People in Greece and Italy consume lots of wild fish, avocados, and nuts and seeds such as almonds, cashews, pecans, and sunflower seeds. Despite their high fat intake, people in these Mediterranean countries suffer from the lowest rates of heart disease—including other metabolic diseases such as elevated cholesterol, high blood pressure, and diabetes.

Monounsaturated Fats

Besides nuts and seeds, monounsaturated fats are found in meat, especially wild meat like fowl, venison, buffalo, duck, and bone marrow. For our pre-agricultural ancestors (hunter-gather societies) monounsaturated fats accounted for about half of total fat intake and sixteen to twenty-five percent of their total fat intake came from wild meat, bone marrow, and nuts. Many of the hunter-gather tribes that roamed our planet thousands of years ago broke the bones of the animals they caught and sucked out the fatty marrow, which is more than fifty percent monounsaturated fat. Modern grain fed meats do not have as much monounsaturated fat as wild or game meat. This is due to modern agriculture that involves a lot of grain in the feed of livestock—which reduces healthy monounsaturated fat considerably. Eating more monounsaturated fats greatly benefits your heart and cardiovascular system, which is why many cardiologists recommend the Mediterranean Diet. Even the AHA (American Heart Association) agrees that higher intakes of monounsaturated fats are directly related to healthy cholesterol levels, lower levels of LDL oxidation (which is responsible for the LDL causing damage to your body), and less risk of stroke and blood clots.

Monounsaturated fats are a rich source of vitamin E and several other antioxidants. They improve insulin sensitivity, reduce diabetes and breast cancer risk, reduce pain in people with rheumatoid arthritis, reduce belly fat, and promote weight loss. Be aware that some monounsaturated fats are produced in a way that makes them unhealthy and even toxic to the body. Canola oil, which has been touted as a healthy oil for many years is produced with high heat and harsh chemical solvents during the refining process. The Watson A. Price foundation, in an article titled "The Great Con-ola" states, "Like all modern vegetable oils, canola oil goes through the process of caustic refining, bleaching, and degumming—all of which involve high temperatures or adding chemicals of questionable safety. And because canola oil is high in omega-3 fatty acids, which easily become rancid and foul-smelling when subjected to oxygen and high temperatures, it must be deodorized." Due to the heavy refining process which degrades omega-3s and turns the oil rancid, stay away from canola oil and stick to extra virgin olive oil, avocado oil, and unrefined coconut oil. Choose organic when possible.

Polyunsaturated Fats (PUFA) Omega-3 & Omega-6 Fatty Acids

Unless you don't own a television and don't read magazines, you've been hearing and reading about the health benefits of omega-3s. TV advertisements for various foods and supplements display products such as fish oil capsules, omega-3 modified snacks, and other health foods (some of which are not healthy but disguised as such through clever marketing). Considering the fact that most of the fat—about ninety percent total fat calories—Americans consume is the inflammation-promoting omega-6 type, eating foods that are high in omega-3s will balance out your omega-3 to omega-6 ratio and do wonders for your cholesterol levels, insulin levels, energy levels, and fat loss. As we've already gone over, our modern diet provides us with far too many omega-6s from processed foods, safflower, corn, canola oil, and conventionally raised meats. Simply put, too many omega-6s and too few omega-3s is bad news. An imbalance has been shown to depress your immune system and contribute to weight gain and inflammation.

It's important to know that omega-3 fats are found in polyunsaturated fats (PUFAs), which also contain omega-6 fats. Omega 3 fats are one type of PUFA, with the other type being omega-6. You see, omega 6 fatty acids are *not* bad for you when they're in their natural, unprocessed, and unrefined state. They are only toxic and inflammatory to your health when they're refined with chemicals and processed.

Polyunsaturated fats are considered "essential" by scientists as your body cannot produce them on its own, so they must be consumed through diet or supplementation. PUFAs play an important role in hormonal and immune functions, including your cellular health. They are potent regulators of health and disease. Omega-3 fats, one type of PUFA, are found in most of your cell membranes and regulate inflammation, insulin function, and your neurotransmitters. They are crucial in preventing and treating diabetes, arthritis, depression, and autoimmune disease. Some of the best sources of PUFA (so long as these foods are not processed) include the seeds from sunflower, sesame, pumpkin, and chia. Walnuts and fatty fish are also great sources of PUFAs.

It's also important to be aware that, as with monounsaturated fats, the processing or cooking of polyunsaturated fats affects their ability to promote disease or health. Polyunsaturated fats that aren't refined and/or processed are an essential part of a whole foods-based diet. The two essential fatty acids found in food that you need every day are:

ALA: Alpha linolenic acid is a type of omega-3 found in walnuts, flaxseeds and flaxseed oil, macadamia nuts, and organ meats.

LA: Linoleic acid is a type of omega-6 fat found in vegetable oils and commercial seeds. It's found in various nuts and seeds in addition to vegetable oils. Your body needs LA omega-6 fats in small amounts, but only from whole food sources or from cold/expeller-pressed vegetable oils in small amounts.

Apart from these two essential fatty acids, there are other longer-chain omega-3 and omega-6 derivatives that your body can create on its own. The following are considered "conditionally essential fatty-acids" that are not necessary to consume through diet. However, I highly recommend you get these fats through your diet as most people's bodies are not effective at converting ALA into the active forms of the omega-3 fats DHA and EPA, thus they can be considered essential:

EPA: Eicosapentaeonic acid is an omega 3 that can be derived from ALA and is a great anti-inflammatory fat. It's abundant in fish and wild and pasture-raised animals.

DHA: Docosahexaenoic acid is another omega-3 that can be derived from ALA, but only about five to ten percent of ALA can be converted to DHA. It's found in fish, pasture-raised and wild animals, and algae.

AA: Arachidonic acid is an omega 6- fatty acid that can be derived from LA. AA helps with your cell membrane flexibility and it's found in most animal foods (fish, chicken eggs, and other meats).

GLA: Gamma linolenic acid is an omega-6 fatty acid derived from LA. GLA is found in hemp oil, evening primrose oil, and borage oil.

Medium-Chain Omega-3: Alpha Linolenic Acid (ALA)

Alpha linolenic acid is found in walnuts, hemp seeds, flaxseed oil, flaxseeds, canola oil, and chia seeds. Small amounts of ALA are also found in plants such as green leafy vegetables. Mayonnaise and salad dressings that contain soybean oil are the greatest source of ALA, but unfortunately are accompanied by large amounts of omega-6 linoleic acid (LA); therefore, I recommend avoiding these foods. If you can't go without salad dressing or mayonnaise, you can buy these products in low-fat versions which usually contain olive oil instead of soybean oil as the main fat/oil ingredient. These are often labeled as low fat, low calorie, or omega-3 enriched. To be sure that what you're buying is olive-oil based and not soybean-oil based, read the ingredients list when buying mayonnaise and salad dressing. The first one or two ingredients needs to read "virgin or extra virgin olive oil." Food manufacturers are required by law to list the ingredients of a product from most to least in the ingredients list. Omega-3 fats from ALA are health-protective even though only about five to ten percent can be converted by your body into the more beneficial long-chain omega-3s (EPA and DHA).

Medium-Chain Omega-6s: Linoleic Acid (LA)

Linoleic acid is highly abundant in vegetable oils and seed oils such as corn, safflower, sunflower, and cottonseed oils. LA is the most-consumed fat in most people's diets and has been consumed in enormous quantities over the last one hundred years. Consumption of the health-sabotaging soybean oil has increased by a factor of one thousand since 1900, and this consumption is showing no signs of reversal. As soybean oil is high in linoleic acid, consuming it can quickly lower your LDL or bad cholesterol levels and most doctors recommend it, advising patients to swap it for saturated fat. But this is erroneous advice, as too many omega-6 fats from soybean oil and other processed vegetable and seed oil compete with omega-3 receptors in your body and, therefore, interfere with the health-protective benefits of omega-3. What is worse, these oils are easily damaged by oxygen and become oxidized, which turn your LDL rancid and dangerous. These oxidized fats are called OXLAMs, or oxidized linoleic acid metabolites. This is why I highly recommend to never cook with these oils, especially when frying carbohydrate foods such as potatoes

(French fries) which makes them even more toxic to your health. Linoleic acid from soybean oil accounts for about ninety percent of all PUFA intake or about seven percent of total energy intake. This is high, considering that our ancestors in the pre-agriculture era consumed only about three percent of total calories as LA from wild meat—and some tribes living in coastal areas consumed only one percent. The amount of LA we are currently consuming is astoundingly high when compared to not only our pre-agricultural ancestors, but also our relatives who were alive just one hundred years ago. The massive amount of LA we're consuming now has been called a "massive uncontrolled human experiment."

In less developed parts of the world and in indigenous populations, LA intake is very low compared to modern Western diets—thus rates of heart disease are also very low. While there are conflicting studies, high LA intake alone seems to elevate the risk of heart disease independent of omega-3 intake. In one large randomized controlled study that reduced LA intake to pre-industrial levels, a whopping seventy percent reduction in heart disease and death occurred. Foods and oils high in LA cannot be a part of your daily diet if longevity is important to you, despite common recommendations to replace saturated fats with omega-6 heavy vegetable oils.

Long-Chain Omega-3's: EPA and DHA

Sadly, more than ninety percent of Americans are deficient in EPA and DHA. A lack of these essential omega-3 fats in your diet significantly increases your chances of developing every major disease—from depression to heart disease, to colon and breast cancer. Omega-3s are abundant in cold water fatty fish including herring, trout, mackerel, salmon, anchovies, shrimp, oysters, and tuna just to name a few. Avoid tuna if you are elderly, pregnant, or breast feeding as tuna contains the highest amounts of mercury compared to other fish. Consistently eating foods high in EPA and DHA is vital for good health, along with taking a high-quality omega-3 fish or krill oil supplement. Be aware that most omega-3 supplement capsules can become rancid at room temperature, meaning the healthy fats are essentially destroyed. To avoid this, keep your fish oil and krill oil refrigerated. Further benefits and dosage recommendations for fish and krill oil is outlined in the supplements chapter. The benefits of omega-3 fats have been well studied for decades.

Here are some conditions that these beneficial fats help:

ADHD

Asthma

Bipolar disorder

Breast cancer

Colon cancer

Cognitive decline

Depression

Diabetes

High blood pressure

High cholesterol

Heart disease

Inflammatory bowel disease

Osteoporosis

Prostate cancer

Rheumatoid arthritis

Schizophrenia

Omega-3 fatty acids are essential for proper brain function and provide proper fluidity for your brain-cell membranes. A study done on omega-3s and depression demonstrated that they were more effective than placebo (fake omega-3) in treating depression in adults and children. What's more, a study published in the *Australian and New Zealand Journal of Psychiatry* that compared the effects of fluoxetine (Prozac) and EPA in major depressive disorder showed that EPA is as effective as Prozac in treating depressive disorder. This study proved that omega-3s are a powerful tool against major depression and are just as effective as anti-depressants. Anti-depressant pills are the most widely prescribed drugs in America and have side-effects, sometimes severe, whereas omega-3s are natural and benefit your mind and body in dozens of ways, all without any side-effects!

CHAPTER 6: LONGEVITY SECRETS

Why Your Liver Matters

Your liver, which is your body's largest solid organ that weighs around three pounds and is roughly the size of a football, is vital to your body's metabolic functions along with keeping your immune system functioning smoothly. Since you'll be consuming whole unprocessed foods and staying away from excess alcohol while you're on the Fit Body 4 Life 21-Day Meal Plan and hopefully for the rest of your life, your liver will have plenty of protection and all the nutrients it needs to function properly.

From an anatomical view, your liver is located in the upper portion of your stomach, just below the diaphragm with a portion of your liver going into the upper left of your abdomen. Compared to the rest of your body, the liver has a significant amount of blood flowing through it, with an estimated thirteen percent of your body's blood flowing through it at any given time. Your liver's main purpose is to filter toxins from your blood and remove them from your bloodstream.

The cells located in your liver are known as hepatocytes, which accept and filter blood and act as storing centers, determining which nutrients should be processed and which should be stored. Your liver stores vitamins as well as minerals such as copper and iron, releasing them when your body needs nutrients. Your liver also helps to break down the fats from the food that you eat, and either stores fats or releases them to be used for energy. Your liver creates an estimated 800 to 1,000 milliliters of bile every day, which gets transported through the bile duct into the small intestine. The small intestine uses the bile to further break down fats; any extra bile that's unused gets stored in the gallbladder.

Additionally, your liver breaks down protein from the foods you eat, where some of it gets converted into ammonia. Ammonia can be toxic to your body in large amounts. Fortunately, your liver turns the potentially toxic ammonia into a substance called urea, which releases it into the blood where the kidneys excrete it when you urinate. Your liver breaks down alcohol in the blood including any medications you take. In addition to breaking down protein and converting ammonia into urea, your liver plays a major role in the following bodily functions:

- It creates proteins that are necessary for blood clotting.

- It creates immune-system defenses that help your body fight off infections.

- It stores extra blood sugar as glycogen (which is used for supplying your body with energy).

- It breaks down old and damaged red blood cells.

When you are aware of all that your liver does to keep the systems in your body operating in top order, you will gain a brand-new appreciation for it. It's one of the hardest working and amazing organs in your body! Unlike other organs, your liver is the only organ that has the ability to regenerate or rebuild itself. What this means is that if you injure your liver or its function is affected by surgery, its tissue can grow back— sometimes one hundred percent depending on the type of injury.

The liver grows back by enlarging its existing cells, and afterwards, the new cells start to multiply. Within a week after surgically removing two-thirds of the liver, it returns to the same or original weight it was before surgery. Even more amazing, the liver has been known to regenerate one hundred percent after as many as twelve surgeries where a part of the liver was removed. An unhealthy lifestyle and substance addiction can lead to a number of conditions that affect the function of the liver. Some of these conditions are:

Autoimmune hepatitis – This condition leads the body's immune system to attack itself and destroy healthy liver tissue, which leads to cirrhosis (severe liver scarring, see next condition).

Cirrhosis—This is a condition where scar tissue, which is weak and not the same as normal liver tissue, takes over and replaces healthy tissue throughout the liver. Cirrhosis is caused by heavy alcohol consumption, chronic hepatitis and a rare genetic disorder called Wilson's disease.

Hemochromatosis—A condition caused by excessive iron buildup in the body. Too much iron in your blood can lead to liver damage.

Hepatitis A, B, and C—Hepatitis A is a viral infection that causes the liver to become inflamed. It's more common in developed countries that lack basic sanitation systems and clean drinking water. In most cases, hepatitis A is reversible and does not cause long-term complications or liver failure.

Hepatitis B can cause both short- and long-term infection and is the most commonly spread hepatitis through sexual contact. It's also contracted through the sharing of dirty needles used for tattooing, drug injections, or accidental injection with contaminated needles. If you are concerned about contracting hepatitis B, I recommend getting vaccinated to prevent developing the disease.

Hepatitis C can be a chronic or acute infection and is most commonly spread by coming in contact with blood containing the hepatitis C virus, which can also be contracted from sharing unclean needles to inject drugs or apply tattoos. Having unprotected sexual contact with an infected person can transmit the infection as well. Hepatitis C can cause inflammation that can lead to liver failure, cirrhosis, and liver cancer.

Nonalcoholic fatty liver disease and NASH – These are conditions where fat builds up in the liver to the point where it causes inflammation and eventual liver damage. NASH, or nonalcoholic steatohepatitis, is a form of nonalcoholic liver disease that causes fibrosis or scarring. Being obese and having health complications due to obesity such as type 2 diabetes greatly increases your chances of developing NASH.

Symptoms of a Damaged and Diseased Liver

There are many (more than 100) types of liver diseases. Many conditions start out as flu-like symptoms and advance to more severe signs of liver damage, including dark colored urine and jaundice, which is characterized as the yellowing of the skin and eyes. Apart from jaundice, which is one of the more prominent and severe symptoms of liver disease, the following symptoms are commonly associated with liver damage: Note, while these conditions are common in most cases of liver damage, you may not experience any of these symptoms if your liver is damaged. If you're experiencing any of these symptoms and you haven't been diagnosed with liver disease, go see your doctor. In most cases liver disease starts out with some of these symptoms:

Weakness

Chronically itchy skin

Joint pain

Chronic nose bleeds

Low sex drive

Lack of appetite

Vomiting

Abnormal blood vessels of the skin

Stomach pain

Fatigue

More serious symptoms of liver damage and liver disease include:

Jaundice (yellowing of the skin and eyes)

Dark colored urine

Confusion and difficulty thinking clearly

Impotence

Abdominal swelling

Edema (swelling of the legs)

Enlarged liver

Pale-colored stools

Experiencing any of these symptoms is a sign of serious liver damage. Go see your doctor immediately if you have any of the above symptoms more than once or twice a week. If you are concerned about your liver, consider getting a liver function test. A liver function test will determine if your liver is functioning properly.

How to Keep Your Liver Healthy

Apart from a whole-foods diet high in fiber, healthy fats, and low in total carbohydrates, you can take the following steps to ensure your liver stays in top operating shape:

Never share needles or personal items.

Get vaccinated for hepatitis A and B.

Limit the amount of alcohol you consume.

Speak with your doctor about any medications that may affect your liver.

Practice safe sex.

Eat plenty of foods high in fiber.

In addition to the above steps, there are several natural dietary supplements that are proven to help cleanse your liver and keep it functioning effectively. See the dietary supplements section for more on the supplements that can help with liver health.

Protecting Your Heart

Just like the liver, your heart is a magnificent organ that you couldn't survive a second without. Your heart is responsible for pumping blood to your body every second of your life. It pumps oxygen-rich blood through your circulatory system, providing your body with oxygen and nutrients, as well as assisting in the removal of metabolic waste. Your heart is located between your lungs, in the center compartment of your chest underneath the ribcage. Your heart valves are responsible for delivering blood to your body and ensuring backflow does not happen, which is when blood goes back towards the heart into the valves the other way. The heart pumps blood with a rhythm that is determined by a group of pacemaker cells in the SA node or sinus node. When you are at rest, (not walking or running but not sleeping), your heart beats close to seventy-two beats per minute. Exercise temporarily increases your heart rate, but lowers your resting heart rate in the long term, in addition to strengthening the muscles of your heat.

Cardiovascular disease or CVD is the most common cause of death, not only in the United States but also globally, accounting for thirty percent of all deaths. More than three quarters of total deaths are caused by stroke and coronary artery disease. Being inactive, not exercising, smoking, having high cholesterol, being overweight, and having poorly-controlled diabetes are the greatest risk factors for developing heart disease. What's alarming is that in most cases, cardiovascular disease has no symptoms, with a heart attack being the first and only symptom. Heart attacks and strokes are usually acute events and are mainly caused by a blockage that prevents blood from flowing to the heart or brain. Specific conditions that affect the proper functioning of the heart and put you at risk for suffering a heart attack and stroke are:

Coronary Heart Disease – This is a disease of the blood vessels that supply blood to the heart. Coronary heart disease, also known as ischemic heart disease, is caused by atherosclerosis, which is a build-up of plaque along the inner walls of the arteries. This plaque causes a narrowing of the coronary arteries, reducing blood flow to the heart. This narrowing is known as stenosis, and, if minor, does not cause any symptoms. Moderate and severe stenosis causes chest pain known as angina and breathlessness during exercise and while at rest. When the thin covering of an atherosclerotic plaque ruptures, it exposes the fatty center to circulating blood, in which case a blood clot can form, blocking the artery and restricting blood flow to an area of the heart, causing a myocardial infarction or heart attack. Cardiac arrest, which is a sudden loss of output from the heart can also occur in some cases. Obesity, smoking, high blood pressure, high LDL cholesterol and poorly controlled diabetes all significantly increase your risk of developing atherosclerosis and coronary artery disease.

Cardiomyopathies – Cardiomyopathies are diseases that affect the muscles of the heart. Some can cause abnormal thickening of the heart muscle, known as hypertrophic cardiomyopathy, while others cause the heart to abnormally expand and weaken, which is known as dilated cardiomyopathy. Restrictive cardiomyopathy is when the heart muscle becomes stiff and is unable to fully relax between contractions. Abnormal heart rhythms are known as arrhythmogenic cardiomyopathy and are often genetic and inherited. Dilated cardiomyopathy can be caused by damage from alcohol and other toxins, while hypertrophic cardiomyopathy is linked to a sudden risk of cardiac death, with athletes having the highest risk. Most cardiomyopathies can lead to heart failure as the disease progresses.

Cardiac Arrhythmias – Cardiac arrhythmias are abnormal heart rhythms that sometimes do not have any symptoms and sometimes cause breathlessness, palpitations and blackouts. When the heart is healthy, waves of electrical impulses originate in the sinus node before spreading to the rest of the atria (the upper two cavities of the heart where blood is passed to the ventricles), atrioventricular node (which controls heart rate), and the ventricles. This is known as a normal sinus rhythm and when disrupted, it's considered an arrhythmia. Certain types of arrhythmias such as atrial fibrillation, can increase the long-term risk for suffering a stroke. Some arrhythmias can cause the heart to beat slowly, which is known as a bradycardia, and some cause the heart to beat rapidly at an abnormal rate. The most dangerous form of heart racing is called ventricular fibrillation, where the ventricles quiver rather than contract, leading to instant death if not quickly treated.

Congenital Heart Disease – When someone is born with a heart that is abnormal and not developed like a regular or normal heart, it's called a congenital heart defect. Congenital heart defects range from relatively minor to serious and life-threatening. Some common abnormalities are defects in the tissue that separate the two sides of the heart, known as a "hole in the heart" or ventricular septal defect. Other defects include those affecting the heart valves or the main blood vessels that lead from the heart. Some congenital heart defects are more complex and can affect more than one part of the heart. More minor forms of congenital heart disease can remain undetected throughout a person's life and only reveal themselves in more mature age.

Pericardial Disease – When the sack that surrounds the heart called the pericardium becomes inflamed, it causes a condition known as pericarditis. This condition usually causes chest pain that may spread to the upper part of the back. Pericarditis is often caused by a viral infection such as cytomegalovirus, coxsackievirus, or glandular fever. Fluid can build up within the pericardial sack, which is known as a pericardial effusion and these effusions usually occur secondary to pericarditis, kidney failure, or tumors, and usually, do not cause symptoms. However, large effusions which accumulate rapidly can compress the heart in a condition known as cardiac tamponade, which leads to breathlessness and potentially-fatal low blood pressure. Fluid can be removed from the pericardial area in order to diagnose the condition or to relieve cardiac tamponade using a syringe in a procedure called pericardiocentesis.

Heart Failure – Heart failure is a condition where the heart can't pump sufficient blood to meet the body's demands. People with heart failure often experience breathlessness when lying down along with swelling of the ankles. Heart failure is the end result of various diseases that affect the heart, but is most commonly associated with chronically-elevated blood pressure, ischemic heart disease (coronary artery disease), and valvular heart disease, which occurs in the elderly. Heart failure is frequently associated with weakening of the heart muscle but is also seen in heart-disease patients whose heart muscle is strong but very stiff. Heart failure patients have a much higher risk of developing dangerous heart rhythms.

Heart disease has become a global epidemic and is currently the most frequently diagnosed health condition throughout the world. An ECG, known as an electrocardiogram, is used to diagnose heart disease. Additional diagnostic tests may include a chest x-ray, an MRI, or an echocardiogram. The costs associated with treating heart disease are some of the most expensive of any medical treatment and are on the rise. For example, a typical emergency room visit for heart-related conditions ranges from $150 to $3000 or more depending in the severity of the heart condition and treatment administered. According to the Agency for Healthcare Research and Quality, the average length of hospitalization and related costs for heart-attack patients is 5.3 days, at $21,500 per stay. Bypass surgery costs range between $70,000 and $200,000, with stents costing between $11,000 and $41,000 or more. If you are currently undergoing heart-disease treatment, it's imperative that you speak with your doctor first before you consider coming off or lowering your medications.

Along with regular exercise and a whole-foods diet that includes plenty of wild-caught fish and other seafood, taking a high-quality omega-3 fish oil supplement is one of the simplest and most important things you can do to protect your heart, especially if fish isn't your favorite dish. The benefits of omega-3s have been well documented and have been covered in-depth in this book. Apart from fish oil, there are several other natural supplements that I recommend taking if your risk factor for heart disease is elevated.

Even if your risk factor is low, you should still supplement with fish oil at the very minimum. It's far wiser to take small steps with nutrition and supplementation to prevent heart disease from developing, than it is to allow the disease any chance to take over your health. The financial and physical burdens associated with treatments and medications against the disease far outweigh the small price of taking preventative measures, which includes a health club membership and supplementation with heart-protective nutrients.

What About Plant Based Diets & Heart Disease?

Doctors and scientists have made observations and performed research which has shown that low-fat diets void of meat (vegetarian diets) may be highly effective for preventing heart disease. Doctor Dean Ornish, who's a proponent of the Diet-Heart hypothesis, has done some impressive research through his Preventative Medicine Research Institute on low-fat plant-based diets and heart-disease reversal. His research has demonstrated that low-fat plant-based diets work when it comes to treating and preventing heart disease. His pursuit of finding a reversal for the disease has been passionate and tireless, and he has had a positive and profound impact on the lives of many people. However, Dr. Dean's heart disease research has been controversial in the medical community. His studies involved a small sample of thirty-five men which he studied over a span of five years. The interventions were rather complex, involving stress reduction, exercise, group support, a ten percent very low-fat plant-based diet (vegetarian), and smoking cessation. There was an improvement in blood flow of the arteries and fewer heart attacks in the treatment group, but it's very difficult to determine which of those interventions were the most important. It's unknown whether it was a reduction in stress, smoking cessation, group support, or exercise that was the cause of arterial blood-flow improvement and heart-attack reductions.

What's important to know is that there were some indications that the low-fat diet had adverse consequences on weight and lipids. The low-fat group *gained* an average of seven pounds throughout the study, while their total cholesterol and LDL (bad cholesterol) decreased, their triglycerides went up and their HDL (good cholesterol) went down. These changes are all signs of a higher-carb diet linked to pre-diabetes and insulin resistance. The real question to ask is how this study would have compared to the effectiveness to all the same interventions but with a diet that included ample healthy fats from foods high in omega-3s and unprocessed monounsaturated fats, including natural saturated fats and grass-fed meats. Unfortunately, a study like this has never been done so we can't know for certain. Dr. Ornish took men who were eating the typical standard American diet full of processed, nutrient-deficient foods and put them on a low-fat whole-foods plant-based diet. Health improvements are expected with this type of change in diet but it does not answer the question of whether this is the best diet for disease prevention and weight loss. What we know is that in most studies of low-fat vs low-carb diets for weight loss, the low-carb, high-fat diet prevails. In a study called the A TO Z Weight Loss Study comparing the Atkins and Ornish diets (high-fat vs low-fat) in 311 postmenopausal women for a year, the high-fat diet group achieved the fastest and most dramatic loss in weight and had better improvements in cardiovascular risk factors such as diabetes and heart disease. The evidence points overwhelmingly to the fact that it's our processed high-sugar diet and not the fat that's the driving factor behind disease, weight gain, and obesity.

The key is to switch to a whole-foods diet that is high in unprocessed fats, wild and grass-fed meats, plants, and nuts and seeds. Dr. Ornish, who is a huge proponent of restricting fat, is also an advocate of adding omega-3 fats as part of his program. His low-fat diet clearly worked for reducing diabetes, heart attacks, and other metabolic markers for heart disease for people who were on the standard American diet, and there is no disputing what was found in his study. What would be interesting to know is how his diet would compare to a higher-fat diet that's made up of mostly whole-foods such as coconut oil, grass-fed and wild meats, olive oil, nuts and nut butters, avocado, and other natural, unprocessed foods high in fat. A study is needed to compare Dr. Ornish's findings. Due to genetic differences, some people tend to do better on a low-fat diet, while others do well on a high-fat diet. What we know is that regardless of the percentage of fat calories in one's diet, everyone does better on a whole foods diet compared to the standard American diet, which is the worst diet on the planet (and is becoming popular in many countries around the world).

When you switch from the standard American diet to a whole foods diet, you will experience dramatic changes to your health and weight, regardless if you eat less fat or more of it (from healthy sources). You see, kicking processed foods to the curb and restricting your sugar intake is the single most important change you can make to rapidly lose excess pounds and improve every marker for disease. What we know for certain is that your body prefers to use fats for energy and runs more efficiently on a high-fat diet. Think of quality high-fat foods such as wild salmon, cage-free eggs, avocado, extra virgin olive oil, walnuts and other nuts, grass-fed meats, and butter as premium gasoline for your body. This premium fuel energizes you, cleanses your body, sharpens your mind, and keeps many diseases at bay. Now think of high carbohydrate foods, regardless if they are labeled as "whole-grains" or not, as cheap, low-grade fuel that does not give you the same results as high-grade fuel. You can certainly put low-grade gasoline into a high-performance car like a Ferrari and it will run, but don't expect it to last. The low-grade fuel will degrade every component of the Ferrari's engine, and the car will soon cease to function. It's the same with your body. You can run on sugar and carbs, but you will eventually pay the price when your health goes south.

Can Heart Disease Be Reversed?

The answer to this question is yes—in most cases—and it's based on the type and stage of the disease. Many cases of heart disease (coronary artery disease) can be reversed with proper intervention. Reversing coronary artery disease is possible when the factors that led to its development (a high-sugar and high-carb diet, processed foods, a lack of whole foods, lack of exercise, etc.) are addressed properly via nutrition, lifestyle modifications, and supplementation. Heart disease is caused by plaque that develops in the arteries and blood vessels that lead to the heart. This plaque blocks vital nutrients and oxygen from reaching the heart, and, if the buildup is severe enough, causes a heart attack or stroke.

The plaque that builds up in the arteries is a waxy substance made up of cholesterol, fatty molecules, and minerals. Over time, plaque accumulates when the inner lining of an artery is damaged by high blood pressure, cigarette smoking, elevated LDL (bad) cholesterol, or triglycerides. The good news is that this plaque can be cleared or removed from the arteries. Reducing your alcohol intake, quitting smoking, being more active, eating more plant foods, and limiting sugar and carbohydrate intake will lower your chances of suffering a heart attack or stroke by reducing arterial plaque and reversing its buildup. It's important to know that the damage that occurs to the heart—whether through genetics, lifestyle choices, or both—is not solely caused by genes or diet, but also by mitochondria-induced oxidation and inflammation that happens within your arteries.

You see, your heart is shaped like a twisting muscle that looks like the coiled back of a boa constrictor. The twisting motion of your heart is designed to keep you alive by delivering nutrients your body needs at any given time. The heart muscle is stimulated by pacemaker cells to eject blood through the aortic valve. Picture a towel being wrung out of water, that's how your heart pumps blood. That blood pulsates the aorta, which is the body's largest artery, delivering oxygen-rich blood to the rest of the body, as well as to the coronary arteries surrounding the heart. Much of heart disease happens in your arteries—which are the tunnels that feed both nutrients and toxins to all your organs—rather than in your heart itself. Arteries are made up of three layers of tissue: a cellophane-like exterior shell, a muscular middle, and a thin smooth inside layer that allows blood to slide through. Your arteries serve as the site of the inflammatory process that's responsible for most types of heart disease.

It all starts with cholesterol which as you know comes in healthy HDL, or high-density lipoproteins and bad LDL, or high-density lipoproteins. The smooth inside layer of your arteries is pummeled by various things: cigarettes, high blood pressure, excess sugar, etc. When that happens, your body sends bad LDL cholesterol to damaged areas in an attempt to heal the wounds or damage. Your immune cells in the damaged area absorb the LDL cholesterol and burrow into the inner layer of your arteries. Your body then reacts to the wounds and the cholesterol with low-grade inflammation. Inflammation is how your body deals with various stressors to your system like bacterial infections, splinters, insect venom, and other foreign invaders. Meanwhile, your healthy HDL cholesterol works to clear the LDL cholesterol out of the area. As you are aware, cholesterol comes in different sizes, but the most dangerous type is the smaller kind. The smaller the cholesterol particle, the more likely it is to nestle itself into the artery wall, where it causes damage and triggers the inflammatory process.

To clear the arteries of plaque, the function as well as the size of the healthy HDL cholesterol needs to be increased. This can be done by supplementing with omega-3 fatty acids, niacin (vitamin B3), and Vitamin B5, as well as some of the newest fibrate and statin drugs. Other supplements that can help reduce inflammation are bromelain, nettle leaf extract, ginger, and curcumin. Refer to the supplements section for dosages and frequency for these supplements.

The low-grade inflammation that occurs in response to LDL cholesterol calls on your body's reinforcement immune cells called macrophages. These macrophages eat the LDL cholesterol, becoming engorged with fat and literally blowing up, then attaching themselves to the walls of your arteries. Pathologists call them foam cells, as they clog the artery walls, leading to the birth of arterial plaque. As the plaque grows, it reduces the nutrient-rich blood supply through the arteries, and when the plaque runs out of blood supply – there's a big-time explosion as a clot fills up the plaque. The sudden clot formation then closes off the artery, and the artery dies. To give you a picture of how the process works, think of a six-lane bridge going into a city: If one of the lanes is shut down, traffic can still get through, but a bit slower. But if an explosion on the bridge takes out all of the lanes, no traffic can get through. That's why arterial plaques are so dangerous. No test can tell whether just one of your lanes is closed, or if a lane will potentially explode. When heart disease is discussed, you often hear the word *calcification*. Calcification in the arteries is your body's attempt to heal those inflammatory plaques in your body.

The calcium stabilizes the plaque-like cement reinforcement of a plaster wall. About ninety percent of men with atherosclerosis have calcified arteries compared to thirty percent in women. Women respond better to heart disease reversal compared to men, since their arteries are not lined in a cast of calcium. However, because of this, women's arteries are more precarious and more prone to rupture and sudden clot formation than men's arteries. The meaning of all this is that you can't become healthy by testing yourself; you have to live healthfully to prevent any sudden explosions that cause heart disease and strokes. Inflammation plays a huge role in many types of heart disease and must be greatly reduced to reverse the disease.

For example, in atrial fibrillation (abnormal heart rhythm), the heart's small upper chambers, which are supposed to receive blood and gently propel it downstream, start looking like bags of worms. Because blood is not pushed completely out of the atria, it may pool and clot. Atrial fibrillation is frequently caused by inflammation of the heart wall, and the damage is done by oxygen-free radicals which are produced by inefficient mitochondria. Arrhythmias can also be caused by other things, including pressure on the walls of the atria or abnormal hormone function, which can be linked to general inflammation of the heart. Regardless of the cause, the delicate cables that conduct electricity throughout your heart become swollen and start short-circuiting. Arrhythmias can actually be felt as a fluttering of the heart, compared with most other heart conditions which you can't feel. Avoid trans fats, saturated fat, processed omega-6 laden fries, and other fried and baked foods such as pie. Occasionally indulging (once per week) in these foods is fine, but being in the habit of eating fried and baked goods on a regular or daily basis puts your arteries under heavy stress and contributes to significant arterial plaque build-up over time.

Your goal to protect your heart and prevent heart disease is not only to cut down on the foods and habits that damage and clog your arteries, but also to take action to strengthen your heart muscle to further decrease your risk of cardiovascular disease. This is done by taking in antioxidants and being physically active. As you age, consistent exercise is a must in order to prevent the onset of heart disease. That being said, there are a few (rare) cases of people having lived well into their 80s and 90s who never undertook a planned exercise routine and who did not consume a strict diet high in antioxidants, but these people are not the norm and are exceptions. Antioxidants are vital in heart-disease prevention, as they keep oxidation from wounded mitochondria in check. While medicine helps too, it should not be your first resort because drugs come with unpleasant side-effects. Statin drugs tend to have the least side effects and they work by decreasing inflammation in the plaque, which slows the progression of the clogging process and reduces sudden closure of the arteries.

Think of my recommendations for preventing heart disease as a firefighting unit. Adding antioxidants in the form of supplements, eating antioxidant-rich fruits and vegetables, being physically active on most days, and avoiding cigarettes, excessive alcohol and processed foods are all factors that you add to your firefighting unit so that it stays fresh and can extinguish the small fires and occasional flare ups that occur within your arteries. The stronger your firefighting unit, the better your body is able to fight arterial plaque buildup and heart disease.

Coronary Artery Disease (CAD) Prevention Tips:

While it would be easy for me to instruct you to never eat M&M's again, no more burgers and fries, no more fried chicken, no more milk shakes, no more smoking and alcohol, I believe that, by this point, you're fully aware that fried foods, candy, chips, and baked pastries are not heart-healthy. My goal is not to take away all your life's joys when it comes to food. Life would certainly be very dull without the foods that we desire the most. So, without taking away most of your joys, here are the steps you should take so your heart can perform its main job: moving blood through all areas of your body— without obstructions.

You don't have to be a dietician to know that certain foods will create roadblocks in your arterial highways. Foods containing processed vegetable oils and trans fats are at the top of the list of foods that accelerate and trigger inflammation. You see, *every* time you eat, you are either contributing to plaque build-up and inflammation in your arterial walls and stimulating genes to produce more inflammatory proteins to make the tissue irritation a lot worse, or you are delivering heart-healthy nutrients to your arteries which block and *prevent* inflammation and promote the clearing of arterial plaque.

Base your diet around fruits and vegetables: If your dinner plate is loaded with potatoes, rice, bread or pasta, and only contains a miniscule amount or no veggies on the side, with parfait, ice cream, or cake as desert and no fruit in sight, you are headed straight towards the inflammatory highway of coronary artery disease. While it's okay, but not ideal, to eat small amounts of carbs in the form of bread, pasta, potatoes, and rice with each meal, most of your plate should contain veggies and your dessert needs to be fruit most of the time. If you don't eat dessert, then fruits should be part of your between-meal snacks at least twice a day. Most fruits and vegetables—especially cranberries, red grapes, onions, tomatoes and tomato juice—contain powerful antioxidants called flavonoids and carotenoids. Carotenoids and flavonoids are vitamin-like nonessential substances that help to reduce inflammation by handcuffing damaging oxygen free-radicals and stimulating your body to eliminate or throw them from your system through urine.

Eat Garlic: While there is still some debate on this in the scientific community, eating a clove of garlic once a day can help thin your blood and lower your blood pressure. If you don't like the taste or don't want to alienate people with the less-than-pleasant aroma of garlic, you can take it in pill form. Refer to the supplements section for dosage and frequency.

Eat Dark Chocolate: Recent studies have shown that eating dark chocolate may lower your blood pressure as effectively as the most common antihypertensive medications and may increase HDL cholesterol and lower LDL cholesterol. Dark chocolate contains high amounts of flavonoids, which are powerful compounds that help smooth the lining of your arteries and benefit your cholesterol levels. An interesting fact: The Kuna Indians, who live on islands near Panama, have very little age-related hypertension. They drink more than five cups of flavonoid rich cocoa a day. When selecting dark chocolate, go with a minimum of seventy percent cocoa content, as the higher the cocoa content the more flavonoids the chocolate will contain and the less sugar it will have.

What's more, a study done in 2018 at Loma Linda University Health in California showed that dark chocolate had a very positive effect on memory and recall. Lee Berk, PH, associate dean of research at the School of Allied Health Professions at Loma Linda University, along with his researchers, used 48-gram bars of dark chocolate that were made from 70 percent cocoa beans, stating that the consumption of antioxidants has the capability to change your brain frequency—a beneficial brain frequency called gamma. "The gamma frequency is up-regulated, enhanced, turned on by virtue of the chocolate antioxidants."

Cook with Olive oil: Extra-virgin olive oil contains lots of healthy monounsaturated fats and phytonutrients which help raise your good HDL cholesterol. Aim for a minimum of twenty-five percent of your diet to come from healthy fats like olive oil. You can achieve this by cooking all your meals with olive oil and using it as part of salad dressing.

Drink alcohol (Red Wine is best): While this tip contradicts what I specified earlier about avoiding and reducing your alcohol intake to prevent heart disease, small amounts of alcohol can be beneficial to your arteries. To benefit from alcohol, *moderation* is key. Drinking it in moderation is fine if you don't have a problem with alcohol;

having one alcoholic drink every other night (twelve ounces of beer, four ounces of wine, or one and a half ounces of spirits) for women and up to two for men, can have a beneficial effect on your heart by raising levels of good HDL cholesterol. Alcohol also helps you wind down at night, which can lower your blood pressure. Go with red wine because it contains the highest number of antioxidants compared to other alcoholic drinks.

Eat Foods High in Omega-3s and Take an Omega 3 Supplement: Essential fatty acids are found abundantly in fish, especially in fatty fish like salmon and trout. Other great choices are mahi-mahi, whitefish, swordfish, and shrimp. Choose wild over farmed fish and seafood whenever possible and go with baked or smoked instead of fried to avoid extra fat. When it comes to choosing the right omega-3 supplement, go with a high-quality fish oil, salmon oil, or krill oil product. Take two to three soft gels per day. Refer to the supplements section for more on choosing the right omega-3 supplement.

Eat Foods High in Magnesium: Non-GMO soybeans, lima beans, avocados, raisins, cashews, and beets help lower blood pressure and reduce arrhythmias by dilating (expanding) your arteries. Get at least four hundred milligrams of magnesium a day. A serving of lima beans contains about one hundred milligrams, one cup of spinach contains about one hundred sixty milligrams, and twelve cashews contain fifty milligrams.

Sweat: By this I am referring to cardiovascular activity, more specifically walking fast and jogging, either outside at the park when the weather is nice or on a treadmill. The way to improve heart function is to sweat more. You see, cardiovascular activity lowers both the top systolic (the pressure being exerted when your heart contracts) and the bottom diastolic (the pressure in the arteries when the heart is at rest) numbers of your blood pressure. Cardio helps strengthen your heart because it makes your blood vessels more elastic by forcing them to dilate. In addition to at least thirty minutes of daily walking, shoot for a minimum of sixty minutes a week of cardiovascular activity that makes you sweat—in which you raise your heart rate to eighty percent or more of its age-adjusted maximum (two hundred twenty minus your age) for an extended period. Mix up your cardio by doing low-impact activities like swimming, using an elliptical trainer, and cycling. All of these cardio activities are considered low-impact as they don't put an excessive amount of stress on your joints. I also highly recommend interval training, which is alternating periods of maximum effort with periods of minimal effort. If you are over the age of forty, check with your doctor first before undertaking interval training. Your doctor may want to try it in a controlled setting of a stress test first. Interval training does not have to be very intense to benefit your heart. Even doing one minute at the end of every nine or ten minutes with maximum effort can be beneficial. For example, after warming up, go for maximum effort for a minute, then slow down to sixty percent of maximum (recover) for two minutes. Then go eighty percent of maximum for seven minutes. Cool down afterwards. As you progress, you can do intervals alternating between intense effort and effort that allows you to recover—one minute fast, two minutes slow, and so on.

Take Aspirin: While pharmaceutical drugs should not be your first resort in treating and preventing heart disease, taking a low-dose aspirin can be an exception if you're over thirty-five years of age. As a very potent anti-inflammatory agent, aspirin works to combat your body's inflammatory response when it's triggered by foods and stressors. Be sure to speak with your doctor first before you start taking it on a regular basis. I recommend half a regular aspirin or two baby aspirins (162 milligrams total) daily if you're a man over thirty-five or a woman over forty. Several studies of primary prevention have shown that two baby aspirins decrease the risk of heart attack by thirty-six percent. Aspirin works by making blood platelets less sticky, which prevents clotting, and by decreasing arterial inflammation. Some people experience gastric discomfort from aspirin. You can avoid this by drinking half a glass of warm water before and after taking aspirin (the pills dissolve faster in warm water and are less likely to cause stomach irritation). A word of caution on aspirin: as aspirin is a blood thinner, you may notice more bleeding from flossing or a shaving cut or become more susceptible to bruising. If you notice these effects, it's most likely from the aspirin. Cut back on your aspirin intake and speak with your doctor.

Take the Following Supplements: B-Vitamin Complex, Coenzyme Q10, Vitamin D, and D-Ribose. Refer to the supplements section for dosage and frequency.

Beating Stress

Thousands of years ago, stress was something that our ancestors dealt with constantly, just like we do today. However, the stress we deal with today is a very different type of stress compared to the stress our ancestors had to deal with. You see, in the hunter-gatherer days, there was only one type of stress and it involved life or death. Stress may have come from evading a predator or enduring a twenty-day famine. Human life in the hunter-gatherer days was *far* different than it is today, and the stresses our ancestors had to deal with were very simple.

Now days, your energy and attention are pulled in more directions than you can possibly deal with at one time, and most of the stress you deal with day to day isn't life or death. Your boss needs you, your kids want you, your smartphone goes off every few minutes, be it a text message or an app notification; you have bills, appointments, and deadlines to meet. Most of us are used to dealing with life's stressors daily, and most of us are so beaten, bruised, and burdened by stress that we've come to accept it as a normal part of life, something that we just live with. After all, stress is intangible, so it can't be bad for us, right?

Wrong. Understand: stress is a concrete condition that if poorly managed and left unchecked, makes your body age *far* faster and kills your life contentment and happiness. Stress is not like a pair of shoes, where one size fits all. Either you're stressed out or you're not. Modern stress comes in many different sizes, shapes, and levels of intensity. Some people are more prone to worry than others, and some of us are more quipped to deal with both small and large circumstances and life events that lead to stress. Learning how to manage stress and keep it low is vital to your short- and long-term health and happiness.

The danger with stress is that it increases as we age, and it becomes a major driver of health problems. Stress impacts your immune system, affects every cell in your body, and alters the variability of your heart, which can lead to arrhythmias and fatal heart problems. Most of the stress we deal with is considered ongoing, low-level stress. Work, family, and interacting with others all generate low-level stress, no matter your gender, age, or what you do for a living. Expecting to eliminate stress completely is very unrealistic, unreasonable, and even unhealthy as you'll find out in a minute—your ability to deal with stress can make you stronger.

The other type of stress comes from nagging or unfinished tasks. One of the most persistent forms of stress comes in the form of something that chips and chisels at you piece by piece until you can't take it anymore. This would be a cluttered closet, cracked bathroom tiles that have been staring at you for years, or weekly paperwork that eats away at you every Friday, etc. These nagging or unfinished tasks are much more destructive and harmful to your health than low-level stress that comes from being alive.

Finally, there is stress that occurs when you go through a major life event such as a divorce, moving to another city, a job change, a death in the family, bankruptcy, or being diagnosed with a life-threatening illness. This type of stress is not the same level as the stress you feel from a dead cell phone battery or from a sudden splash of water from a puddle that soils your pretty pants. Statistics show that experiencing three major life events in a single year will make your body feel and act as if it's *thirty years* older in the following year. This is an eye-opening finding, making it especially important to develop sound coping strategies and support systems to carry you through in times of a major life crisis.

These different types of stressors affect you on different levels. The first kind of stress (low-level stress) wears you down and fatigues you but is not harmful to your health. The last two kinds of stress outlined above are the most harmful and dangerous. Understanding how they happen is the first step to understanding how to stop dangerous, killer stress from occurring.

The Biology of Stress

A certain amount of stress is good for you. Yes, you read that right—stress is good. You see, stress heightens all your biological systems so that your body can deal with an impending threat, be it a natural disaster, an enemy, or a fire. When you're stressed, changes occur inside your body that gives you the strength to either combat the stressful situation or leave. This is commonly referred to as the "flight or fight" response. Your concentration becomes laser focused, your strength increases rapidly, and you react faster. Stress is good, as long as you can survive it. However, the major difference between the stress that we feel today and the stress our ancestors felt thousands of years ago in caveman times is that their stress was fleeting. They had periods of high-intensity stress followed by low (or no) stress. This is considered acute stress, and your body is well equipped to deal with it when it occurs. Now days, we're drowning in an ocean of chronic stress with constant waves coming at us and knocking us over. As our bodies are not equipped to deal with chronic (on-going and repetitive) stress, we suffer from it in the form of declining physical and mental health. With acute (short-term) stress, our biological reactions work in our favor to eliminate the stressful situation, but when we're chronically stressed out over long periods, those same biological reactions turn against us.

Chronic stress is a major contributor to cardiovascular disease, heart attacks, cancer, and disabling accidents. Stress also destroys your sleep patterns, which can lead to unhealthy addictions to food, in the form of late-night binge eating, overeating, excessive snacking, and alcohol addictions. Your stress system initiates the production of a series of chemicals that travel through the blood affecting every system in your body. This is known as the stress circuit, which is the interaction between your nervous system and your stress hormones. More specifically, the hypothalamic-pituitary-adrenal (HPA) axis is responsible for initiating the stress feedback loop. When you're faced with a major danger like a mugger, a tight deadline, or a shortage of food, the hypothalamus at the base of your brain releases CRH (corticotrophin releasing hormone), which then triggers your pituitary gland, stimulating it to release another hormone called ACTH (adrenocorticotropic hormone) into your bloodstream.

ACTH signals your adrenal glands to release cortisol and carries out the production and release of norepinephrine, also known as adrenaline—the fight-or-flight chemical. Adrenaline increases your blood pressure and heart rate, while cortisol releases sugar in the form of glucose to fuel your muscles and brain. Then, to close the loop, cortisol travels back to the hypothalamus to stop the production of CRH. At this point, the stress is considered over and the body's hormones return to normal, but only if the stress stops as well. In addition to giving your body the tools it needs to combat stress when it occurs, stress hormones also work throughout various regions of the brain to influence everything from your mood and memory to your appetite. These hormones also interact with hormonal systems that control reproduction, metabolism, and immunity.

The hormones that run through your HPA axis are only bad for your health when they run out of control and when the HPA becomes overactive. An overactive HPA means that your body is not able to turn off its stress response, which leads to anxiety and depression. Anxiety and depression are further manifested through low sex drive and high blood pressure – both of which are associated with aging. Also, when the HPA axis is flooded, we experience other potentially fatal health problems like elevated LDL cholesterol combined with reduced HDL cholesterol. Part of this risk comes from a stress-related surge in chemicals called cannabinoids which increase your appetite and can eventually lead to diabetes and obesity. Excessive cortisol (a major stress hormone) prevents the release of chemicals that strengthen your immune system. This is one of the reasons why you tend to get sick when you're stressed out. Too much cortisol suppresses your immune system and decreases your ability to fight infections. Stress also makes you more susceptible to diseases that rely on your immune system to prevent or fight off diseases like cancer. In general, men have a faster rebound from cortisol release during stress compared to women.

CRH (corticotrophin releasing hormone) prevents the release of a hormone that controls all the hormones responsible for sexual behavior and reproduction, including those that control sperm release and ovulation. Stress reduction techniques are one of the tactics used by couples with fertility issues. Relaxation is done not due to some spiritual or emotional reason but to make their bodies better equipped hormonally for conception. What's important to know is that if the HPA axis is activated for too long it inhibits the release of growth hormone. As you're aware, growth hormone is essential for your body to combat aging-related diseases and other health conditions, and it's essential to building lean muscle tissue. If your HPA axis is active for too long, it will lead to an exhausted response, which produces a wiped-out feeling when stress does come.

The Role of Stem Cells in Stress

Stress is all about adapting to the challenges of life. It's not the strongest or fastest person who wins in the game of life, but rather it's the most adaptable. When stress hormones damage tissues, cells, or organs in your body, stem cells replace damaged cells and make the repairs. Stem cells play a huge role in the body's repair and healing process. For example, if you consume toxic food (processed foods), stem cells swoop in to rescue the organs that sustained stress and damage; in the case of consuming processed foods, your heart and liver are stressed the most. Stem cells come to the rescue and rebuild you as good as you were before the stress occurred or the toxic food was consumed. Stress has a cascading effect on many aspects of our health. It damages your immune system, accelerates arterial aging, and makes you more likely to be involved in a life-altering or life-ending accident. Many accident victims admit to having been stressed or angry prior to a mishap. Stress also has a huge impact on your mental health by making you more likely to be in a negative or pessimistic state of mind. Stress is not just something you write off as a need for spa treatment; it's a major biological contributor to aging.

Realize that your response to stress is somewhat determined by your genetics. Everybody has differences in genes that control the HPA axis, which means that some people never have a strong response to a threat, while some people have a strong response to even minor threats. The genetic predisposition can be altered at any time by extreme stresses. When you have major stresses early in life, your responses to stress are stronger as you age, making you better able to handle future stresses. To give you an example of this, when exposed to extreme heat (known as heat shock), all animals, including humans, learn to adapt to the extreme temperature so they can respond to it the next time it's encountered. It's the biological mantra of what does not kill you makes you stronger.

You see, when our ancestors faced periods of famine, they stored fat in their bellies with an organ called the omentum. The same thing happens to us when we are faced with chronic stress. Being chronically stressed out causes you to eat more food than you need, which causes the food to be stored in the omentum for quick access to energy. The steroids that your body releases through the HPA axis are also sucked up by the omentum and help grow it. This is a very damaging process to your body as not only does it expand the size of your belly, but also because the toxins from your omentum fat are pumped directly into surrounding organs. If you tend to store a lot of fat in your belly, it's a sign of high-stress levels and you need to take steps to reduce your stress levels. To help minimize the internal damage that external stressors cause, adopt the following strategies:

Manage Your Anger: It's no secret that anger does not help anyone. Yelling at the car in front of you in traffic or going off on your kids won't help you or the people whom you're directing your anger towards. Anger has been shown to lead to a higher incidence of heart disease and other health problems. Part of the problem is that we're misinformed about the best way to handle our anger. While you may think that punching the pillow or a punching bag helps you release pent-up aggression and stress, the opposite is true. It teaches you to develop a behavior pattern where you punch something every time you're mad. You can't nor should you harbor stress until it eats away at you like termites through wood. What you need to do instead is use behavioral and mental techniques that have been proven to reduce anger and anxiety—including chronic heart problems that are associated with them.

Reduce Your Intake of Caffeine: Caffeine is found in coffee, tea, and energy drinks and has positive effects on your health by increasing your energy levels and productivity; unfortunately, it can also have negative effects on your health by contributing to or amplifying stress. You see, when you consume caffeinated beverages, your body starts pumping out the fight-or-flight hormones adrenaline and norepinephrine, which increases your heart rate and temporarily raises your blood pressure. These side-effects of caffeine consumption make it more difficult to stay calm when a stress-triggering event or situation occurs, which further amplifies the stressed-out feeling. For example, excessive caffeine consumption would be having a large cup of coffee in the morning, then downing an energy drink in the afternoon or early evening. While everyone has different levels of tolerance for caffeine, you should not have to rely on caffeinated beverages to keep you going throughout the day. Staying away from processed foods and excessive sugar will keep your energy levels stable throughout the day. Ultimately, the foods you eat (and stay away from) play the biggest role in your energy levels, and caffeinated beverages should only be consumed on top of a wholesome, nutrient-dense diet, not as a replacement for real food.

Go Outside: Being outdoors, especially when it's sunny, is a fail-proof stress-reduction strategy. Sunshine provides your body with natural vitamin D, which is essential for your health and well-being. The next time you feel very stressed out or overwhelmed by your routine, take a thirty-minute walk outside, preferably in a park. Try not to listen to music and don't use your cell phone while walking, but rather just focus on the scenery around you and maintain a brisk pace. Take deep breaths and take your mind off work, bills, and other commitments while you are walking. You'll notice an instant reduction in stress and you'll feel focused, calmer, and clearer minded. Drinking pure, fresh water while you're out walking or before your walk will contribute to relaxation as water nourishes your brain cells and muscles and is essential for every bodily function. Go with spring water as it's free of contaminants and additives, does not contain fluoride (a potentially harmful additive found in tap water) and has naturally occurring essential trace minerals.

Take a Nap: While napping may be the last thing on your mind during a busy day at the office and when running errands, it will work wonders to reduce and eliminate stress. Dozing off for just twenty to thirty minutes in the afternoon will re-energize you and clear your mind, which has a direct impact on your stress levels. Napping slows down your heart rate and temporarily reduces your blood pressure, which lowers stress levels and leaves you feeling refreshed.

Try Meditation: Meditation does not have to be a drawn-out event that takes up an hour or more of your day to be effective. Meditating for just five to ten minutes a day has been shown to reduce stress and induce a sense of calm and tranquility, allowing you to be more productive and focused.

Take a Quiet Day: You do not have to go on vacation to enjoy some down time. Once a week, take a day and don't do anything stressful. Listen to music that relaxes you, go swimming at the pool or lake, and just take it easy by not focusing on or worrying about work, bills, and other commitments. Taking a quiet day will re-charge your mental batteries and allow you to function more effectively at work the following day.

"STRESS KILLS. NO MATTER HOW PAINFUL IN THE SHORT-TERM, REMOVE ALL CHRONICALLY STRESSFUL SITUATIONS, PEOPLE AND ENVIRONMENTS FROM YOUR LIFE."

CHAPTER 7: What You Need to Know about Dietary Supplements

When it comes to dietary supplements, there are endless options to choose from. Walk into any health store, supplement shop, or the nutritional products section of your local grocery store and you are instantly dazed by the wide array of pills, powders, and bars neatly packaged sitting on shelves waiting to be picked up. Being aware of how specific nutrients affect your body and contribute to fat loss and longevity will go a long way towards choosing the right supplements that will enhance your quality of life. You see, dietary supplements are made from nutrients that are found inside the foods you eat every day. However, due to soil erosion caused by modern agriculture practices, many fruits and vegetables now contain fewer vitamins and minerals overall compared to just two or three decades ago.

Soil erosion by water, tillage, and wind affects not only the nutrient density of farmed foods but also the entire agriculture industry and our natural environment. Soil loss and its associated environmental impact is one of the most important of today's environmental problems and is affecting the nutrient density of our food. Fruits and veggies used to be loaded with vitamins and minerals and fewer plant foods were needed to obtain enough nutrients for health. Now days, the amount of nutrients we get from eating five to seven servings of fruits and veggies a day may still not be enough, especially if you are very active and/or exercise vigorously several times a week. This is where dietary supplements come into play, as they can help close any nutritional gaps you may have in your diet.

However, it's important to know that supplements can *never* compensate for a good diet that consists of various foods from plant and animal sources. You see, many of the shortcomings in the modern American diet are linked to economics. Fast food is popular because it's cheap, and processed and packaged foods cost less and stay fresh longer. The U.S. Preventative Service Task Force (USPSTF), an independent group of doctors, opted in 2013 not to recommend the use of any herbal supplements, and advised consumers to stay away from beta-carotene (Vitamin A) and Vitamin E supplements amid concerns of increased heart disease risk in men who've suffered a heart attack prior to supplementing with Vitamins A and E.

A 2011, Iowa Woman's Health study found that when other variables were excluded, those who took vitamin supplements died sooner than those who did not. Only vitamin B and calcium had a minor positive effect on longevity. The study followed more than 38,000 women over a twenty-year period. A long-term study conducted by Stephen P. Fortmann and colleagues failed to come up with evidence to suggest there's any reason to take multivitamins or any of the common single-letter vitamins as a preventative measure against heart-disease and cancer. On the other hand, a study done by Doctor J. Michael Gaziano and colleagues found that multivitamin supplements reduced the risk of cancer in an older and largely male population of physicians.

So, what do these findings mean for your health? Simply put, taking multivitamins and single nutrient vitamins will *not* guarantee that you will not get cancer, heart disease, and other serious conditions. Rather, multivitamins and other supplements can work and be recommended under specific circumstances. For example, vegans and those over fifty may want to consider adding vitamin B12, which is abundant in animal products and can be difficult for older people to digest. Women who are pregnant or may become pregnant are advised to take folic acid to guard against natural birth defects. The USPSTF recommends vitamin D supplementation for people over sixty-five who are at risk of falls. Some doctors recommend Vitamin D products for younger patients because sunscreen and more time spent indoors limit our natural production of the vitamin.

Consuming ample amounts of fruits and veggies along with animal products will ensure that your risk of being nutrient-deficient remains low. Eat more vegetables and fruits every day and you'll instantly reduce your risk factor for disease. The more color your plate contains, the better. Most of your plate should be filled with veggies, with the remainder being meat, and a small amount of starchy carbohydrates. Eat fruit as dessert most of the time instead of cake, cookies, and other sweets and pastries. Eating fast food several times a week, skipping veggies (or eating very little), and eating low amounts of fruit will certainly put you at risk for a nutrient-deficiency and will increase your risk of developing cancer and heart disease. Eating nutrient-rich foods means your body will have all the tools it needs to combat disease and maintain healthy and vibrant cells that function at an optimal rate as you age. Skipping veggies and fruits, feeling bad about doing so, and then taking a multivitamin to compensate for poor nutritional choices and saying "at least I'm doing that" simply won't do if you are serious about transforming your health and body.

The Supplement Industry Lacks Regulation

While I am an advocate of nutritional supplements in the presence of a nutrient-dense diet, I cannot recommend most nutrition supplements as the supplement industry lacks regulation. You see, literally no one inspects supplements before they hit store shelves, which means that your protein powder and multivitamin can contain other nutrients, fillers and dangerous contaminants, and you won't even be aware. Supplement makers must adhere to the FDA's (Food and Drug Administration) good manufacturing guidelines, which means they are required to accurately state the ingredients their products contain. But, as with any industry, the supplement industry is not immune from corruption.

In 2015, the FDA, along with the New York State Attorney General's office, conducted tests on several top-selling store brands of herbal supplements at four national retailers—Walmart, GNC, Target, and Walgreens. What they found was shocking. Four out of five of the products tested *did not contain any* of the herbs on their label. Some of them contained substances that could be hazardous to people with allergies and food sensitivities. The test showed that pills labeled as medicinal herbs often contained little more than cheap fillers like asparagus, house plants and powdered rice. Among the Attorney General Office's findings was a popular store brand of ginseng pills at Walgreens, marketed for "physical endurance and vitality" that contained only powdered garlic and rice.

At Walmart, they found that its gingko biloba, a Chinese plant promoted as a memory enhancer, contained little more than powdered radish, wheat, and houseplants—despite a claim on the label that the product was wheat and gluten-free.

Three out of six herbal products at Target—St. John's wort, ginkgo biloba, and valerian root, a sleep aid—tested negative for the herbs on their labels. They contained only powdered rice, beans, peas, and wild carrots.

The New York Attorney General's investigation was triggered by an article in the *New York Times* in 2013 that raised questions about widespread labeling fraud in the supplement industry. The article pointed to research done at the University of Guelph in Canada, which found that as many as a third of herbal supplements tested did not contain the plants listed on their labels, but rather only cheap fillers. Due to budget limitations, the FDA only tests about one percent of the more than 65,000 dietary supplements on the market, according to Todd Runestad, editor of the publication *Functional Ingredients and the Engredea* reports. Dietary-supplement manufacturers are not required to prove (via controlled studies) that their products have any effects on health and performance. Only when a supplement results in "adverse" health effects can the FDA pull it from shelves. In 2004, the FDA banned the popular weight-loss ingredient ephedra after it led to eight deaths. In 2013, the FDA recalled a top selling fat-loss product after it led to several cases of liver failure.

What's important to know about the FDA is that it's a wholly-owned subsidiary of Big Pharma, and they exist to protect the interests of the multi-billion dollar pharmaceutical industry. Yes, you read that right. Big Pharma *owns* the FDA. There's a huge conflict of interest when it comes to testing dietary supplements. Due to this fact, the supplement industry is in direct competition with the prescription and over-the-counter drug industry in the United States.

While the right supplement combination can work wonders in treating and preventing disease in conjunction with a whole-foods diet and a health-promoting lifestyle, there are many supplements on the market that are poor quality and don't contain the ingredients stated on the label. This is a very unfortunate fact and something that has put the industry into a negative light in recent years. Choosing to buy supplements only from reputable and established manufacturers is paramount to benefiting from nutritional products.

There have bene numerous efforts by the FDA to develop tighter regulatory control. For example, in 1976, the FDA pushed to regulate vitamins that contained more than one hundred fifty percent of the recommended daily allowance as drugs. However, congress stepped in and stopped the agency from doing so. In the early 1990s, Congress considered several bills that would have expanded the powers of the FDA. *The Nutritional Labeling and Education Act*, passed in 1990, imposed stricter labeling rules on food products. At the urging of Senator Orrin Hatch, a Utah Republican, the law exempted dietary supplements. Utah is home to many dietary supplement companies, whose combined value exceeds five billion dollars, according to NASDAQ.

In 1994, regulations were loosened under the Dietary Supplement Health and Education Act (DSHEA), which was a big win for the supplement industry. The DSHEA was sponsored in large part by Tom Harkin, a now-retired Iowa Democrat whose largest corporate donor over the course of his career was the dietary supplements conglomerate Herbalife. Passage of the law led to an explosion of new manufacturers in the industry. But it didn't go so far as to allow herbal supplements to claim on their labels that they cure, treat, or prevent any diseases, as pharmaceutical drugs can. Rather, more general health claims, such as "supports healthy immune function" are allowed to be stated on labels. There are currently more than 1,000 companies across the globe making more than 29,000 herbal products, with medicinal herbs being the fastest-growing segment of the North American alternative medicine market. Choosing the right dietary supplements from established and reputable manufacturers is key to getting the health and nutritional boost that supplements can provide.

Synthetic Vs Natural Supplements

It's important to know that there are two forms of supplements: synthetic and natural. Synthetic supplements are known as isolated nutrients, which are usually made artificially via an industrial process. Natural supplements are obtained from whole-food sources and have no synthetic or "man-made" nutrients. On the other hand, natural supplements, sometimes referred to as "whole-food supplements" are made from concentrated and dehydrated whole foods. Most supplements that you see on shelves today are synthetic or artificial, largely because synthetic nutrients are cheaper to source and formulate. To figure out if your supplement is synthetic or natural, check the label. Non-synthetic or natural supplements usually list whole food sources in the ingredients list or are labeled as one hundred percent plant or animal-based. Products that list individual nutrients such as ascorbic acid (vitamin C) are almost certainly synthetic. Synthetic nutrients are chemically identical to natural nutrients or those found in food; however, due to the production process of synthetic nutrients, which is different from the way nature creates nutrients, your body may react differently to synthetic vitamins and minerals.

Despite the numerous studies that have been done to date on the effectiveness and safety of synthetic nutrients, we still don't know how well synthetic nutrients are absorbed and used by the body. Some synthetic vitamins may be more easily absorbed than others, depending on different factors such as the presence of other co-nutrients that help with the absorption of a particular vitamin or mineral. You see, when you eat real food, you're not consuming single nutrients, but rather a whole range of vitamins, minerals, and co-factors and enzymes which allow your body to process and absorb each nutrient optimally. For example, eating a sweet potato, which is a rich source of Vitamin A, will almost certainly guarantee that your body will absorb most of the vitamin A as sweet potatoes contain other nutrients such as potassium and fiber, which help with the absorption of co-nutrients. Taking a Vitamin A pill or capsule with a glass of water is very different from eating a sweet potato which naturally contains the vitamin along with many other nutrients. Without these other nutrients, synthetic vitamins are not likely to be used by the body the same way as their natural compounds. A study done by researchers published in 1998 in the *American Journal of Clinical Nutrition,* showed that natural Vitamin E is absorbed twice as effectively as synthetic Vitamin E.

It's important to know that there are two types of synthetic supplements: beneficial synthetically-produced micronutrients and potentially dangerous synthetically produced micronutrients. Beneficial synthetically produced micronutrients are most often extracted from whole-food ingredients and are molecularly and chemically identical to their whole-food counterpart. In some cases, they are delivered in what's known as an active form, which allows superior absorption of the nutrient. Some examples of beneficially produced micronutrients:

Lutein: Lutein is a synthetically produced, lab-made nutrient designed for eye health. Many quality multivitamin supplements will include lutein, and while whole food supplements may get their lutein source from spinach or kale, there is no way of knowing exactly how much lutein is in each bushel and therefore these food sources cannot be standardized. Lutein can be safely and effectively extracted from the marigold flower, and this synthetically-produced source is a natural compound that allows supplement manufacturers to include specific quantities of this beneficial nutrient into their formulations, without the inherit anti-nutrients that are present in whole-food supplements. Anti-nutrients are chemicals found in plants that keep your body from absorbing essential nutrients from food. Anti-nutrients are found in the highest concentrations in beans, grains, legumes and nuts. More on anti-nutrients in just a bit.

Vitamin C (Ascorbic Acid): Ascorbic acid is a synthetic version of Vitamin C and comes in two forms, L-ascorbic acid and D-ascorbic acid. L-ascorbic acid has all the benefits while the D form does not. If the synthetic form of ascorbic acid is all L-ascorbic acid, it has the exact same effect on the body as natural ascorbic acid found in whole foods. According to the Linus Pauling Institute at Oregon State University: "Natural and synthetic L-ascorbic acids are chemically identical, and there are no known differences in their biological activity."

Vitamin B9 (L-5-MTHF): Finally, let's look at a synthetically produced, lab-made, and, in some cases, a patented form of folate (Vitamin B9) called L-5 MTHF. This nutrient is where synthetically produced ingredients really shine and are superior to their whole-foods counterparts, but it's also where the lines can be blurry regarding the benefits of synthetic supplements. There are two forms of synthetically produced folate: L-5-MTHF and folic acid. For years, many supplements—especially prenatal vitamins—utilized synthetic folic acid as the form of vitamin B9, due to folic acid's superior absorption rate over whole-food folate. Recently, folic acid got a twin called L-5-MTHF—a synthetically produced form of folate that is better than folic acid because it's delivered in the active form the body needs. This is important because folate from whole food and folic acid is difficult for some people to convert into its active form due to a genetic mutation of the MTHFR gene. This gene interferes with the production of the MTHFR enzyme that is required to convert food folate and folic acid into its active form (5-methylenetetrahydrofolate). It's estimated that sixty percent of the population may have this genetic mutation. Due to this, many doctors and nutritionists are hesitant to recommend synthetic folic-acid supplements. People with the MTHFR mutation cannot utilize folic acid, and it can build up in the body to the point of elevating levels of homocysteine, which is a risk factor for cardiovascular disease. Synthetic folic acid could be dangerous and falls into the potentially dangerous synthetic definition. It's due to this that synthetic L-5-MTHF is not only beneficial but also superior to whole-food folate.

When you understand that synthetically-made, lab-produced vitamins have the exact same chemical structure as their natural counterparts, it becomes easy to see how all synthetic nutrients are not the evil that some whole-foods vitamin manufacturers would have you believe. With that said, synthetic vitamins that are potentially dangerous are *usually* not extracted from their whole food counterparts and are usually not similar on a chemical and molecular level as natural vitamins, making them potentially dangerous and un-absorbable when consumed. Some examples of potentially dangerous, synthetically produced micronutrients are:

Vitamin E (dl- alpha-tocopherol): There are two forms of synthetically produced vitamin E—a natural source vitamin E (d-alpha-tocopherol) typically derived from vegetable oils and a synthetic vitamin E (dl-alpha-tocopherol) typically derived from petroleum products. While both are synthetically produced, lab-made, standardized versions of vitamin E, the difference between why one is beneficial and the other potentially dangerous has everything to do with the differences in the molecular structures of the two forms. These molecular structures affect how well the vitamin is retained in the body and in turn, its biological availability. Synthetic vitamin E is a mixture of eight alpha-tocopherol stereoisomers in equal parts or amounts. However, only one of these stereoisomers, about twelve and a half percent of the total mixture is d-alpha-tocopherol, the natural form. The human body is confused by this new synthetic vitamin E. The carrier protein in the liver prefers the molecular makeup of the natural vitamin E, d-alpha-tocopherol (the natural form), as it's retained better and for a longer time in the body when compared to the synthetic form. The bioavailability is approximately two to one for natural-source vitamin E over synthetic vitamin E. To compensate for the lower retention of synthetic vitamin E, you would have to ingest two times the amount of synthetic vitamin E (by weight) to match the bioavailability of the natural form.

The main concern with synthetic vitamin E is that it goes beyond bioavailability. Studies show that there's real danger of negative health consequences when products contain the synthetic petrochemically-derived form of dl-alpha tocopherol. Research shows that high doses—400 IU's a day or more of synthetic vitamin E (dl-alpha tocopherol)—may increase your risk of prostate cancer by seventeen percent. When shopping for a Vitamin E or multivitamin supplement, make sure the product does not contain any dl-synthetic vitamin E.

Vitamin B12 (cyanocobalamin): While cyanocobalamin is the standard or most-typically delivered source of B12 in most vitamin supplements, it's not a natural source. You see, cyanocobalamin is not found anywhere in nature. The potential danger of this synthetic form of B12 is that, just like folic acid, it must be converted by the liver into the active form of B12 (methylcobalamin) in order to be utilized in humans and all other animals. Just like in the example of folic acid in individuals with a mutation of the MTHFR gene, supplementing with cyanocobalamin could lead to a B12 deficiency, which on its own could lead to permanent brain and nerve damage but could also increase homocysteine levels, increasing the potential for heart disease. Instead, well-formulated supplements should source methylcobalamin, a beneficial synthetically-produced micronutrient.

Vitamin D2 (Ergocalciferol): As with vitamin E, there are two forms of synthetically produced lab-made vitamin D available in supplemental form: vitamin D2 (ergocalciferol) and vitamin D3 (cholecalciferol). This is another case where the two forms should not be considered the same. D2 is made in plants and fungus exposed to ultraviolet light, synthesized in laboratories, and has a different molecular formula. Vitamin D3, the preferred beneficial source, is formed in your skin when exposed to sunlight and has a separate molecular formula than D2. Because of its different molecular formula,

D2 does not behave the same in your body and is not as effective as D3. Despite this fact, vitamin D2 is still added to milk, cereal, and other fortified products. For example, a 2008 study involving thirty-two older women found that a single dose of vitamin D3 was nearly twice as effective as vitamin D2 at raising blood calcifediol (vitamin D) levels. When choosing a vitamin D supplement, always go with vitamin D3 for best results. Note that while milk fortified with D2, or the poorly-formulated supplement that includes D2, isn't going to cause any immediate danger to your health, ingesting this particular form of synthetically-produced vitamin D could set the stage for a future vitamin D deficiency and the formation of any number of health conditions and diseases associated with vitamin D deficiency—including Alzheimer's disease, cardiovascular disease, osteoporosis, and diabetes.

How Synthetic Supplements Solve the Drawbacks of Whole Food Supplements

On the surface, it would appear that whole food supplements are superior to synthetic supplements. But as you are about to find out, it's a little more complicated than that. You see, the way natural or whole food supplements are marketed and advertised can lead you to imagine that they're directly extracted from fruit, veggies, and other foods and neatly and conveniently infused into a capsule or powder. However, the term "Whole Food" does not mean what most people think it does on a supplement label. The term does not mean that "whole food" vitamins and minerals are free from synthetically-produced nutrients. First, let's define what the term "whole foods" or "natural" actually means on a supplement label. No matter how neatly these words appear on the package of a supplement, make no mistake, whole food supplements are *not* the same as fresh whole foods that you buy at the grocery store or your local farmers' market.

Whole food supplements are pulverized, dehydrated, and highly processed versions of fruits and vegetables. This would not be a bad thing if that's all whole foods supplements underwent during their transformation from food to supplement. To get to the truth about whole food supplements, you must look further—past the shiny and pretty packaging of whole foods nutritional products. In a word, you must investigate the ingredients and supplement facts stated on the label. What you will find is that the majority of "whole food" supplements start out with a "food" base but then add synthetic, lab manufactured USP vitamins and minerals. This in itself means that these products, which are advertised as "natural" and "whole" are anything but, and they aren't much different than their purely synthetic counterparts. This would not be an issue if whole food product manufacturers were truthful in their marketing and advertising. What most people aren't aware of is that a vitamin can be marketed as natural or whole-foods based so long as a minimum of ten percent of its ingredients are from natural, plant-derived ingredients—the other ninety percent can be and, in most cases, are synthetically made in a laboratory. When choosing a whole foods supplement, read the ingredients and vitamins list carefully. What you will find is that most of these products (which are advertised as coming from whole-foods and non-synthetic), contain the same synthetic ingredients as their purely synthetic counterparts. Again, this would not be an issue or concern if whole foods nutrition products were advertised truthfully, but as you are now aware, that is not the case. Additionally, whole food products are more expensive than synthetic supplements and can contain anti-nutrients, making them anything but superior to synthetic products.

You see, manufacturers know that you as a consumer are willing to pay more for a whole-foods based supplement, even though they often use synthetic ingredients (to ensure potency). Apart from the cost, whole food supplements can contain harmful anti-nutrients such as tannins, oxalates, and phytates. While these substances are naturally occurring in food, they are classified as anti-nutrients because they deplete your body of nutrients and can block your body from absorbing the very vitamins and minerals you're ingesting from a multivitamin supplement. While these anti-nutrients are impossible to avoid in everyday foods, consuming them in concentrated supplement form on top of the food you're eating will greatly reduce your chances of absorbing the vitamins and minerals the whole foods multi is promising to provide.

It's counterproductive to have foods that contain oxalates (which reduce absorption of calcium, magnesium, or iron it comes into contact with), phytates (reduce the absorption of vitamin B3 (niacin), calcium, chromium, copper, magnesium, manganese, iron, and zinc, and accelerates the metabolism of vitamin D), and lectins (can cause leaky gut and make it difficult to properly absorb micronutrients) in a product that is meant to deliver those very same micronutrients. In other words, the whole food bases in whole food supplements contain anti-nutrients that have been proven to reduce micronutrient absorption. Whole-food supplements can be especially problematic in people who have food sensitivities and a damaged gut. Some products blend in wheat, potato starch, nightshades (which are found in veggies such as peppers, tomatoes and eggplant), and other ingredients that not only contain anti-nutrients such as lectins and trypsin inhibitors (a type of serine protease inhibitor that reduces the biological activity of trypsin, an enzyme involved in the breakdown of many different proteins, including as part of digestion in humans), but can also cause negative reactions in people with food sensitivities. Lab-created, or synthetic nutrients, do not have this issue.

People with a compromised gut lining can find whole-food supplements more difficult to absorb; thus, synthetic micronutrients may be more easily digestible and, therefore, more easily used by the body. Another large drawback to whole-food supplements is that they can only supply non-specific dosages as they contain many different nutrients from pulverized whole foods, which means their potency cannot be guaranteed (unlike standardized, synthetically-produced USP vitamins and minerals). Additionally, all the vitamins and minerals from a whole food supplement are delivered at once (in the same capsule, pill or powder) which means that many of the nutrients compete with each other for absorption, thus greatly reducing the number of micronutrients these supplements are actually delivering. According to Wendy Myers (FDN-P, NC, CHHC), an expert in detoxification and minerals:

> "Suppose we wish to take twenty-five mg of zinc to a person. In a food-based product, the zinc will be combined in a food or herbal form that most likely contains a little copper, manganese, selenium, chromium and other minerals. However, the other minerals directly compete with zinc for absorption. So no matter what the label says, you will not be getting the same amount of zinc as you would if there were no antagonistic or competing nutrients present. Additionally, food-based vitamin companies may add herbs to their products without realizing that the minerals in the herbs can and do also compete with the desired advertised mineral in the product. This can also reduce the effective dose of the desired mineral."

Whole-food-based supplements are more expensive compared to synthetic ones; this issue alone means that the extra money you're spending does not necessarily mean you're getting a superior product. Ultimately, it's up to you whether you choose a whole-food supplement or a synthetically-based one. Now that you are aware of the drawbacks of whole-foods-based supplements and how most are not what they're advertised and marketed to be, you can make better decisions when shopping for multivitamins and herbs to supplement your diet. Read supplement labels carefully so that you don't end up buying a product that may work against your body by inhibiting nutrient absorption instead of enhancing it. To put it simply, don't fall victim to misleading marketing and hype. Before buying any supplement, do some research on the brand you're considering and only buy products from respected and reputable manufacturers who are well established in the nutrition field.

Supplement Recommendations

Instead of steering you toward or against certain supplements, I will outline nutritional supplements and herbs that have a research-proven and established track record for effectiveness and safety, and let you decide which products (if any) to add to your cabinet based on the facts. You see, when it comes to dietary supplements, there is no such thing as "one size fits all." Every person has a distinct biological structure and different levels of hormones, nutrient receptors, and unique genetic profiles. What this means is that a supplement with a proven record may work exceptionally well for your co-worker, who may be like you in many ways on the outside, but won't produce the same results or benefits for you. Although you can be reasonably confident that a product will work for you if it's backed by solid research and it has worked well for thousands of people who've used it, there are never any guarantees. I strongly suggest, before you take any new supplement, that you clear your system of any products that you may be currently taking which may interfere with or lessen the benefit of the new supplement you are considering. For example, adding a new fish oil product to your regiment while you're already taking a fish oil product is not an effective way to measure the effectiveness of the new product. Another example would be taking two different multivitamins of different brands at the same time. For example, taking brand A one day and brand B the next and so on. When it comes to supplements, keeping things simple by sticking to products that are backed by plenty of research and have been around for a while is the absolutely best way to ensure that you're getting your money's worth.

Supplements with a Proven Track Record

#1. Fish Oil: Fish oil supplements are high in omega-3 fatty acids, which, as you are aware, are vitally important to your health. The best way to get enough of these essential fatty acids is to eat foods that are high in omega-3—especially fatty fish, several times a week. If you do not eat fish often, an omega-3 supplement in the form of fish oil will provide you with the same health benefits as eating fatty fish. However, there are hundreds of fish oil products available on the market, so choosing the best one for you is key to benefiting from this essential fat. Fish oil comes in processed and natural forms. The processed form can affect how well your body absorbs the omega-3, which is important because some forms are better absorbed than others. The different forms of fish oil are:

Processed Fish oil: When fish oils are processed, either to purify or concentrate them, they become something called ethyl esters, which are not found in nature.

Natural Fish Oil: In conventional (non-processed) fish oils, omega-3 fatty acids are mostly present as triglycerides.

Reformed Triglycerides: The ethyl esters in processed fish oil can be converted back into triglycerides, which are then considered "reformed" triglycerides.

Fish: In whole fish, omega-3 fatty acids are present as free fatty acids, triglycerides, and phospholipids.

While all these forms of fish oil are beneficial, studies have shown that the absorption of omega-3 from ethyl esters is inferior to the other forms. In general, the absorption of omega-3's in the form of free fatty acids (found in food) is about fifty percent better than triglycerides, and the absorption of triglycerides is fifty percent better than ethyl esters. When shopping for a fish oil supplement, go with a product that is derived from natural fish oil to get the most benefits.

Processed Fish Oil: Processed fish oil is usually purified and/or concentrated, transforming the fats into the ethyl ester form. On the ingredients list of processed fish oil products, you will see the words "purified" or "concentrated" as one of the first ingredients. This is how you know that the product contains a processed form of fish oil. The benefit of purification is that it rids the oil of potential harmful contaminants such as mercury and PCBs. Concentrated fish oil can also increase EPA and DHA levels. Some high-quality processed fish oil products may contain fifty to ninety percent of pure EPA and/or DHA. Processed fish oils make up the majority of the fish oil products you see on the shelves of supplement stores and in grocery stores. They are cheap to produce and usually come in capsule form.

The main drawback of processed fish oil is that it's not absorbed as well as natural fish oil because it's in ethyl ester form. However, some manufacturers go a step further and process the oil until it converts back into a synthetic triglyceride form which is better absorbed. These oils are also known as reformed or re-esterified triglycerides, and are the most expensive fish oils, making up only a very small percentage of the market. Due to processed fish oils' (the non-reformed or standard type) tendency to oxidation, I recommend keeping your fish oil refrigerated after purchase, especially the liquid form. Cool temperature slows down the oxidation process of the oil.

Natural Fish Oil: Natural fish oil supplements are the closest you can get to real fish. About thirty percent of the oil in natural fish oil products is in the form of EPA and DHA omega-3 fatty acids, while the remaining seventy percent consists of other fatty acids that can help with the absorption of EPA and DHA. Natural fish oil also contains vitamins D and A. Salmon, sardines, and cod liver oil are among the most common sources from which natural fish oils products are manufactured. These oils are usually found in liquid form and are the most resistant to oxidation (turning rancid) than processed oils.

#2. Krill Oil: Krill oil is extracted from Antarctic krill, which is an animal very similar to shrimp. Krill oil contains omega-3s in both triglyceride and phospholipid form. Multiple studies have shown that the omega-3s from krill oil are absorbed just as effectively—and sometimes even better— as those from fish oil, even at a lower dosage. Unlike fish oil, krill oil is highly resistant to oxidation due to being high in the antioxidant astaxanthin. What's more, as krill are very tiny and have a short lifespan, they don't accumulate many contaminants during their lifetime. This means the oil does not need purification and is rarely found in the ethyl ester form. Krill oil is an excellent omega-3 supplement due to its highly absorbed EPA and DHA forms, low contaminate levels, and antioxidant contents. The only drawback to supplementing with krill oil is that it's usually more expensive than fish oil products.

#3. Algal Oil: Algal oil is a great alternative to fish oil and is derived from various types of micro-algae. The EPA and

DHA in fish originate from algae, which are eaten by smaller fish and move up the food chain. Algal oil is an excellent source of omega 3 and a great alternative to fish-oil capsules and fish oil in liquid form. In a small study published in 2008 in the *Journal of the American Dietetic Association*, researchers recruited thirty-two healthy adults to consume either algal-oil capsules or cooked salmon with an equivalent amount of DHA every day for two weeks. The groups showed similar increases in their blood levels of DHA, leading the authors to conclude that "algal-oil DHA capsules and cooked salmon appear to be bioequivalent in providing DHA to plasma and red blood cells," and accordingly, "algal-oil DHA capsules represent a safe and convenient source of non-fish-derived DHA." As with krill oil, one downside of algal oil supplements is that they are significantly more expensive than conventional omega-3 capsules from fish. The upside is that Algal oil does not contain any heavy metals and other contaminants that can be found in fish. If your budget permits, add Algal oil into your supplement cabinet.

What to Look for When Buying an Omega-3 Supplement:

As with any supplement, read the label of any omega-3 supplement you are considering purchasing to ensure that what you're buying is actually what it's advertised and marketed to be. Be sure to check the following:

Freshness: Omega-3s are very prone to going rancid. Once they go bad, they will have a foul smell, and become less potent and can even be harmful. Always check the date and smell the product and see if it contains an antioxidant like vitamin E. Vitamin E helps extend shelf life of fish oil by slowing down oxidation. Oxidation is a process where chemicals start to fall apart due to light, heat, or moisture exposure.

Type of Omega-3: Many omega-3 products contain very little DHA and EPA, the most beneficial parts of omega-3. A high-quality omega-3 product will contain a few hundred milligrams of EPA and DHA per serving. Make sure your omega-3 product contains plenty of EPA and DHA.

Amount of Omega-3: While a product's label may state on the front that it contains 1,000 mg of fish oils per serving, on the back it may state EPA and DHA as only 200 mg or 300 mg per serving. A quality fish oil or omega-3 product will contain far higher amounts of EPA and DHA per serving than this.

Form of Omega-3: For better absorption, look for FFA (free fatty acids), TG, rTG (triglycerides and reformed triglycerides), and PLs (phospholipids), rather than EE (ethyl esters).

Sustainability: Try to buy fish oil that is certified by the Marine Stewardship Council (MSC), the Environmental Defense Fund, or a similar organization. Small fish with shorter lifespans tend to be more sustainable than larger fish.

Authenticity and Purity: Opt for products that have either the GOED standard for purity or a "third-party-tested" stamp on them. That shows they are probably safe and actually contain what they say on the front and back of the label.

To benefit from fish oils' heart-protective effects, take a minimum of 2g of fish oil per day containing at least 600 mg of EPA and at least 400 mg of DHA. It's best to take omega-3 products with meals that contain fat, as fat increases the absorption of omega-3s. Note that omega 3 products containing only ALA do not have the same health benefits as omega-3 products high in EPA and DHA. Finally, keep in mind that omega-3 products are highly perishable, just like fresh fish, so avoid buying in bulk and always store them in the refrigerator.

#4. Turmeric: Turmeric is a culinary spice used in Indian dishes as well as in traditional Indian medicine. The main component of Turmeric is curcumin, which has been shown in studies to be a potent anti-cancer compound. According to a study done in 2008 published in the *Journal of the National Cancer Institute* (JNCI), curcumin is effective at preventing cancer cells from multiplying, slowing existing tumor growth, and killing breast, colon, melanoma, and prostate cancer cells. Quite simply, there are very few supplements in existence today that can match the disease-fighting power of turmeric. Curcumin works its magic in the body by reducing inflammation and, as you're aware, inflammation promotes everything from heart disease to cancer and arthritis.

Unlike chemo-therapy cancer drugs, curcumin can kill cancer cells in many ways, which means cancer cells have a difficult time becoming resistant to curcumin. Additionally, unlike cancer drugs, curcumin targets only cancer cells, leaving healthy cells unaffected. A 2008 study concluded that curcumin can help fight pancreatic cancer cells at very high doses. To address the issue of needing high dosages to fight cancer, a highly bioavailable form of curcumin called Theracurmin was developed. The widely available supplement is designed to deliver higher levels of curcumin to people with cancer without an increase in side effects from very high curcumin dosages. Although promising, more research is needed on people with pancreatic and other cancers to determine Theracurmin's effectiveness.

A 2017 study published in the *Journal of Exercise Rehabilitation* demonstrated Theracurmin's effectiveness on alleviating pain when walking and exercising in patients with osteoarthritis. Osteoarthritis is a degenerative joint disease which gradually destroys the joints over time. Patients with osteoarthritis suffer from decreased mobility, joint pain, and joint deterioration. Patients who received Theracurmin for four weeks showed a marked improvement in mobility, suffered less pain in the knees and other joints, and saw enhanced muscular and balancing function. These positive effects can be considered significant or dramatic, considering how debilitating osteoarthritis is to people who are afflicted by the disease. Turmeric works by acting like a natural pain killer, directly inhibiting and reducing inflammation throughout the body, without the potentially deadly side-effects of over the counter anti-inflammatory drugs like ibuprofen and acetaminophen.

To benefit from turmeric supplementation, take a minimum of 200 mg of ninety-five percent or higher Curcminoids (the active compound in turmeric) every day in capsule format. Be aware that taking too much turmeric can lead to gastrointestinal side-effects such as gas and nausea. If you have gallstones or another bile condition, talk to your doctor before adding turmeric to your diet. Turmeric is available in powder form, as a tea, in capsules and the raw cut root that you can buy at the produce department in your grocery store and at health food stores. The most optimal and convenient way to get an effective dose of curcumin is to take curcumin supplements. Alternatively, cooking with turmeric can be a flavorful way to get the benefits of curcumin, with or without additional intake from a turmeric supplement.

#5. Guarana: Guarana is a common ingredient used in energy drinks. It's an excellent source of natural caffeine and contains several antioxidants including theobromine, saponins, tannins and catechins. Guarana's antioxidant profile is similar to green tea, which makes it an excellent health and metabolism booster. Studies have found that the antioxidants in guarana may combat cancer cell growth and reduce heart disease risk and skin aging. Thanks to its caffeine content, guarana helps improve focus and concentration, while reducing fatigue. Unlike synthetic caffeine which is the base ingredient in many energy drinks, energy shots and caffeine pills, guarana is generally tolerated better by most people with less negative effects. Studies have shown guarana to be effective in combating mental fatigue in people undergoing chemotherapy cancer treatment, without negative side-effects such as jitters and anxiety.

What's more, guarana has been shown to help improve your mood and learning capacity. A study published in the *Journal of Psychopharmacology* in Oxford England, looked at the effects of guarana on learning and mood. What the researchers found was that study subjects who received either 37.5 mg or 75 mg of guarana achieved the highest test scores. The lower the dose of guarana, the less caffeine is consumed, thus other compounds found inside guarana (apart from caffeine) are believed to be responsible for the mood and learning improvements seen in this study. In addition to improving your cognitive abilities and reducing fatigue, guarana is also a powerful weight loss aid. Caffeine has been shown to boost your metabolism by up to twelve percent over a twelve-hour period. A faster metabolism equals more calories burned while you are at rest, which equates to more fat loss. Guarana triggers weight loss because it suppresses genes that aid in fat cell production, while at the same time promoting genes that slow down fat accumulation around your belly, arms, legs and other areas. It gets even better; guarana has been shown to reduce your risk of heart disease by improving blood flow and inhibiting clots, while reducing the oxidation of LDL (bad cholesterol). Oxidized LDL can contribute to plaque accumulation in your arteries. To get the most out of guarana supplementation, take a minimum of 40 mg of guarana once a day, preferably in the morning. Many guarana supplements contain only guarana seed extract, while some products contain a blend of guarana along with other cognition and energy enhancers like ginseng, B vitamins and yerba mate, a type of tea with similar energizing effects as guarana.

#6. Green Tea: Green tea has been around for centuries but has only recently gotten widespread attention as a potent health booster, weight loss aid and disease fighter. Green tea contains many bioactive compounds that boost your mood, energy levels, and metabolism. It's rich in polyphenols that act as an anti-inflammatory and cancer fighter. Green tea contains about thirty percent polyphenols by weight, which includes a large amount of caetchins called EGCG (Epigallocatechin Gallate). Caetchins are natural antioxidants that protect your cells against damage and provide many other benefits, including reducing the formation of free radicals and shielding cells from molecule damage. Reducing free radical damage is critical for preventing disease and inhibiting cell turnover (aging). EGCG has been studied to treat different diseases and it's one of the main reasons why green tea is such a powerful disease-fighting compound.

The other main ingredient in green tea is caffeine. While green tea does not contain as much caffeine per cup as of coffee, it has just enough to stimulate you without causing side effects that too much coffee consumption brings on like the jitters and nervousness. Thanks to its caffeine content, green tea has been shown to have multiple benefits in improving brain function including faster reaction time, improved mood, vigilance, and memory. In addition to its caffeine content, green tea also contains the amino acid L-theanine, which increases the activity of the inhibitory neurotransmitter GABA. GABA has anti-anxiety effects and increases dopamine levels in your brain, which leads to a calm, positive mood. Studies have shown that caffeine and L-theanine have synergistic effects, improving brain function better than caffeine or L-theanine alone. Because of the abundant L-theanine and the smaller dose of caffeine, green tea can give you a much milder and different kind of "buzz" than coffee. Most people report having more stable energy levels and being much more productive when they drink green tea, compared to drinking coffee.

When it comes to aiding weight loss and improving metabolism, green tea is one of the top fat-burning aids that helps you get rid of excess body fat. In controlled human trials, green tea has been shown to elevate metabolism and increase fat burning by four percent. Another study showed that fat oxidation (burning) was increased by seventeen percent when green tea consumption was combined with thirty minutes of cycling exercise. These results were impressive considering that green tea is a natural compound that does not have any side effects, unlike a lot of weight-loss-specific products on the market. If that wasn't enough, the antioxidants in green tea have been shown to help lower your risk of getting cancer.

The antioxidants in green tea can help combat breast, colon, and prostate cancer. A meta-analysis of observational studies found that women who drank the most green tea had a twenty to thirty percent lower risk of developing breast cancer, which is the most common cancer in women. Other studies have shown green tea to be effective at reducing prostate cancer risk by forty-eight percent. Finally, in an analysis of twenty-nine large studies, green tea has been shown to reduce colon cancer risk by an impressive forty-two percent.

Drink at least one cup of green tea several times a week to benefit from this one-of-a kind, natural weight loss aid. If you are not a fan of drinking tea, take an EGCG supplement in capsule format. Green tea capsules have all the same benefits of green tea in its liquid form.

#7. PPQ: PPQ (pyrroloquinoline quinone) is a powerful mitochondria and nerve cell boosting compound that is slowly emerging as a potent health protective supplement. One of the top benefits of PPQ supplementation is that in can help protect the brain from damage caused by high blood-sugar. A study found that brain blood cells that were exposed to high blood sugar concentrations in the lab were protected from glucose damage (PPQ suppressed cell death and reversed production of harmful reactive oxygen species). Animal studies have also shown impressive results with a 100mg dose (equivalent to 20mg for humans) significantly lowering cell death damage in mice with diabetes.

As you age, your brain undergoes damage from multiple factors and natural stressors. As this stress increases and accumulates, neurodegenerative disorders such as

Alzheimer's, Dementia, Parkinson's and Huntington's disease can develop, and your risk of stroke increases as blood vessels lose their strength and integrity. Additionally, suffering any type of brain trauma can seriously disrupt the fragile structure of brain cells, which leads to a loss in agility, function, and cognition.

Unfortunately, main-stream medicine tends to focus on managing and treating debilitating brain disorders only after they have developed. A far more effective approach is to reverse and inhibit the underlying degenerative process and damage before it occurs. The best way to protect yourself from crippling brain disorders is to eat a diet rich in plant foods (especially green leafy vegetables and a variety of fruits). If you do not like plant foods or do not digest them well (I would still strongly recommend consuming them via smoothies and other liquid forms), I highly recommend supplementing with PPQ. You will only increase your protection from brain cell injury and greatly reduce your chances of developing a debilitating degenerative disease with a combination of PPQ supplementation and a diet rich in plant foods.

Promising Supplements
(further research studies needed)

While the following supplements aren't backed by heavy scientific research, they've so far been shown to have a lot of potential for treating different health ailments, reducing cancer risk, and improving numerous health markers such as high cholesterol and elevated blood sugar, along with reducing heart-disease risk.

#1. Apple Cider Vinegar: Apple cider vinegar does not fit the standard definition of a supplement and is not considered a supplement by many. However, you would be foolish not to add this potent disease fighting and immune boosting vinegar into your daily diet. Apple cider vinegar or ACV is a type of vinegar that's made by fermenting apples with bacteria and yeast. Its main active compound is called acetic acid, which gives it its sour taste. Apple cider vinegar has many uses for cooking, but its potent disease-combating and immune-boosting effects have just recently started to emerge. In the early 1900s, renowned scientist and Nobel Prize winner Otto Warburg suggested that cancer was caused by low levels of oxygen and high levels of acid within the body's cells. His observations led him to discover that cancer cells produced an acid called lactic acid as they grew and expanded.

If you're not familiar with Otto Warburg, his work has had a significant impact in the scientific field and his contributions have led to our present knowledge of energy and metabolic processes in cells. His innovative thinking and his experimental breakthroughs set the framework for his numerous scientific achievements. The term "Warburg effect" was coined to denote a metabolic process that is typical of many tumor cells, specifically the increased activity of lactic acid, even in the presence of sufficient oxygen. Apple cider vinegar has been shown to reduce lactic acid production by lowering the body's acidity, while being alkalizing, meaning that it reduces acidity. This acidity-reducing effect of apple cider vinegar makes it different from other vinegars, which increase acidity instead of reducing it. Acid levels in the body are measured with something called the PH scale, which ranges from zero to fourteen. The lower the PH, the more acid is present, where a higher PH means something is more alkalizing. Most of the research on Apple Cider Vinegar has been done on animals and tissue samples rather than on living humans, but several studies have shown that cancer cells grow more aggressively in an acidic environment.

In one study involving a test tube which contained stomach cancer cells from rats and humans, the main ingredient in ACV (apple cider vinegar) called acetic acid, effectively killed the cancerous cells. While these findings are certainly exciting, researchers were applying acetic acid directly to cancer cells in a laboratory and not into living humans. Further research is needed on ACV's anti-cancer effects on living humans. A 2003 study published in the *Asian Pacific Journal of Cancer Prevention* found a link between regular ACV consumption and a lower risk of esophageal cancer in Chinese people. Researchers found that along with consumption of apple cider vinegar, a diet high in vegetables and low in salt intake were all associated with a decreased risk of esophageal cancer. It's important to understand that increasing PH levels in the blood doesn't necessarily mean you will be cancer proof. There are more factors involved in the development and growth of cancer apart from PH levels. While it's true that cancer cells produce lactic acid as they grow, this alone does not increase acidity in the body. Your blood requires a PH between 7.35 and 7.45, which falls into a slightly alkaline level or range. Blood levels of PH that fall even a small margin outside this range can have a severely negative effect on your organs.

You see, your body has its own system for maintaining a specific blood PH regardless of what you eat or drink, which makes it difficult to significantly affect your blood PH levels through diet. While there are no studies proving that cancer cells don't grow in an alkaline environment, what we do know is that low PH levels could increase your risk factor for cancer where other risk factors are present (a diet low in veggies and fruit, excessive salt intake, and processed food consumption).

In addition to the potential anti-cancer effects of apple cider vinegar, studies have shown that it promotes fat loss, increases insulin sensitivity, lowers blood sugar levels, and improves cholesterol levels. In one Japanese study published in the *Japan Society for Bioscience*, ACV was shown to reduce total body weight, body fat mass, and serum triglyceride levels in obese people.

To benefit from ACV and reduce negative side effects (due to its high acidity, apple cider vinegar can cause tooth enamel erosion and burns to the throat), be sure to dilute it with water. Start with one tablespoon a day diluted with an eight-ounce cup of water and work your way up to two to three tablespoons per day. For many people, apple cider vinegar diluted in water tastes like unsweetened apple juice, which makes it palatable. In one unfortunate case, a twenty-eight-year-old woman developed dangerously low levels of potassium by consuming excessive apple cider vinegar. Note that this was an extreme case where consumption was well above the recommended two to three tablespoons a day. What's more, the woman was diagnosed with osteoporosis, a condition where bones become brittle, something that's rarely seen in young people. Doctors who treated the woman believe the large daily doses of apple cider vinegar led to minerals being leached from her bones to buffer the acidity of her blood. They also noted that high acid levels reduced the formation of new bone. Of course, the amount of apple cider vinegar in this case was much more than most people would consume in a single day—plus, she did this every day for many years.

Apple cider vinegar can in some cases interfere with certain medications. If you are taking diabetes medicine, blood potassium lowering drugs such as Digoxin or diuretic drugs, speak to your doctor before taking apple cider vinegar. If you prefer to use apple cider vinegar as a salad dressing instead of diluting it in a glass of water and drinking it, limit the amount you put on your salad to two tablespoons to avoid side effects such as tooth enamel decay and throat burns. Also, don't drink ACV and put it on your salad on the same day. Only consume it in one form or the other.

#2. Garlic: Just like apple cider vinegar, most people would not consider garlic a disease-fighting food and supplement. Unless you are eating at least one clove of garlic a day, I highly recommend supplementing with a quality garlic product to reap the powerful health benefits of this amazing herb. The ancient Greek physician Hippocrates, often called the father of Western medicine, used to prescribe garlic to his patients to treat a variety of medical conditions. Here's what garlic can do for your health:

Garlic Improves Bone Health - In one study done on rats, garlic has been shown to minimize bone loss by increasing estrogen levels. In a separate study published in 2012 in the *Journal of Dietary Supplements,* a daily dose of garlic extract (equal to about two grams of raw garlic) significantly decreased a marker of estrogen deficiency in menopausal women. In addition, garlic is also a powerful weapon against osteoarthritis

Garlic Can Help Detoxify Your Body of Heavy Metals - At high doses, the sulfur compounds of garlic have been shown to protect against organ damage from heavy-metal toxicity. A four-week study of employees from a car battery plant who were suffering excessive exposure to lead, found that garlic reduced lead levels in the blood by nineteen percent. It also reduced many clinical signs of toxicity, including headaches and elevated blood pressure. Just three daily servings of garlic outperformed the drug D-penicillamine in reducing symptoms.

Garlic Can Improve Athletic Performance - Before the words "performance enhancing" became common in sports circles and amongst both recreational and competitive bodybuilders and powerlifters, garlic was used in traditional ancient cultures to reduce fatigue and enhance the work output of laborers. Additionally, garlic was given to Olympic athletes in ancient Greece to help boost their athletic prowess, which drew larger crowds to ancient Olympic games. Studies have shown that exercise-induced fatigue can be reduced with garlic intake, including in patients with heart disease, by as much as twelve percent.

Garlic May Help Prevent Dementia & Alzheimer's Disease - Garlic contains powerful antioxidants that support the body's protective mechanisms against oxidative damage. High doses of garlic supplements have been shown to increase antioxidant enzymes in humans, including the reduction of oxidative stress in people with high blood pressure. Garlic contains the compounds allicin, diallyl disulfide, and s-allyl cysteine, all of which are unique antioxidants that have been shown to have potent biological effects in the human body. The unique antioxidant profile of garlic makes it a potent natural weapon against debilitating diseases like Alzheimer's and dementia.

Garlic Can Help You Combat a Cold - A large twelve-week study from 2001, published in the peer-reviewed journal *Advances in Therapy*, found that a daily garlic supplement reduced the number of colds by sixty-three percent compared to a placebo (fake supplement). The average length of cold symptoms was also reduced by a whopping seventy percent, from five days in the placebo group to just one and a half days in the garlic group. Study volunteers who received the placebo were much more likely to suffer from more than one cold during the treatment period. These findings demonstrated that an allicin (the main compound in garlic) containing supplement can prevent a common cold virus from occurring during cold season. Another study found that supplementing with aged garlic extract improved cell immunity and reduced the severity and length of cold and flu symptoms.

Garlic Can Help Improve Your Cholesterol Levels & Lower Heart Disease Risk - Garlic has been shown to have a cholesterol-lowering effect, reducing LDL (bad cholesterol) by up to fifteen percent in people with elevated cholesterol levels. In addition, garlic supplements were shown to prevent oxidative damage to DNA in subjects with essential hypertension, which is a type of high blood pressure with no known cause. While garlic does not appear to have any direct effects on heart disease, its effect on LDL cholesterol and reducing high blood pressure makes it a great weapon for improving heart disease risk factors.

Garlic can be taken in several forms - Fresh/raw garlic, aged garlic, garlic oil and boiled garlic. Boiled garlic prevents alliin from creating its sulfur-containing metabolites, and garlic oil, while effective as a supplement, has a potentially high level of toxicity. All the beneficial components of garlic can be found in fresh garlic, which makes aged garlic supplements and fresh garlic the two best ways to supplement garlic. Always crush, slice, or chew garlic (prior to cooking) to ensure maximum allicin production (allicin is responsible for garlic's positive effects on health). Take up to 1200 mg of garlic extract per day in divided doses for optimal benefits.

#3. Resveratrol: Resveratrol is an antioxidant found in blueberries, grapes, red wine and other fruits with purple skin. Resveratrol supplements may help reduce inflammation in people with insulin resistance, heart disease, gastritis, and other serious conditions. Studies have demonstrated that resveratrol lowers inflammatory markers, blood sugar, and triglycerides in obese people in a similar manner as calorie restriction. The resveratrol in red wine may have health benefits, but you would need to consume a very excessive amount, about 3 liters (which I definitely don't recommend) in order to benefit from the resveratrol in red wine. Red wine contains only about 13 mg of resveratrol per liter (34 oz), but most studies have shown that at least 150 mg needs to be consumed per day to experience health benefits.

To benefit from resveratrol's powerful ant-inflammatory effects, take between 150 mg and 500 mg per day in supplement form in divided doses. Resveratrol supplements have been shown to be very safe unless you are taking blood thinning medications. Speak to your doctor before supplementing with resveratrol if you are taking any type of blood thinners.

#4. Spirulina: Spirulina was consumed by the ancient Aztecs hundreds of years ago to treat various ailments and strengthen the immune system. It's a type of blue-green algae that grows in both fresh and salt waters throughout the world. It has been shown to have powerful antioxidant effects when taken in supplement form. Spirulina has been shown to strengthen the immune system, combat aging, and reduce deadly inflammation. Spirulina became popular when NASA found that it could be grown in space and used by astronauts. Spirulina is a nutrient-packed powerhouse that contains four grams of protein, Vitamins B1 (eleven percent of RDA), B2 (fifteen percent of RDA), B3 (four percent of RDA), copper (twenty-one percent of RDA) and Iron (eleven percent of RDA), along with decent amounts of magnesium, potassium, and manganese per seven grams (1 tablespoon) powder serving. Spirulina delivers all of this with only twenty calories and less than two grams of carbohydrates per serving. Gram for gram, this makes spirulina the single most nutrient dense food on the planet. The protein in spirulina is very high quality when compared to animal protein sources such as eggs, cheese, and milk—containing all the essential amino acids you need. Spirulina's main active antioxidant component is called phycocyanin, which gives it its unique blue-green color. Phycocyanin fights free radical production and has impressive ant-inflammatory effects.

Thanks to its high and unique nutrient profile, spirulina can lower LDL and triglyceride levels, reducing your risk of heart disease. Spirulina lowers LDL cholesterol while raising HDL (good) cholesterol). In a study involving twenty-five people with type 2 diabetes, two grams of spirulina per day had a significant impact on lipid profiles. In one study, just one gram of spirulina per day lowered triglycerides by an impressive 16.3% and LDL levels by over 10%. Other studies have shown favorable effects with higher doses between four and eight grams per day. What's more, spirulina can protect you against cancer. In a study done on eighty-seven people in India suffering from pre-cancerous lesions, spirulina was shown to regress lesions in forty-five percent of the study participants, with only one gram of spirulina taken every day for a year. When the study participants stopped taking the spirulina, almost half of them developed lesions again the following year.

In another study comparing the effects of spirulina to Pentoxyfilline, an anti-inflammatory drug used to treat muscle pain in people with peripheral artery disease, just one gram of spirulina per day led to greater improvement in symptoms compared to the drug. These results are very impressive considering that spirulina is plant-derived and has no side effects, compared to pharmaceutical drugs, which can have a whole host of unwanted effects ranging from mild to severe. In addition to lowering LDL cholesterol, reducing pre-cancerous lesions and lowering inflammation, spirulina can also lower your blood pressure. High blood pressure is a pre-cursor to heart attacks, chronic kidney disease, strokes, and other deadly diseases. Spirulina in higher doses (4.5g) per day has been shown to reduce blood pressure in people with normal blood pressure levels. This is thanks to spirulina's nitric-oxide-boosting effects. Nitric oxide is a gas that helps blood vessels dilate and relax. Finally, spirulina can help boost your muscle strength and endurance. Two studies have shown that spirulina enhances muscle endurance and delays fatigue, with another study showing increased muscle strength from spirulina supplementation prior to a workout. To sum up, spirulina is an incredible superfood that's well tolerated by the body, is packed with disease-fighting nutrients and antioxidants, and has numerous health benefits. Take one to four grams of spirulina in divided doses once a day.

FIT BODY 4 LIFE FOODS

The Fit Body 4 Life meal plan has been designed to be simple to implement into your day and easy to follow. I have designed it to give you a great example and template of what and when to eat for optimal health, energy, fat loss, and well-being. The foods outlined in the meal plan are designed to nourish, energize, and replenish your body while providing you all the essentials your cells need to function at peak capacity.

What to Eat

Protein: Apart from between-meal snacks, every meal you eat needs to contain quality protein, ideally from animal sources unless you are a vegetarian. Eat a minimum of four ounces of protein from fish, chicken, turkey, and other lean meats and fish twice a day. Protein is essential to rebuilding muscle tissue, maintaining a fast metabolism, and helping you recover from illness. Strive to consume at least 0.6 grams of protein per pound of lean bodyweight per day. Ask your doctor or a certified fitness coach for a simple body fat test to determine your lean body weight. For example, if you weigh 200 pounds and your lean body weight is 155 pounds, you should consume a minimum of 93 grams of high-quality animal-based protein every day. You may need to up that amount by an additional twenty to forty grams per day if you are very active—for example, your job requires physical movement for an extended period of time and you exercise vigorously several times a week. The best way to gauge how much protein you need is to pay attention to how your body feels from day to day. If you feel fatigued, sluggish, and hungry on most days despite getting adequate sleep, increase your protein intake slightly and see how you feel.

Fats: As you are now aware, healthy fats are critical to optimal health, weight loss, and well-being. They are so important that being even slightly deficient in omega-3 fats can quickly put a halt to your fat loss and fitness progress and make it more difficult to burn fat. Consume only good fats as outlined in chapter two. Ensure that you are eating ample healthy fat foods as listed in the Best Healthy Fat Foods section.

Carbohydrates: Keeping your starchy carbohydrate intake low has been proven to be the most beneficial to your health, mood, and energy levels. Starchy carbohydrates are foods like bread, rice, pasta, potatoes, bagels, cookies, and other baked goods containing flour. Eat mainly fibrous carbs such as broccoli, green beans, asparagus, kale, and cabbage. Vegetables are full of essential minerals, vitamins, fiber, and other plant nutrients that keep you full and help with digestion. Keep in mind that foods such as nuts, seeds, and fruits contain carbohydrates, so eliminating starchy carbs does not mean you won't be eating any carbohydrates at all.

Snacks: Only consume snacks if needed, up to two times a day. Unless you missed a meal during the day, avoid having snacks late at night or before bed, as your body has very little need for extra calories before bed, which increases your risk of gaining body fat. Snacks should be kept small, just enough to hold you over to your next meal. A great example is a handful of mixed nuts along with a small piece of fruit such as an apple, orange, or other fruit. Raw veggies, avocados, nut butters (almond or cashew), and tahini are all great snacks.

Coffee & Tea: Coffee and tea have numerous health benefits in addition to containing caffeine which gives your day a kick. If you enjoy coffee, drink one to two cups daily. Be sure your coffee comes from the highest quality beans you can purchase. Same goes for tea—preferably green tea as it's highest in antioxidants and has numerous health benefits. The best time to consume coffee and tea is in the morning before your first meal. Do not add any caloric or artificial sweeteners to your coffee or tea. If you must have it sweet, choose a natural non-caloric sweetener such as Stevia or Xylitol. Apart from tea and coffee, you should be drinking water only.

Supplements: Refer to the supplements section for info on which supplements to take and when. Supplements should never be used as a substitute for real food. In certain instances, for example, when you cannot eat your usual food and do not have access to it due to extended traveling, driving, etc., a protein powder or meal replacement or protein bar is okay to have.

What Not to Eat

Grains: While grains such as rice, quinoa, corn, buckwheat, and others can be part of your diet, they should be limited, especially if weight loss is one of your goals. You see, all grain foods cause a large spike in your insulin levels when consumed—due to their starchy nature. Grains are pure carbohydrate foods that increase blood sugar and can cause inflammation and other gut issues. I recommend eliminating most grains initially (see 21-day meal plan), then re-introducing them later when you have lost a decent amount of body-fat and have already achieved your 30-day goal, at a minimum. If your primary goal is not weight loss, keep grains in your diet but have several low-grain or no-grain days throughout the week and see how you feel. Chances are good that you will feel more alert, focused, and energized during the day without grains.

Grains can have a negative impact on your brain chemistry by reducing cognition, reaction time, and lowering your overall mental capacity. If you are used to eating grains on a daily basis, significantly reduce your consumption or eliminate them altogether for at least twenty-one days. The Fit Body 4 Life 21-Day Meal Plan does not contain any grains.

Dairy: The only dairy products that I recommend while on this plan and beyond is grass-fed butter and ghee. Small amounts of Greek yogurt and kefir are acceptable as they contain beneficial bacteria that can improve digestion. Dairy contains an allergen called lactose, a milk-sugar which many people cannot tolerate and are sensitive to.

Gluten: Gluten is an antibody that's part of the wheat plant. It's hidden in many different foods, making it very difficult to avoid. Be sure to read labels carefully to look for hidden gluten and wheat and be vigilant when you go to restaurants. Ask for a gluten-free menu and whether gluten-free options are available. Even a slight amount of cross-contamination can set off reactions in your body. A great resource for finding hidden names and sources of gluten is www.celiac.org. Gluten is found in rye, oats, barley, soy sauce, and other condiments.

Beans: While beans are high in protein and fiber, they unfortunately contain a high number of lectins, which are inflammatory compounds that cause gastric distress and other issues associated with inflammation. Since the goal is to reduce inflammation as much as possible, you'll want to eliminate, or at the very minimum, drastically cut down your intake of inflammation-promoting foods for at least twenty-one days.

All processed foods: Avoid foods that contain additives, preservatives, artificial flavoring and coloring, dyes, and MSG. This means processed meats like hot dogs, salami, bacon (a small amount of uncured, natural bacon is OK to have). Cured and processed meats are the only meats that have been linked to increased cancer risk as well as other diseases. Occasionally consuming a bit of salami or enjoying a hot dog once or twice a month is fine, but eating processed meat and other processed foods on a daily and weekly basis is a big No-No.

Artificial sweeteners: Artificial sweeteners have been linked to diabetes, obesity, and neurological problems. Stay away from these or suffer the consequences. Replace artificial sweeteners with natural sweeteners. Xylitol and Stevia are two of my favorites. Allulose and Monk-Fruit extract are also great alternatives.

Refined vegetable oils: This includes canola, corn, soybean, safflower, and others. These contain excessive omega-6 fats which are highly inflammatory. Replace these with extra-virgin olive oil, unrefined coconut oil, grass fed butter, ghee, and avocado oil.

Fruit: While fruit is high in antioxidants and most contain decent amounts of fiber, fruit also contains fructose, which is the natural sugar found in fruit. The problem with fruit is that your liver can handle and process only small amounts of fructose at any given time, with the remaining fructose being sent to your blood stream and converted into dangerous LDL cholesterol particles. Once your body converts fructose into LDL, all sorts of bad things start to happen, with weight gain being one of them. This is why high fructose corn syrup

(HFCS) is considered one of the worst health-destroying additives in processed foods. Your body is simply not capable of processing large amounts of fructose, so you must limit your intake of fruit. Go with fruit that contains less fructose overall and more fiber per serving such as apples (with skin), kiwi, blueberries, strawberries, blackberries, and plums. Fruits that are higher in fructose (sometimes called tropical fruits) are bananas, grapes, oranges, pineapple, figs, watermelon, dates, and peaches. Once you have re-set and accelerated your metabolism, you can gradually add higher fructose or tropical fruits back into your diet.

THE FIT BODY 4 LIFE 21-Day Meal Plan

Some important guidelines before you get started:

This meal plan can be followed two ways: The first way is to follow it exactly as it's outlined meal by meal and day by day.

The second option is if you want to mix things up for more variety, you can eat the meals on different days and in a different order. For example, you can have "Day 1 Breakfast" on day two and "Day 2 Lunch" on day three. You can also eat breakfast meals for lunch and lunch meals for dinner and vice versa, if you prefer.

All of the meals in this meal plan are designed to boost your metabolism and teach your body to use fat for energy, plus encourage more fat burning throughout the day and during your workouts. If you prefer option two above, you cannot go wrong with switching up the order of the meals and the days on which you eat them if you wish to do so.

You will see best results when you prepare each meal exactly as outlined. DO NOT add ingredients that are not listed for a meal as adding ingredients off the menu will hinder fat burning. Seasonings, spices, and herbs that do not contain MSG or artificial flavorings are OK to use.

As most of these meals call for fresh foods that spoil quickly, only buy three to four days' worth of food at a time when you go shopping for groceries. Two to three days is even better.

Refer to the "Recipes" section for instructions on how to prepare the meals where indicated as "see recipe."

If your schedule is very busy and don't have time to cook every day, cook the meals on a Saturday or Sunday so that you have enough food to last you until Tuesday or Wednesday. Then cook enough food again mid-week to last you until Saturday or Sunday.

If you are doing intermittent fasting, your first meal can be either breakfast or lunch. If you choose to start with breakfast, your second meal would be lunch followed by dinner. If you start with lunch, your second meal will be dinner. If dinner falls early in the day for you— several hours before going to bed—I highly recommend you choose a healthy snack listed in the "Healthy Snacks" guide and eat it two to three hours before bed so that you meet your daily nutrient and calorie requirements.

*Remember to drink at least eight to twelve glasses of water every day. Spring or Artisan Well water is best and highly recommended.

**For males, if you are highly active (3-5 workouts per week or work a physically demanding job), double the ounces of protein listed for each meal.

***If you have a lot of body fat to lose (25 pounds or more), after every 6-7 days of following the meal plan, have one cheat meal + one cheat snack of whatever you desire. High carbohydrate foods are recommended for cheat meals to accelerate fat burning and prevent metabolic stagnation.

Note: All meals serve one unless otherwise indicated.

Day 1

Breakfast

Ingredients

- 15 almonds
- 2 whole eggs + ½ cup egg whites
- 1 tablespoon of coconut oil
- 1 cup of blueberries

Directions:

- Scramble the eggs using the coconut oil. Enjoy the almonds and blueberries on the side.

Lunch

Ingredients

- Dijon Almond Crusted Salmon (see recipe)
- Large green salad with vegetables of choice
- ½ cup of cooked sweet potatoes
- ½ tablespoon of Extra Virgin Olive Oil
- ½ tablespoon of Apple Cider Vinegar

Directions:

- Toss the cooked sweet potato into the salad or have it on the side with the salmon.
- Mix the Extra Virgin Olive Oil together with the apple cider vinegar and use as the salad dressing.

Dinner

Ingredients

- Slow-cooked Pork Loin

- Butternut Squash Soup (see recipe)

- 1 Cup Steamed Broccoli

Directions:

- Enjoy the broccoli as a side dish with the pork loin or mix it into the soup.

Day 2

Breakfast

- Creamy Chocolate Shake (see recipe)

Lunch

Ingredients

- 4 ounces of chicken, cooked with seasonings
- Grapefruit and Avocado Salad (see recipe)

Directions

- Enjoy the chicken separately or chop it into the Grapefruit and Avocado Salad.

Dinner

- 4 ounces of ground turkey, browned
- 2 cups of raw coleslaw mix
- 1 cup of broccoli
- 15 walnuts, chopped
- 1 tablespoon sesame seed oil
- 1 cup medium salsa

Directions

- Brown the turkey in a large skillet.
- Once it is cooked, add in the coleslaw mix, broccoli, sesame seed oil, and salsa.
- Stir-fry until the vegetables are tender, but not limp.
- Remove the mixture from the heat and add walnuts on top.

Day 3
Breakfast

- 1 cup of plain Greek Yogurt

- 1 cup of mixed berries

- 2 tablespoons of shredded coconut

- 1 tablespoon of chopped raw almonds

Directions:

- Mix the berries and shredded coconut into the yogurt.

- Sprinkle the chopped raw almonds on top.

Lunch

Ingredients

- Chicken Waldorf Salad (see recipe)

- 1 cup of blueberries

Directions

- Have the blueberries on the side of the salad.

Dinner

Ingredients

- Curried Fish and Vegetables (see recipe)

- Cauliflower Mash (see recipe)

Day 4

Breakfast

Ingredients

- Eggs with Avocado and Salsa (see recipe)
- 1 cup of berries

Directions:

- Enjoy the berries on the side of the eggs with avocado and salsa

Lunch

Ingredients

- Shrimp Cakes (see recipe)
- 2 cups of spinach
- ½ cup cherry tomatoes, chopped
- ½ cup cucumbers, chopped
- ½ cup red pepper, sliced
- 1 ounce of goat cheese, crumbled
- 1 tablespoon apple cider vinegar

Directions:

- Combine all salad ingredients together.
- Pour in apple cider vinegar and mix.
- Sprinkle goat cheese on top.

Dinner

Ingredients

- Ginger Beef and Broccoli (see recipe)
- Cauliflower Mash (see recipe)

Directions:

- Enjoy the Cauliflower Mash on the side of the Ginger Beef and Broccoli.

Day 5

Breakfast

- 1 serving Breakfast Smoothie (see recipe)

Lunch

Ingredients

- 4 ounces turkey burger (see recipe)

- Large Portobello mushroom, grilled (use mushroom instead of bun)

- 1 cup apple cider coleslaw (see recipe)

- 1 tablespoon olive oil—½ used to grill mushroom and the other ½ used in the coleslaw

- Use Dijon mustard, sliced onions, tomatoes, and lettuce as toppings

Directions:

- Place the turkey burger on top of the Portobello mushroom.

- Add additional condiments as desired.

- Eat with a knife and fork.

- Enjoy the coleslaw on the side.

Dinner

Ingredients:

- 4 ounces of grilled chicken breast—cut into strips and seasoned with salt and pepper

- 1 cup of grilled vegetables—onions, peppers, shredded kale, and mushrooms

- ¼ cup avocado—cut into chunks

- 10 large olives

- ¼ cup salsa

Directions:

- Cook chicken breast.

- Mix all ingredients together for fajitas on a plate.

Day 6

Breakfast

Ingredients

- 2 whole eggs plus ½ cup egg whites
- ½ cup sautéed kale, mushrooms, onions, and tomatoes
- 1 tablespoon coconut oil; use to sauté vegetables and scramble eggs

Directions:

- Use 1 tablespoon of coconut oil to sauté vegetables in a frying pan.
- Once the vegetables are almost done, add in the 2 whole eggs and ½ cup of egg whites.
- Scramble all together.

Lunch

Ingredients

- Turkey Vegetable Meatballs (see recipe)
- 1 cup spaghetti squash
- ½ cup tomato sauce (sugar free)
- 1 cup broccoli

Directions:

- Prepare the vegetable meat balls according to the recipe.
- Cook the spaghetti squash according to the instructions.

- Steam the broccoli and mix into the cooked spaghetti squash.

- Top with the tomato sauce and meatballs.

Dinner

Ingredients

- 4 ounces of tilapia—grilled with lemon, garlic, salt, and pepper

- 10 black olives—cook with tilapia

- 8 spears of asparagus

- 1 cup steamed broccoli

Directions:

- Bake tilapia at 350 in the oven for 10-15 minutes in a glass dish with garlic, lemon, salt, and pepper to taste.

- Add in black olives.

- Bake asparagus separately and steam broccoli to have on the side.

Day 7

Breakfast

Ingredients:

- 1 cup Greek yogurt, plain
- Sprinkle of cinnamon
- 1 cup berries
- 1 tablespoon chia seeds
- 1 cup sliced cucumber and tomatoes (on the side)

Directions:

- Mix the berries and chia seeds into the yogurt.
- Sprinkle cinnamon on top.
- Have the veggies on the side.

Lunch

Ingredients

- 1 serving Butternut Squash Soup (see recipe)
- 4 ounces of grilled chicken breast
- Large green salad made with 2 handfuls of lettuce plus 1 cup mixed raw veggies
- ½ avocado, chopped
- 1 tablespoon olive oil plus 1 teaspoon aged balsamic

Directions:

- Chop the chicken up and toss into the salad along with the avocado or eat the chicken separately.

- Enjoy the meal with soup on the side.

Dinner

Ingredients

- Sausage & Tomatoes (see recipe)

- Sautéed Sweet Potato Hash (see recipe)

Directions:

- Prepare recipes as instructed.

Day 8

Breakfast

Ingredients

- Blueberry Carrot Smoothie (see recipe)

Directions:

- Add extra ice if desired

Lunch

Ingredients

- Ground Turkey Casserole (see recipe)
- 1 cup of oven-roasted vegetables of your choice

Directions:

- Bake the vegetables on a baking tray at 375 for 10 - 15 minutes or until tender.
- Have the Ground Turkey Casserole on the side.

Dinner

Ingredients

- 4 ounces of grilled salmon, seasoned with lemon juice, garlic, salt, and pepper to taste
- 2 tablespoons of pistachio nuts sprinkled on top of salmon
- 2 cups of mixed vegetable stir-fry
- 1 tablespoon of sesame seed oil to stir-fry vegetables

Directions:

- Bake salmon with seasonings in a glass dish in the oven at 350 for 8-12 minutes or until opaque.

- Remove when done and sprinkle pistachios on top.

- While the salmon is cooking, stir-fry the vegetables in sesame seed oil.

Day 9

Breakfast

Ingredients

- Coconut Flour Pancakes (see recipe)
- 1 tablespoon of raw almond butter

Directions

- Make coconut flour pancakes according to the recipe.
- Top with raw almond butter.

Lunch

Ingredients

- 1 serving No Fry Salmon Patties (see recipe)
- 3 handfuls of baby spinach plus 1 cup chopped mixed vegetables of your choice
- 10 olives—pitted and cut in half
- 1 tablespoon of apple cider vinegar—as salad dressing

Directions:

- Make the No Fry Salmon Patties according to the recipe and enjoy with the salad on the side.

Dinner

Ingredients

- Sweet and Smokey Chicken (see recipe)
- Rosemary Green Beans (see recipe)

Directions:

- Make dishes according to the recipes.

Day 10

Breakfast

Ingredients

- Tex-Mex Egg Scramble
- 1 cup of mixed berries

Directions:

- Make the Tex-Mex Egg Scramble according to the recipe and enjoy with the berries on the side.

Lunch

Ingredients

- Real Healthy Egg Salad
- 2 cups of Spinach
- 1 cup of raw pepper, sliced

Directions:

- Make the Real Healthy Egg Salad according to the recipe and place on top of the bed of spinach.
- Have the sliced raw peppers on the side.

Dinner

Ingredients

- Fully Loaded Lettuce Wrap Turkey Bacon Burgers (see recipe)
- Sautéed Sweet Potato Hash (see recipe)

Directions:

- Follow the Recipe Instructions.

Day 11

Breakfast

Ingredients

- Low Carb Green Smoothie

Directions

- Follow the recipe instructions.
- Add extra ice if desired.

Lunch

Ingredients

- Balsamic Asparagus & Steak Salad (see recipe)

Directions:

- Make the Balsamic Asparagus & Steak Salad according to the recipe.

Dinner

Ingredients

- Fish Tacos (see recipe)
- 1 cup of broccoli

Directions:

- Make the recipe according to the instructions.
- Steam the broccoli and have it on the side.

Day 12

Breakfast

Ingredients

- 2 whole eggs
- 1 tablespoon coconut oil
- 1 piece of bacon, cooked
- 1 grilled tomato

Directions:

- Scramble the eggs in coconut oil.
- Sear the tomato in a frying pan.
- Enjoy the scrambled eggs, with the tomato and bacon on the side

Lunch

Ingredients

- 1 cup spaghetti squash
- Turkey Vegetable Meatballs (see recipe)
- ½ cup tomato sauce
- 2 handfuls spinach
- 1 tablespoon of shredded Parmesan cheese

Directions

- Cook the spaghetti squash according to the directions.

- Top the squash with the cooked Turkey Vegetable Meatballs, spinach, hot tomato sauce, and sprinkle parmesan cheese on top.

Dinner
Ingredients

- Halibut with Dijon and Almonds (see recipe)
- Stir Fried Rice (see recipe)

Directions:

- Make the recipes according to the instructions.

Day 13

Breakfast

Ingredients

- Smoked Salmon Scrambled Eggs (see recipe)

Directions

- Make the recipe according to the instructions.

Lunch

Ingredients

- Grilled shrimp and vegetables on a stick (see recipe)

- Avocado Salsa (see recipe)

Directions

- Make the recipes according to the instructions.

Dinner

Ingredients

- Sausage and Artichokes (see recipe)

- Real Healthy Zucchini Cakes (see recipe)

Directions

- Make the recipes according to the instructions.

Day 14

Breakfast

Ingredients

- Creamy Chocolate Shake (see recipe)

Directions

- Make according to recipe.

Lunch

Ingredients

- 4 ounces of grilled chicken, baked with garlic

- 8 asparagus spears

- Olive Tapenade (see recipe)

Directions

- Have the cooked chicken with the asparagus on the side.

- Top with the Olive Tapenade.

Dinner

Ingredients

- Halibut with Dijon and Almonds (see recipe)

- Kale Chips (see recipe)

Directions

- Prepare the recipes according to the instructions.

Day 15

Breakfast

Ingredients

- Tex-Mex Egg Scramble

- 1 cup of mixed berries

Directions:

- Make the Tex-Mex Egg Scramble according to the recipe.

- Enjoy with the berries on the side.

Lunch

Ingredients

- Real Healthy Egg Salad

- 2 cups of Spinach

- 1 cup of raw pepper, sliced

Directions:

- Make the Real Healthy Egg Salad according to the recipe and place on top of the bed of spinach.

- Have the sliced raw peppers on the side.

Dinner

Ingredients

- Fully Loaded Lettuce Wrap Turkey Bacon Burgers (see recipe)

- Sautéed Sweet Potato Hash (see recipe)

Directions

- Follow the recipe instructions.

Day 16

Breakfast

Ingredients

- Coconut Flour Pancakes
- 1 tablespoon raw nut butter
- 1 small grapefruit

Directions:

- Make the Coconut Flour Pancakes according to the recipe and top with raw nut butter.
- Have the grapefruit on the side.

Lunch

Ingredients

- Real Healthy Egg Salad (see recipe)
- 3 stalks celery
- 1 green pepper

Directions:

- Prepare the Real Healthy Egg Salad according to the recipe.
- Use the raw vegetables to scoop the egg salad.

Dinner

Ingredients

- 4 ounces of grilled chicken breast, cut up into strips and seasoned with salt and pepper
- 1 cup of grilled vegetables—onions, peppers, shredded kale
- mushrooms
- ¼ cup avocado—cut into chunks
- 10 large olives
- Flour tortillas
- ¼ cup salsa

Directions:

- Cook the chicken breast.
- Mix all ingredients together for fajitas on a plate.

Day 17

Breakfast

Ingredients

- 2 whole eggs
- 1 tablespoon coconut oil
- 1 slice of bacon, cooked
- 1 grilled tomato

Directions:

- Scramble eggs in the coconut oil.
- Sear the tomato in a frying pan.
- Enjoy the scrambled eggs, with the tomato and bacon on the side.

Lunch

Ingredients

- 1 cup spaghetti squash
- Turkey Vegetable Meatballs (see recipe)
- ½ cup tomato sauce
- 2 handfuls spinach
- 1 tablespoon shredded Parmesan cheese

Directions:

- Cook the spaghetti squash according to the directions.

- Top the squash with the cooked Turkey Vegetable Meatballs, spinach, hot tomato sauce, and sprinkle parmesan cheese on top.

Dinner

Ingredients

- Halibut with Dijon and Almonds (see recipe)
- Stir Fried Rice (see recipe)

Directions:

- Make the recipes according to the instructions.

Day 18

Breakfast

Ingredients

- Eggs with Avocado and Salsa (see recipe)
- 1 cup of blueberries

Directions:

- Prepare the Eggs with Avocado and Salsa according to the recipe.
- Have with the blueberries on the side.

Lunch

Ingredients

- 4 ounces of light tuna (less mercury) packed in water
- 2 large handfuls of spinach
- 1 tomato, cut into chunks
- 2 pieces of bacon, cooked and crumbled
- 1 tablespoon of apple Cider vinegar

Directions:

- In a large bowl, mix all the ingredients and top with apple cider vinegar for dressing.

Dinner

Ingredients

- 4 ounces grass-fed beef, cooked and cut into chunks
- 1 cup of broccoli florets
- 1 cup of cauliflower florets
- 1 tablespoon of coconut oil

Directions

- Lightly steam the broccoli and cauliflower.
- Drizzle the liquid coconut oil on top.
- Serve with the cooked beef.

Day 19

Breakfast

Ingredients

- 1 cup of plain Greek Yogurt
- 1 cup of mixed berries
- 2 tablespoons of shredded coconut
- 1 tablespoon of chopped raw almonds

Directions:

- Mix the berries and shredded coconut into the yogurt.
- Sprinkle the chopped raw almonds on top.

Lunch

Ingredients

- Chicken Waldorf Salad (see recipe)
- 1 cup of blueberries

Directions:

- Have the blueberries on the side of the salad.

Dinner

Ingredients

- Curried Fish and Vegetables (see recipe)
- Cauliflower Mash (see recipe)

Directions

- Prepare the recipes according to the instructions.

Day 20

Breakfast

Ingredients

- 2 whole eggs
- ½ cup egg whites
- 1 ounce of goat cheese
- 6-8 cherry tomatoes
- 1 handful of spinach
- 1 tablespoon coconut oil

Directions

- Mix the whole eggs with the egg whites and beat together in a bowl.
- Pre-heat a skillet and add coconut oil.
- Pour egg mixture in the skillet and let it set for one minute.
- Add the rest of the omelet ingredients onto the egg mixture.
- Fold the egg over the ingredients and cook for one more minute.

Lunch

Ingredients

- Grilled shrimp and vegetables on a stick (see recipe)

- Avocado Salsa (see recipe)

Directions:

- Make the recipes according to the instructions.

Dinner

Ingredients

- Dijon Almond Crusted Salmon (see recipe)

- Large green salad with vegetables of choice

- ½ cup of cooked sweet potato

- ½ tablespoon of extra virgin olive oil

- ½ tablespoon of apple cider vinegar

Directions

- Toss the cooked sweet potato into the salad or have on the side of the salmon.

- Mix the extra virgin olive oil together with the apple cider vinegar as the salad dressing.

Day 21

Breakfast

Ingredients

- Tex-Mex Egg Scramble
- 1 cup of mixed berries

Directions:

- Make the Tex-Mex Egg Scramble according to the recipe and enjoy with the berries on the side.

Lunch

Ingredients

- 1 cup spaghetti squash
- Turkey Vegetable Meatballs (see recipe)
- ½ cup tomato sauce
- 2 handfuls spinach
- 1 tablespoon shredded Parmesan cheese

Directions:

- Cook the spaghetti squash according to the directions.
- Top the squash with the cooked Turkey Vegetable Meatballs, spinach, hot tomato sauce, and sprinkle parmesan cheese on top.

Dinner

Ingredients

- 4 ounces of grass-fed beef hamburger patty
- Large spinach salad with tomatoes, cucumbers, and onion
- 1 cup steamed broccoli
- Use Dijon mustard as a condiment

Directions

- Cook the hamburger.
- Enjoy with condiments and vegetables on the side.

Breakfast Recipes

Coconut Flour Pancakes

Ingredients

- 4 eggs, cage-free (organic is best)
- 1 cup unsweetened coconut milk
- 2 teaspoons vanilla extract
- 1 tablespoon raw honey
- ½ cup coconut flour
- 1 teaspoon baking soda
- ½ teaspoon sea salt
- Coconut oil or grass-fed butter for frying

Directions

- Preheat griddle over medium-low heat. In a small bowl, beat eggs until frothy—about two minutes. Mix in milk, vanilla, and honey.

- In a medium-sized bowl combine coconut flour, baking soda, and sea salt—whisk together. Stir wet mixture into dry until coconut flour is incorporated.

- Grease pan with butter or coconut oil. Pour 2-3 tablespoons of batter into pan for each pancake. The pancakes should be 2-3 inches in diameter and fairly thick. Cook for a few minutes on each side, until the batter starts to bubble. Flip and cook an additional 2-3 minutes.

- Serve hot with butter, coconut oil, honey, syrup, or fruit.

Sausage Stir-Fry Breakfast

Makes 2 Servings

Ingredients:

- 1 teaspoon coconut oil

- ½ yellow onion, diced

- ½ cup mushrooms

- ½ pound of chicken or turkey sausages (nitrite free), sliced

- 2 cups of spinach plus 2 cups of shredded kale

Directions:

- Heat a skillet over medium heat; add coconut oil when hot.

- Add diced onions and sauté until they soften. Then add mushrooms and sauté until both are tender.

- Remove onions and mushrooms from the heat and set aside.

- Add sausage and cook until browned, tossing frequently.

- Add greens, onions, mushrooms, and sausage; reduce heat to medium-low and cover.

- Serve when the greens are wilted and soft (about 5 minutes).

Eggs with Avocado and Salsa

Makes 2 Servings

Ingredients:

- 4 eggs
- 1 teaspoon olive oil
- ½ sliced avocado
- ½ cup sliced or slivered raw almonds
- 4 tablespoons of salsa (Garden Fresh)
- Season with salt and pepper

Directions

- Heat non-stick skillet over medium-high heat with olive oil.
- Beat eggs in a small bowl and pour them into the skillet.
- Cook for 1 minute and then turn heat to medium-low and add seasonings. Finish cooking (about 2-4 minutes longer).
- Top with almonds, avocado, and salsa.

Tex-Mex Breakfast Scramble

- Makes 2 Servings

Ingredients:

- 1 teaspoon coconut oil

- 4 eggs
- ½ teaspoon cumin
- ½ teaspoon chilli powder (or ground chipotle)
- ¼ teaspoon sea salt (optional)
- 1 tablespoon water
- ¼ red onion, diced
- 1 green bell pepper, diced
- 1 jalapeno, diced (optional)
- 12 ounces of chicken breasts, grilled and chopped (use leftovers)
- 1 medium tomato, diced
- ¼ cup fresh cilantro, chopped

Directions:

- Heat coconut oil in a medium skillet over medium-high heat.
- Scramble eggs in a bowl. Add cumin, chili powder, sea salt, and water.
- Add onions, bell peppers, and jalapeno to the hot skillet. Sauté 3-5 minutes, or until slightly softened.
- Add eggs and chicken, and cook while continuously stirring until eggs are light and fluffy.
- Remove from heat. Stir in tomatoes and top with fresh cilantro to serve.

Breakfast Stir-Fry

Makes 2 servings

Ingredients:

- 8 bacon slices, diced
- 1 tablespoon coconut oil
- ½ yellow onion, diced
- 1 medium sweet potato, diced
- 1 medium zucchini, diced
- 7-8 green beans
- 2 handfuls spinach
- 1 avocado
- Freshly ground black pepper, to taste

Directions

- Cook chopped bacon in a medium skillet over medium-low heat. Drain fat when done.

- Meanwhile, heat a large sauté pan over medium-high heat. Add coconut oil and, when hot, add sweet potato—stirring often for about 10-15 minutes.

- Once potatoes are softened, add in onions and sauté until they turn translucent.

- Add zucchini and green beans to the sweet potato mixture and cook just until they turn bright green.

- Combine bacon, vegetables, and spinach. Season with freshly-ground black pepper; top with avocado to serve.

Fruit Salad with Cinnamon

Makes 2 Servings

Ingredients

- 1 cup mixed strawberries and blueberries
- 1 apple, diced
- ½ cup pecans or walnuts, chopped (optional)
- ½ teaspoon cinnamon

Directions

- Place the fruit evenly into two bowls.
- Sprinkle with chopped nuts (optional) and cinnamon.

Breakfast Smoothie

Makes 2 Servings

Ingredients

- 2 cups frozen berries
- 1 cup unsweetened almond milk (canned coconut milk if you want more calories/fat)
- 4 tablespoon hemp seeds

- 2 tablespoon chia seeds
- 2 servings of protein powder

Directions

- Fill a blender (or magic bullet) with the frozen berries.
- Add chia, hemp seeds, protein powder, and almond milk.
- Continue to blend until smooth; divide into two servings.

Cashew Strawberry Cream Smoothie

Makes 1 serving

Ingredients

- ½ cup coconut water
- ½ cup of water
- ½ cup raw cashews
- ½ cup ice cubes
- ¼ cup frozen strawberries
- 1/8 teaspoon pure vanilla extract
- 2 dates

Directions

- Place the cashews with water in a blender along with the ice cubes, strawberries, vanilla, and dates.

- Blend until smooth.

Blueberry Carrot Smoothie

Makes 1 serving

Ingredients

- 1 cup frozen blueberries
- 1 carrot (peeled and sliced)
- 2 tablespoons cashews
- 1 cup spinach
- 1 serving protein powder
- ½ cup unsweetened almond milk
- ½ cup ice cubes

Directions

- Place all the ingredients in a blender and blend on high until smooth.

Smoked Salmon Scrambled Eggs

Makes 2 Servings

Ingredients

- 1 teaspoon olive oil
- 4 eggs
- ½ cup egg whites
- 4 ounces of smoked salmon, sliced or broken into small pieces
- ½ avocado

- Freshly-ground black pepper, to taste

- 4 chives, minced—or use 1 green onion, thinly sliced

Directions

- Heat a medium skillet over medium heat. Add olive oil to pan when hot.

- Meanwhile, crack eggs into a small bowl and mix in egg whites.

- Add eggs and smoked salmon to the hot skillet.

- Stir continuously, cooking eggs until they are soft and fluffy.

- Remove from heat. Top with black pepper, avocado, and chives to serve.

Low Carb Green Smoothie

Makes 1 Serving

Ingredients

- 1 cup coconut water
- 1 tablespoon almond butter
- ¼ cup wheat grass
- 2 cups spinach
- 1 serving of high-quality, low-carb protein powder
- 1-inch slice of banana
- Optional pinch of Stevia
- ½ cup of ice

Directions

- Place all ingredients in the blender and blend until smooth.

Creamy Chocolate Shake

Makes 2 Servings

Ingredients

- 2 bananas
- ½ cup unsweetened coconut milk
- 1/8 raw cocoa powder
- 2 tablespoons of raw honey
- 2 tablespoons of raw almond butter
- Dash of sea salt
- Dash of fresh, ground cinnamon
- 2 cups ice

Directions

- Place all ingredients into the blender and blend on high until smooth.

Lunch/Dinner Recipes

Delicious Chopped Salad

Makes 4-6 Servings

Ingredients

- 1 bunch of chopped asparagus
- 4 large carrots, chopped
- 5 green onions, chopped
- 1 green zucchini
- 1 yellow zucchini
- 1 teaspoon olive oil
- dash of salt and pepper
- 1 avocado, chopped
- 2 heads of romaine lettuce, chopped

- ¼ cup Kalamata olives, chopped

- ¼ cup pine nuts, toasted

For the dressing

- 1/8 cup olive oil

- 2 tablespoons of lime juice

- 2 tablespoons of agave nectar

- 1 clove garlic, minced

- 1 teaspoon of Champagne Mustard

Directions

- Preheat oven to 425° Fahrenheit. Place the asparagus, carrots, onions, and zucchinis in a large bowl; mix well with the olive oil and then salt and pepper.

- Place on a baking sheet and roast for 20 minutes, stirring after the first 10 minutes.

- Meanwhile, place the remaining salad ingredients into a large bowl.

- In a small bowl combine all of the dressing ingredients and whisk with a fork.

- Once the veggies are roasted, mix into the salad bowl and toss with the dressing.

Teriyaki Chicken Salad

Makes 4 Servings

Ingredients

- 1 can stevia-sweetened lemon-lime soda (Zevia Brand)

- ½ cup coconut aminos

- ¾ cup brown rice vinegar

- 1 medium yellow onion—half minced and half thinly-sliced

- 4 cloves garlic, smashed

- 1 tablespoons of fresh ginger, grated

- 1 packet of stevia

- 2 tablespoons of cilantro, chopped

Directions

- Combine the soda, vinegar, minced onion, garlic, ginger, and coconut crystals in a bowl. Add chicken and turn to coat. Place in refrigerator overnight.

- Remove chicken from marinade and pat dry. Reserve 1 cup of marinade.

- Heat one teaspoon of coconut oil in a large skillet. Add the chicken and heat on medium high, turning once after 8-10 minutes, until browned. Transfer to a plate.

- Wipe out the skillet. Heat remaining 1 teaspoon of coconut oil. Add the sliced onion and asparagus. Cook for 5 minutes until browned. Add the reserved marinade and boil until slightly reduced. Add the cilantro.

Delicious Egg Salad

Makes 4 Servings

Ingredients

- Eggs
- Celery
- Green Onions
- Greek yogurt
- Mustard
- Lemon
- Salt
- Pepper

Directions

- To boil the perfect egg: place eggs in a large pot and cover with cold water by half an inch.

- Heat the water to a boil; turn off heat and cover the pot. Wait exactly 7 minutes and then place the eggs in a bowl of ice water for 3 minutes.

- Peel and chop hardboiled eggs. Place in the large bowl. Add celery, onion, greens, Greek yogurt, mustard, lemon, salt, and pepper. Mix well.

- Chill and then serve.

Sweet and Smokey Chicken

Makes 4 Servings

Ingredients

- 4 bone-in, organic, skin-on chicken thighs
- 1 teaspoon smoked paprika
- 1 teaspoon garlic powder
- 1 teaspoon ground cumin
- 1 tablespoon olive oil
- ¼ teaspoon Allspice
- ½ teaspoon onion powder
- 1 packet Stevia
- Dash of salt and pepper

Directions

- Preheat oven to 450° Fahrenheit.

- Rinse the chicken and pat dry. Place in a Ziploc bag.

- In a small bowl, combine the remaining ingredients. Add to the Ziploc bag and toss until the chicken is fully coated.

- Place the coated chicken thighs on a broiling pan and bake for 40 minutes.

Fully Loaded Lettuce-Wrapped Turkey Bacon Burgers

Makes 6 Servings

Ingredients

- 8 strips nitrate-free bacon
- ½ yellow onion, sliced
- 1/8 cup blanched almond flour
- 1 pound of organic ground turkey
- 2 teaspoons of balsamic glaze
- 1 teaspoon of tomato paste
- ¼ teaspoon of smoked paprika
- ½ teaspoon of garlic powder
- ½ teaspoon of onion powder
- 1/8 red bell pepper, minced
- 1 tablespoon of fresh chives, chopped

- Large lettuce leaves

- Sliced organic tomato

Directions

- Heat the oven to 400° Fahrenheit. Line a baking sheet with foil and place a metal cooling rack in the center. Arrange the bacon pieces on the rack and bake for 20 minutes, or until crispy. Remove from oven and set aside to cool.

- Grill the sliced onion in a grill pan over medium-high heat with a few drops of olive oil. Grill until tender and caramelized. Remove from heat and set aside to cool.

- Chop 6 of the bacon strips and place in a medium bowl. Chop 1/4 cup of the grilled onions and add to the bowl. Add the almond flour, turkey, balsamic glaze, tomato paste, paprika, garlic powder, onion powder, bell peppers, and chives to the bowl. Mix well with your hands—it's okay to get messy here! Form into 6 patties.

- Place the patties on your grill pan over medium high heat for about 4 minutes per side—until cooked through.

- Serve your Fully Loaded Lettuce-Wrapped Turkey Bacon Burgers on large lettuce leaves and topped with sliced tomato and the extra grilled onions and bacon pieces.

Braised Cabbage and Sausage

Makes 6 Servings

Ingredients

- 1 head green cabbage
- 1 yellow onion, chopped
- 4 large carrots, sliced
- ¼ cup vegetable broth
- 1/8 cup of olive oil
- 1/8 teaspoon of crushed red pepper
- Dash of freshly-ground pepper
- 1 pound of cooked chicken sausage
- ¼ cup balsamic vinegar

Directions

- Preheat oven to 325° Fahrenheit. Lightly grease a large baking pan with olive oil.

- Peel off the outer leaves of cabbage. Cut into 8 equal wedges. Arrange in prepared dish—each wedge should lay flat.

- Sprinkle the onion and carrot pieces over the cabbage. Drizzle with olive oil and evenly apply the seasonings.

- Cover tightly with foil. Bake for 1 hour.

- Turn each wedge with tongs; add a touch of water if cabbage is dry. Replace the foil tightly and bake for another hour.

- Remove the foil; sprinkle the chicken sausage slices over cabbage. Increase the oven temperature to 400° Fahrenheit, and then bake, uncovered, for an additional 10 minutes.

- Remove from oven and drizzle with balsamic vinegar. Serve warm.

Fish Tacos

Makes 4 Servings

Ingredients

- 16 ounces of wild cod fillets
- 1 lime
- 1 head lettuce
- Dressed avocado
- 1 cup shredded cabbage (buy pre-shredded)
- Papaya mango salsa

Directions

- Defrost frozen cod by placing in the fridge overnight.
- Preheat oven to 375° Fahrenheit. Grease a pan with olive oil.

- Place defrosted cod in prepared pan; cut lime in half and squeeze juice over cod. Bake for 15 minutes.

- While cod is baking, separate leaves from lettuce, being careful to keep them intact.

- Enjoy the cooked fish in the lettuce leaves, adding salsa and avocado to taste.

Shrimp and Noodles

Makes 4 Servings

Ingredients

- 4 zucchinis
- ½ cup macadamia nuts
- 2 cups fresh basil leaves
- 2 garlic cloves
- 1/3 cup nutritional yeast
- Dash of sea salt
- Juice of ½ lemon
- ¼ cup olive oil
- 2 dozen large shrimp

Directions

- For the noodles: Run a vegetable peeler along each zucchini until you reach the seeds. Place your zucchini noodles in a bowl.

- For Pesto: Place the macadamia nuts, basil leaves, garlic, nutritional yeast, salt, and lemon juice in a food processor. Pulse until well-combined while drizzling in the olive oil.

- Peel and devein the shrimp, pulling off the tail and then the rest of the shell.

- Heat a pot of water under a steamer basket. Steam your noodles for about 5 minutes, until tender. Remove to a medium bowl.

- Steam the shrimp for 3 minutes, until fully pink.

- Combine the noodles with the pesto and top with warm shrimp. Serve and enjoy.

Buffalo Chicken Wings In "Peanut Sauce"

Makes 2 Servings

Ingredients:

- 1 and 1/2 lbs of chicken wings
- 2 tablespoons of almond butter
- ¼ cup hot pepper sauce
- 1 - 2 tablespoons of tamari sauce
- 2 teaspoons of olive oil
- ¼ teaspoon of sea salt (optional)
- Pepper to taste

Directions:

- Preheat oven to 375° Fahrenheit.
- Line a rimmed baking sheet with parchment paper and spread wings out evenly. Sprinkle salt and pepper over wings. Bake for 20 minutes.
- Meanwhile, soften almond butter in a small saucepan over medium heat. Stir occasionally.
- When soft, stir in hot pepper sauce, tamari sauce, olive oil, and sea salt (if desired). If sauce gets too thick, add a bit of hot water.
- After 20 minutes of cooking, remove wings from the oven. Turn and brush each wing with sauce. Return to oven for 10 more minutes.
- Turn each wing, baste with sauce, and return to oven for 10 additional minutes (or until completely cooked).

Rosemary Chicken and Mushroom Glaze

Makes 2 Servings

Ingredients

- 4 boneless, skinless chicken breasts (4-6 ounces each)

- sea salt (optional) and freshly ground black pepper

- 4 tablespoons of coconut oil, divided

- 2 cloves garlic, minced

- 2 teaspoons of fresh rosemary leaves or 2 teaspoons of dried rosemary

- 2 teaspoons of hazelnuts, chopped

- 10 white button or cremini mushrooms, sliced

Directions

- Season chicken breasts with sea salt (optional) and black pepper (to taste).

- Heat a large skillet over medium heat. Add 1 tablespoon of coconut oil when the pan is hot.

- Add chicken breasts and cook until there is no pink in the center. Set chicken aside.

- In a different heated pan, add the remaining coconut oil. When the pan is hot, add rosemary, hazelnuts, and garlic. Simmer together for 5 minutes.

- Add mushrooms and cook for another 5 minutes, or until mushrooms are browned. Season with sea salt and black pepper if desired.

- Pour mushroom mixture over chicken and heat through.
- When hot, serve.

Turkey Vegetable Meatballs

Makes 2 Servings

Ingredients

- 1 pound of ground turkey or chicken
- 2 medium carrots (or a handful of baby carrots)
- 1 red or green bell pepper
- 5 large mushrooms
- handful of fresh parsley
- 1/2 yellow onion
- 1 clove garlic
- 2 teaspoons of granulated garlic (garlic salt)
- 2 tablespoons of Italian seasoning
- 1/2 teaspoon of freshly ground black pepper
- 3 tablespoons of ground chia seeds

Directions

- Preheat oven to 350° Fahrenheit.
- Combine carrots, bell pepper, mushrooms, onion, garlic, chia seeds, and seasonings in a food processor; blend until well-chopped.

- Empty the food processor into a large bowl, add the ground turkey, and mix together completely.

- Form meatballs and place on a non-greased baking sheet (about 1 1/2" - 2" each).

- Bake for about 25 minutes, or until completely cooked.

Beef and Sweet Potato Chili

Makes 10 Servings

Ingredients

- 2 tablespoons of olive oil

- 1 large yellow onion, diced

- 2 tablespoons of chili powder

- 1 teaspoon of ground chipotle

- 2 teaspoons of sea salt (optional)

- 1 teaspoon of cumin

- 1 teaspoon of garlic salt

- 2 lbs of beef stew meat, cut into one-inch by one-inch chunks

- 2 (28 ounces) cans diced tomatoes

- 2 (4 ounces) cans of diced green chilis

- 1/2 of a 4-ounce can of diced jalapenos (may add more if desired)

- 1/2 teaspoon of oregano

- 1/2 teaspoon of thyme

- 1 bay leaf

- 7-8 medium mushrooms, sliced

- 2 medium carrots, sliced

- 2 medium zucchinis, diced

- 1 large red pepper, diced

- 2 large sweet potatoes—cut into even chunks

- 4 - 6 large kale leaves, shredded

Directions

- Heat large soup pot over medium-high heat.

- When hot, add olive oil and onion to pot and brown slightly.

- Meanwhile, combine chili powder, sea salt, cumin, and garlic salt in a large dish. Roll raw beef-stew meat in the mixture to coat on all sides.

- When onions have browned slightly, add beef and brown on all sides.

- Add the diced tomatoes. Fill the empty can with water and add to the pot. Add sweet potato, green chilis, jalapenos, chipotle peppers, mushrooms, carrots, oregano, thyme, and bay leaf. Make sure the liquid covers all of the ingredients.

- Turn heat down to medium and cook for about 40 minutes, stirring occasionally.

- Add zucchini and red pepper, and cook for another 20 minutes.

- Add kale and finish cooking for 10 more minutes. Season with sea salt if desired.

Ginger Beef and Broccoli

Makes 2 Servings

Ingredients

- 2 tablespoons of coconut oil
- 2 cloves of garlic, minced
- 1 pound of petite sirloin steak, cut into very thin strips
- 2 tablespoons of lemon juice
- 1 tablespoon of ground chia seeds
- 2 teaspoons of freshly-grated ginger
- 2 teaspoons of freshly ground black pepper
- 1/2 teaspoon of red pepper flakes
- 1/4 to 1/2 cup organic low sodium chicken broth
- 2 cups broccoli, cut into florets
- 2 cups carrots, thinly sliced

- 1 cup celery, thinly sliced

- 1 green onion, thinly sliced

- 2 tablespoons of sesame seeds (garnish)

Directions

- Heat the 1-tablespoon of coconut oil and garlic in a large skillet over medium-high heat.

- Add the sliced beef and 1/4 teaspoon of sea salt, and brown it. Remove the beef from the pan to a side dish. Get rid of the excess juice left in the pan.

- In a small bowl, mix lemon juice, ground chia seeds, grated ginger, freshly-ground black pepper, and red pepper flakes with 1/4 cup broth.

- Heat the pan again over medium heat. Add 1 tablespoon of coconut oil when the pan is hot.

- Add broccoli, celery, and carrots to pan. Pour liquid ingredients on top and toss to coat.

- Cook over medium heat until the broccoli is tender.

- Return the beef to the pan and add the green onions. Add the extra chicken broth if preferred.

- Stir beef in until it's coated with sauce, and let simmer for a few minutes until the beef is warmed through.

- Sprinkle sesame seeds on top and serve.

Slowed Cooking Pork Loin

Makes 2 Servings

Ingredients

- 1 and 1/2 pounds of pork loin
- 1 (16 ounces) can tomato sauce
- 2 medium (6"- 8") zucchinis, sliced
- 1 head cauliflower, separated into medium florets
- 1 to 2 tablespoon dried basil
- 1/4 teaspoon of freshly-ground black pepper
- 1/2 teaspoon of sea salt (optional)

Directions

- Add all of the ingredients to a large crock pot.
- Cook on high for 6 - 7 hours.

Sausage and Artichokes

Makes 2 Servings

Ingredients

- 1 pound of high-quality pork sausages (nitrate free)
- 2 tablespoons of olive oil
- 2 medium onions
- 1 clove of garlic, chopped
- 1/4 pound of white button or cremini mushrooms (about 5 medium)

- 1/2 pound of Jerusalem artichokes (also called "sunchokes")

- half of 1 large lemon

- 1 cup of organic low-sodium chicken stock or water to cover

- a small bunch of flat-leaf parsley, roughly chopped

Directions

- Brown the sausages all over in a little oil in a deep cast-iron skillet or pot. Take out of the skillet and set aside.

- Peel the onions and cut them into thick segments, then add to the pan in which you browned the sausages. On medium heat, let the onions soften.

- Add the garlic to the onions. Cut the mushrooms in half and add to the skillet.

- Peel or simply scrub the artichokes, then cut them into 1" pieces. Add them to the pan, pushing the onions aside, and let them color slightly.

- Put the sausages back into the pan along with the cooking vegetables.

- Cut the lemon into fat chunks and mix them in the skillet along with a good seasoning of salt and black pepper.

- Pour over enough stock or water to cover and bring to the boil.

- Turn the heat down and simmer for about 30 minutes, until the vegetables are truly tender. If there is too much liquid, turn up the heat and let it reduce a little.

- Stir in the parsley; season to taste and eat with the steamed greens.

Sausage and Tomatoes

Makes 2 Servings

Ingredients

- 6 large firm tomatoes
- 1 pound of sausage, nitrate-free
- 6 mushrooms, sliced
- 1 medium yellow onion, chopped
- fresh cilantro

Directions

- Preheat oven to 350° Fahrenheit.

- Over medium-high heat, brown onions, sausage, and mushrooms together in a skillet.

- While the above is cooking, cut the tops off the tomatoes. Spoon out the middle and add to the skillet.

- Let all ingredients simmer for 7 – 10 minutes.
- Serve with fresh cilantro.

Lamb and Spaghetti Squash

Makes 2 Servings

Ingredients

- 1 small or medium spaghetti squash
- 1 pound ground lamb
- 1/2 yellow onion, diced
- 1/2 teaspoon of sea salt (optional)
- 1/2 teaspoon of garlic
- 1/4 teaspoon of oregano
- 8 medium white-button or cremini mushrooms, sliced
- 2 tablespoons of coconut oil

Directions

- Preheat oven to 375° Fahrenheit
- Cut the spaghetti squash in half length-wise with a large knife or cleaver. Remove seeds and loose flesh.
- Place cut side down in a shallow baking dish. Add ¾ inch of water to the dish.
- Bake for 45 minutes or so, until the squash is soft to the touch.
- After about 30 minutes of baking, heat a large sauté pan over medium-high heat.
- Add lamb, onions, sea salt, garlic, and oregano.

- Cook 5 minutes, stirring frequently.

- Add mushrooms and continue to cook until lamb is fully done (10-12 minutes). Set aside.

- When squash is done cooking, remove it from the oven and let it cool until it can be comfortably handled.

- Turn the cut side up and remove the flesh from the rind with a fork. This should be done cross-wise, so the strands of squash fall out like spaghetti.

- Spoon lamb mixture over spaghetti squash to serve. If you need a little extra flavor, add some tomato sauce on top.

Grilled Shrimp and Vegetables on a Stick

Makes 2 Servings

Ingredients

- 3/4 pound of shrimp, peeled and deveined

- juice of 1 lime

- 2 teaspoons of minced garlic

- freshly ground black pepper

- 1 medium zucchini, sliced into 1-inch pieces

- 2 cups of button mushrooms

- 1 red bell pepper, sliced into 2-inch pieces

- 1 green bell pepper, sliced into 2-inch pieces

- 1 red onion, cut into eighths

- 4 cloves garlic, minced

- 3 tablespoons of olive oil

- wooden skewers, soaked in cold water for 15 minutes to prevent burning

Directions

- Soak wooden skewers (at least 15 minutes).

- Peel shrimp and put it in a medium bowl. Toss with minced garlic.

- Add lime juice and season the shrimp with pepper. Set it aside for five minutes.

- Wash and chop the vegetables.

- Prepare the grill.

- Add vegetables and garlic to the shrimp, and then toss with olive oil.

- Stack vegetables and shrimp onto skewers and grill until fully cooked.

Curried Fish and Vegetables

Makes 2 Servings

Ingredients

- 1 pound of white fish fillets, cut crosswise into 1-inch

slices

- 1 can unsweetened coconut milk

- 2 tablespoons of red curry paste

- 2 medium carrots, cut into thin matchsticks

- 1/2 small red cabbage, thinly sliced

- handful fresh cilantro, chopped

Directions

- Put the coconut milk and red curry paste in a large sauté pan over medium heat. Cook for 3 minutes, stirring until combined.

- Add carrots and red cabbage to pan. Cover and let simmer for 4 - 5 minutes.

- Add fish and simmer an additional 4 - 5 minutes, or until fish is fully cooked.

- Serve with fresh cilantro.

Dijon Almond Crusted Salmon

Makes 2 Servings

Ingredients

- 3/4 pound of salmon fillet(s), skin on

- ½ cup almond meal

- ¼ cup Dijon mustard

- 1/2 teaspoon of ground coriander

- 1/2 teaspoon of ground cumin

- juice of 1 lemon

- sea salt and freshly ground black pepper

- 2 teaspoons of coconut oil

Directions

- Preheat the oven to 350° Fahrenheit.

- Combine almond meal, coriander, and cumin in a small bowl.

- Season salmon with salt and pepper. Brush on Dijon mustard to coat each piece.

- Coat each fillet with the almond-meal mixture (both sides).

- Place skin side down on a broiler pan, greased lightly with coconut oil.

- Bake for 12 - 15 minutes, or until salmon flakes easily with a fork.

Shrimp Cakes

Makes 12 Cakes (Serving size: 3 cakes)

Ingredients

- 1 pound of shrimp—raw, peeled, and deveined

- 1 red or yellow bell pepper, finely chopped

- 1 clove garlic, minced

- 2 tablespoons of green onions, thinly sliced

- 1 tablespoon of lime juice, freshly squeezed

- 1 tablespoon of raw honey

- ½ teaspoon of sea salt (optional)

- ¼ teaspoon of ground chipotle

- 1 egg

- ½ cup cilantro, finely chopped

- ½ cup almond flour

- 3 tablespoons of olive oil, for sautéing

Directions

- Place shrimp in food processor; pulse until finely chopped.

- In a large bowl, combine chopped shrimp, bell pepper, garlic, scallions, lime juice, honey, sea salt (optional), chipotle, egg, and cilantro.

- Form mixture into 12 (½ inch thick) patties; dip each in almond flour, coating thoroughly.

- In a large skillet, over medium heat, warm 1 tablespoon of oil.

- Add 4 patties to the skillet and cook about 5 minutes per side, until browned; remove and place on paper-towel-lined plate. Repeat with remaining cakes.

Halibut with Dijon and Almonds

Makes 2 Servings

Ingredients

- 1 tablespoon of olive oil

- 1 pound of halibut or other white fish

- 2 tablespoons of Dijon mustard

- Salt and pepper to taste

- 2 tablespoons of almonds, sliced and toasted

Directions

- Preheat the oven to 350° Fahrenheit.

- Lightly grease a baking sheet with olive oil.

- Lay fish in the pan—skin side down.

- Season fish with salt and pepper and then coat with Dijon mustard.

- Bake for 12-15 minutes, or until fish flakes easily with a fork.

- Sprinkle with toasted, sliced almonds.

Mexican Salad

Makes 2 Servings

Ingredients:

- 1 pound of lean ground beef or turkey
- 2 tablespoons of chili powder
- 1 teaspoon of garlic salt
- 1 teaspoon of cumin
- 1/2 teaspoon of oregano
- 1/2 teaspoon of sea salt
- 3/4 cup water
- 1/2 yellow onion, diced
- 1 medium tomato, diced
- 4 roasted red peppers, chopped
- 6 cups baby spinach
- 1 can black olives, sliced
- 1 avocado
- fresh cilantro
- ½ cup salsa (divided into two portions)

Directions

- Heat medium skillet over medium-high heat. Add beef or turkey and onion to pan. Cook for about 10 minutes, or until browned.

- Add chili powder, garlic salt, cumin, oregano, roasted red peppers, sea salt, and water. Let simmer for 5 minutes.

- Meanwhile, separate spinach onto two plates.

- Top with meat, sliced avocado, black olives, tomatoes, cilantro, and salsa.

Chicken Waldorf Salad

Makes 2 Servings

Ingredients

- 2 (4 - 6 ounces) chicken breasts, cooked and diced

- 1 head of romaine lettuce

- 1 large tart apple, cored and diced

- 1 large stalk celery, chopped

- ½ cup walnuts, chopped

- ¼ cup avocado

- 2 teaspoons of lime juice

- 2 teaspoons of raw honey

- Freshly ground black pepper to taste

- Sea salt (optional)

Directions

- In a medium bowl, combine chicken, apple, celery, and walnuts. Set aside.

- In a small bowl, combine avocado, lime juice, and honey. Mix until well-blended. Use extra lime juice if more liquid is needed.

- Season with sea salt and freshly-ground black pepper if desired.

- Spoon dressing over chicken and toss to coat completely. If making salad ahead of time, keep the chicken mixture and dressing separate until just before eating.

- Wash and dry lettuce. Separate the lettuce into two bowls. Spoon chicken salad equally onto the two plates.

Balsamic Asparagus and Steak Salad

Makes 4 Servings

Ingredients

- 1 pound of flank steak
- 1 pound of asparagus, ends trimmed
- 1 tablespoon of red onion, minced
- 1 tablespoon of extra virgin olive oil
- 4 teaspoons of balsamic vinegar
- 1 clove garlic, minced
- sea salt, to taste (optional)
- freshly ground black pepper, to taste

Directions

- Bring a medium pot of water to boil.
- Add asparagus and boil 3 minutes. Drain and rinse under cold water immediately. Dry thoroughly.
- Heat a grill until hot. Trim away excess fat if desired. Cut into 4 steaks. Season with salt and pepper. Place on grill.
- Grill for 4 to 5 minutes per side. Leave medium rare to rare.
- Once it's cooked, set aside and let it rest about 10 minutes.
- Cut each piece into strips after it has rested.

- Mix all other ingredients together. Toss asparagus with balsamic mixture.

- Top with steak slices.

- Serve chilled or at room temperature.

Tasty Tuna Salad (Makes 2 Servings)

Ingredients

- 2 cans of light tuna

- ½ cup green or black olives, chopped

- 1 green onion, chopped

- 1 jalapeno pepper, finely chopped (no seeds and/or less jalapeno if you want less spice)

- 3 tablespoons of capers, rinsed

- 1/2 teaspoon of red chili flakes

- Juice of 2 lemons

- Splash of olive oil

- 6 cups mixed greens (optional)

- 1 avocado, sliced

Directions

- Portion out lettuce onto two plates.

- In a bowl combine all the ingredients and divide onto two plates on top of lettuce.

- Serve with sliced avocado on top.

- Serve immediately or store it in the fridge for a day for more flavor.

Ground Turkey Casserole

Makes 4 servings

Ingredients

- 1 cup coconut milk
- 1 teaspoon of turmeric
- 1 teaspoon of coriander
- 1 teaspoon of salt
- 1 cup low sodium vegetable broth
- Olive oil cooking spray
- 1 pound of extra lean ground turkey (454 g)
- 1 cup sweet onion, diced
- 1 cup baby carrots, thinly sliced
- 1 ½ cup asparagus (cut into 1-inch pieces)
- 2 cups green cabbage (grated)
- ½ cup sliced almonds
- ½ cup aged white cheddar, shredded

Directions

- Preheat oven to 350° Fahrenheit

- Mix half the coconut milk, turmeric, coriander, and salt until smooth and set aside.

- Stir in the rest of the coconut milk and the vegetable broth to the mixture.

- Preheat a non-stick frying pan on medium heat and lightly coat with coconut oil.

- Sauté the turkey in batches until lightly browned, and then transfer it to a large casserole dish.

- Add remaining ingredients—including the liquid mixture—to the casserole dish.

- Stir well to incorporate and bake for 25-30 minutes.

No Fry Salmon Patties

Makes 2 servings

Ingredients

- 1 can sockeye salmon with bones

- 1 whole egg

- 1 small red pepper, finely chopped

- 2-3 celery stocks, finely chopped

- ½ cup brown rice breadcrumbs

- Salt and pepper to taste

Directions

- Preheat oven to 375° Fahrenheit.

- Drain both the tuna and salmon and mix together in a bowl.

- Use a mini processor to chop pepper and celery and drain excess water.

- Mix all ingredients together until the consistency holds together.

- Line a baking sheet with parchment paper.

- Using your hands, make patties and place on baking sheet with space between them.

- Cook time will depend on the size of the patties. The patties should be firm and hold together when cooked—approximately 20 minutes.

SIDES
Bacon Wrapped Scallops

Makes 12 Servings

Ingredients

- 4 tablespoons of coconut oil
- 3 garlic cloves, minced
- Dash of sweet paprika
- Dash of salt and pepper
- 6 slices of nitrate-free bacon; cut in half lengthwise
- 12 fresh scallops

Directions

- Preheat oven to 375° Fahrenheit.

- Grease a baking sheet with coconut oil and set it aside.

- Over very low heat, in a small saucepan, melt the coconut oil. Remove it from heat and pour it into a small bowl. Add the garlic, paprika, salt, and pepper.

- Dip each scallop in the seasoned coconut oil, and then wrap it with bacon and secure it with a toothpick. Place on prepared baking sheet.

- Bake for 15 minutes or until the scallops are cooked through and the bacon is crisp.

Stir Fried Rice

Makes 16 Servings

Ingredients

- 3 cups carrots, chopped

- 2 cups frozen peas

- 4 heads organic cauliflower cut into small pieces

- 4 tablespoons of olive oil

- 6 whole eggs, free range

- 6 tablespoons of coconut aminos

- Salt and pepper to taste

Directions

- Bring a medium pot of water to boil. Add the chopped carrots and boil for 3 minutes.

- Add the frozen peas and boil for another 2 minutes. Drain the water and set the veggies aside.

- Using a food processor with the grating blade, grate all of the cauliflower.

- Heat the olive oil in a large skillet or wok over medium.

- Add the carrots and peas; sauté for 3 minutes.

- Add the 6 eggs; stir to combine. When the eggs have set, add the grated cauliflower and mix to combine.

- Season the rice mixture with coconut aminos, salt, and pepper. Reduce the heat to low, cover, and allow to cook for another 5 minutes.

- Add more coconut aminos, salt, and pepper to taste.

Healthy Zucchini Cakes

Makes 8 Servings

Ingredients

- 1 teaspoon olive oil
- 1 small yellow onion, grated
- 1 garlic clove
- 2 cups grated zucchini
- ½ teaspoon of salt
- 2 eggs
- ¼ cup coconut flower
- 2 tablespoons of flax meal
- ½ teaspoon of baking powder
- 2% Greek yogurt
- Sweet paprika

Directions

- Heat half of the olive oil in a large skillet. Sauté the onion and garlic for 2 minutes, and then set it aside.

- Place grated zucchini in a colander, sprinkle with the salt and allow to sit in the sink for 10 minutes.

- Use a clean paper towel to squeeze excess water from the zucchini.

- In a medium sized bowl, whisk the eggs. Add the coconut flour, flax, and baking powder. Add the onions and zucchini.

- Place the remaining olive oil in a large skillet over medium heat. Drop the dough in heaping tablespoons, and then press each down with a fork.

- Cook each side for 3 minutes or until golden.

Grapefruit, Goat Cheese, and Avocado Salad

Makes 4 Servings

Ingredients

- 1 bunch flowering kale, de-stemmed and cut into chunks

- 1 bunch endive

- 1 red grapefruit

- 1 yellow grapefruit

- 1 avocado

- 3 tablespoons of creamy goat cheese

- 1 teaspoon of olive oil

- ¼ cup grapefruit juice

- 1 teaspoon of poppy seeds

Directions

- Place the kale and endive in a bowl.

- Peel and slice the grapefruits and add to the bowl, reserving ¼ cup juice.

- Chop the avocado and add to the bowl.

- Add the goat cheese in small dollops.

- In a small cup, mix the grapefruit juice, olive oil and poppy seeds. Drizzle on the salad.

Butternut Squash Soup

Makes 8 – 12 servings

Ingredients

- 2 tablespoons salted butter

- 1 medium onion, diced

- 3 carrots, cut into chunks

- 2 medium butternut squash, peeled, seeded, and diced into 2-inch cubes

- 8 cups water or stock

333

Directions

- In a large soup pot, warm the butter.

- Caramelize onion in the pot, sautéing 8 - 10 minutes until golden brown.

- Add the squash cubes and carrots. Cook for 10 more minutes until the outside of the squash cubes are a bit soft.

- Pour the water over the onion/squash mixture.

- Bring entire mixture up to a boil and simmer for 20 - 30 minutes until squash and carrots are soft.

- In a blender, puree soup in very small batches (as not to scorch yourself and have soup splattered on your ceiling) at low, then working up to high speed until mixture is smooth and creamy.

- Serve piping hot

Avocado Salsa

Makes 4 Servings (3 Cups)

Ingredients

- 2 avocados, diced (save the pits)

- 1 jalapeno pepper, seeded and diced

- 3 medium tomatoes, seeded and diced

- 1/4 of a red onion, diced

- 1 bunch cilantro, finely chopped

- Juice of 1 lime

Directions

- Combine all ingredients in a medium bowl.

- Keep the avocado pits in the mixture to serve. This will slow the oxidation of the avocados (what makes them turn brown) and will help the salsa last longer.

Cauliflower Mash

Makes 4 Servings

Ingredients

- 1 and 1/2 large heads of cauliflower
- 3/4 cup unsweetened coconut milk
- 3 tablespoons of coconut oil
- 2/3 cup fresh chives
- 3 cloves garlic
- 2 teaspoons of dried rosemary or 1 sprig fresh rosemary
- Sea salt and pepper to taste

Directions

- Roughly chop the cauliflower, removing all leaves.
- Place in pot of boiling water and cook until it's easy to stick a fork in it.
- Mince the garlic and finely chop the chives. Sauté the garlic, chives, and rosemary in coconut oil until the garlic is light-golden brown.
- Drain cauliflower; use food processor or handheld blender to mash up/puree the steamed cauliflower florets.
- Put the mashed florets into a pot on the stove and add coconut milk and the chive and garlic mixture. Cook through until hot. Use hand blender again if

you want the mixture creamier. Add sea salt and pepper to taste.

Rosemary Green Beans

Makes 2 Servings

Ingredients

- 1 pound of fresh green beans, trimmed
- 1/2 teaspoon of salt, divided
- 1 teaspoon of coconut oil
- 2 green onions, sliced
- 2 teaspoons of fresh rosemary, chopped
- 1/4 cup pecans, chopped and toasted
- 2 teaspoons of lemon rind, grated

Directions

- Heat 1 and ½ inches of water in a medium pot with a steamer basket inserted. Bring to a boil.
- Sprinkle green beans evenly with 1/4 teaspoon sea salt (if desired) and place in the basket.
- Cover and steam 4 - 5 minutes or until crisp-tender.
- Immediately plunge green beans into ice water to stop cooking. Drain them.
- Meanwhile, heat a non-stick skillet over medium-high. Add oil when hot.

- Add green onions and rosemary. Sauté 2-3 minutes or until softened.

- Add green beans, pecans, lemon rind and remaining sea salt (if desired), stirring until thoroughly heated.

Steamed Brussel Sprouts with Ginger and Almonds

Makes 4 Servings

Ingredients

- 1 pound of Brussel sprouts

- 1/2 cup slivered or sliced almonds (or nuts of your choice)

- 4 tablespoons of olive oil

- 1 teaspoon of fresh ginger root, grated

- 2 teaspoons of lemon juice

Directions

- Add 1 inch of water to the bottom of a medium pot with a steamer insert or basket. Add Brussels to the steamer, cover, and cook over medium-high heat for 10-12 minutes, or until just tender and bright green.

- Meanwhile, dry roast the almonds in a small skillet over low heat. Stir constantly and remove from heat when they begin to brown.

- Combine the olive oil, ginger root, and lemon juice in a small bowl. When Brussels are fully cooked, toss with dressing and top with toasted almonds.

Olive Tapenade (*Excellent topping on fish or chicken)

Makes About 2 and 1/2 Cups

Ingredients

- Handful fresh flat leaf parsley (about 1/4 cup)
- Few fresh basil sprigs (about 1/4 cup)
- 2 cloves of garlic
- 1 ounce of sun-dried tomatoes
- 1 cup Kalamata olives, pitted
- 1 cup large green olives, pitted
- 2 tablespoons of capers
- juice of 1/2 lemon
- 3 tablespoons of extra virgin olive oil

Directions

- Rough chop fresh herbs, sun-dried tomatoes, and garlic.
- Add all ingredients to a food processor until rough chopped.

Sautéed Sweet Potatoes Hash

Makes 2 Servings

Ingredients

- 1 tablespoon of olive oil
- 1 large sweet potato, grated
- 1/4 teaspoon of cinnamon

Directions

- Heat a skillet over medium heat. Add olive oil.
- Once the skillet is heated, sauté the grated sweet potatoes until tender (a few minutes or so).
- Sprinkle with cinnamon and mix well.

Zucchini Hash

Makes 5 5-inch or 10 2-inch hash browns

Ingredients

- 2 cups shredded zucchini (about 2 medium zucchini)
- 3 eggs
- 1 tablespoon of coconut flour
- ½ teaspoon sea salt
- ¼ teaspoon freshly-ground black pepper
- 1 – 3 teaspoons of coconut oil

Directions

- Shred zucchini with a box grater or in a food processor and set aside. Blot dry with a paper towel.

- In a large bowl, beat eggs together.

- Sift coconut flour into eggs and beat together. Note: coconut flour often has clumps, which is why sifting is important.

- Mix shredded zucchini, sea salt, and freshly ground black pepper together, and then combine with egg mixture.

- Meanwhile, set a large sauté pan over medium-low heat. When it is hot, add coconut oil to coat the bottom of the pan.

- Spoon the mixture into the pan in desired-sized hash browns. Sauté until light brown and then flip.

- Serve warm or at room temperature.

SNACKS

Kale Chips

Makes 2 Servings

Ingredients

- 1 bunch kale
- 1 teaspoon of olive oil
- 1/4 teaspoon of Celtic sea salt (optional)

Directions

- Preheat oven to 350° Fahrenheit.
- Wash kale and remove tough stems.
- Cut kale into 2 – 3 inch sections and place on baking sheet.
- Drizzle with olive oil and sprinkle with sea salt, if desired. Toss kale to fully coat it with oil.
- Bake for 10-15 minutes, or until kale is crispy. Serve hot.

Apple Cider Coleslaw

Makes 4 Servings

Ingredients

- 1 tablespoon olive oil
- 3 - 4 tablespoons of apple cider vinegar

- 1/4 teaspoon of ground mustard seeds
- 1/8 teaspoon of whole cumin seeds
- 1/4 teaspoon of celery seeds
- 1/8 teaspoon of poppy seeds
- 1/4 teaspoon of freshly-ground black pepper
- 1/4 teaspoon of sea salt (optional)
- 1 teaspoon of raw honey (optional)
- 1 small red or green cabbage (or 1/2 of each)
- 2 cups shredded kale

Directions

- In a small bowl, whisk together all the ingredients except the cabbage and kale to make the dressing. Set aside.
- Finely shred the cabbage and kale and put it in a large bowl.
- Add the dressing to cabbage and mix thoroughly.
- Serve immediately, or store in the refrigerator overnight for more flavor.

DESSERT
Grain Free Chocolate Chip Cookies

Makes 24 - 36 Cookies

Ingredients

- 3 cups of almond flour
- ½ cup coconut oil, melted
- ½ cup raw honey
- 2 large eggs
- 1 teaspoon of baking soda
- 1 teaspoon of sea salt
- 1 teaspoon of vanilla extract
- 1 and 1/2 cups Enjoy Life Semi-Sweet Chocolate Chips

Directions

- Preheat oven to 375° Fahrenheit.

- Line a baking sheet with parchment paper.

- In a small mixing bowl, combine the dry ingredients. Set aside.

- In a medium mixing bowl, beat the eggs, honey, and vanilla extract with a hand mixer, or wire whisk.

- Pour the wet ingredients slowly into the dry ingredients and beat with a mixer or fork until combined.

- Add the melted coconut oil and continue to blend until combined.

- Stir in chocolate chips.

- Drop tablespoon-size balls of cookie dough onto the prepared baking sheet and bake for approximately 8-10 minutes.

ABOUT THE AUTHOR

Adi Crnalic is a certified personal trainer, a nutrition and wellness researcher, and a natural (drug-free) bodybuilder. He passionately believes that the root causes of all modern diseases and illnesses can be reversed and remedied by adequate, whole-food nutrition and supplementation and by the elimination of most man-made processed foods and environments. He believes that preventative nutrition and an active lifestyle are the keys to life-long good health, happiness, and vitality. As a young kid and teen, Adi struggled with being both underweight and overweight within a span of a few years. After kicking an insatiable sweet tooth, Adi began his transformation journey by signing up for a weight-training class in high school. From there, he began competitive bodybuilding at age eighteen, taking second place in the teenage division at his first show and going on to compete in multiple drug-tested shows across the United States with top three placings in every showing to date. Since 2008, his information has been published in numerous national and global health & fitness publications. He is the creator of several top-selling fitness & weight-loss e-courses, eBooks, and other fitness and health information products, helping thousands of people to shed pounds and inches, build lean muscle, and attain their best bodies and health. In his spare time, he enjoys cooking, traveling, swimming, reading, studying philosophy, collecting precious metals, playing sports, and hiking.

ACKNOWLEDGEMENTS

This book began as one big, not-too-organized idea and has evolved into an exciting project spanning several years. I would like to thank the people who've helped me make this book a reality—first, to all my clients who place their trust in me and to all my followers and subscribers who read and share my content. I acknowledge you for your participation and for taking action. To my family - thank you for your faith, support, and trust in me. Thanks to my buddies Rob, Brian, and Aaron for being supportive throughout this project and helping me see it through to completion. Credit to Yanik Silver, Bedros Keulian, John Romaniello, Dr. Michael Greger, Gary Taubes, John Rowley and Craig Ballantyne for your writings, educational platforms, leadership, and Masterminds. You are the mentors and giants whose shoulders I stand upon. Thank you for helping to shape my wisdom, perspective, knowledge, and philosophy - I salute you. Live with passion, dream big, set massive goals, and believe in yourself.

REFERENCES

INTRODUCTION:

2.   The CDC Foundation. Heart Disease and Stroke Cost America Nearly $1 Billion a Day in Medical Costs, Lost Productivity. https://www.cdcfoundation.org/pr/2015/heart-disease-and-stroke-cost-america-nearly-1-billion-day-medical-costs-lost-productivity. April 29, 2015

CHAPTER TWO: FOOD, CALORIES AND DIETS

17.   Willett W. Dietary fat plays a major role in obesity: no. Obes Rev 2002; 3: 59 –/68.

17.   Willett WC, Manson JE, Stampfer MJ, et al. Weight, weight change, and coronary heart disease in women: risk within the "normal" weight range. JAMA 1995; 273: 461 –/5.

18.   Grundy SM. How much does diet contribute to premature coronary heart disease? In: Stein O, Stein Y, eds. Atherosclerosis IX. Proceedings of the 9th International Symposium on Atherosclerosis. Tel Aviv: Creative Communications; 1992. p. 471 –/8.

18.   Indian J Pediatr. 2005 Mar;72(3):239-42. Essential fatty acids, DHA and human brain.

18.   Am J Clin Nutr. 2008 Jun;87(6):1978S-80S. Historical overview of n-3 fatty acids and coronary heart disease.

18.   Indian J Endocrinol Metab. 2013 May-Jun; 17(3): 422–429. doi: 10.4103/2230-8210.11163 A fish a day, keeps the cardiologist away! – A review of the effect of omega-3 fatty acids in the cardiovascular system.

18.   Atherosclerosis. 2007 Jul;193(1):159-67. Epub 2006 Aug 1. Age- and dose-dependent effects of an eicosapentaenoic acid-rich oil on cardiovascular risk factors in healthy male subjects.

18.   Biomed Pharmacotherapy. 2014 Oct;68(8):1071-7. doi: 10.1016/j.biopha.2014.10.008. Epub 2014 Oct 28. Omega-3 fatty acids improve postprandial lipemia and associated endothelial dysfunction in healthy individuals - a randomized cross-over trial.

19.   Nestle M. Corporate funding of food and nutrition research: science or marketing? JAMA Intern Med. 2016;176(1):13-14. PubMedArticle.

19.   White J, Bero LA. Corporate manipulation of research: strategies are similar across five industries. Stanford Law Pol Rev. 2010;21(1):105-134.

19.   Kearns CE, Schmidt LA, Glantz, SA. Sugar industry and coronary heart disease research: a historical analysis of internal industry documents. [published online September 12, 2016]. JAMA Intern Med. doi:10.1001/jamainternmed.2016.5394.

19.   McGandy RB, Hegsted DM, Stare FJ. Dietary fats, carbohydrates and atherosclerotic vascular disease. N Engl J Med. 1967;277(4):186-192. PubMedArticle.

20.   O'Connor A. Coca-Cola funds scientists who shift blame for obesity away from bad diets. New York Times. August 9, 2015. http://well.blogs.nytimes.com/2015/08/09/coca-cola-funds-scientists-who-shift-blame-for-obesity-away-from-bad-diets/?_r=1. Accessed July 11, 2016.

20.   Choi CAP. Exclusive: how candy makers shape nutrition science. Associated Press. The Big Story, June 2, 2016.

http://bigstory.ap.org/f9483d554430445fa6566bb0aa
a293d1.

20. J Clin Endocrinol Metab. 2012 Jul;97(7):2489-96. doi:
10.1210/jc.2012-1444. Epub 2012 Apr.

22. Metabolic slowing with massive weight loss despite
preservation of fat-free mass. Johannsen DL1, Knuth
ND, Huizenga R, Rood JC, Ravussin E, Hall KD.

22. Weight regain in U.S. adults who experienced
substantial weight loss, 1999-2002.

22. Int J Obes (Lond). Author manuscript; available in
PMC 2013 Jun 5. Published in final edited form as:Int J
Obes (Lond). 2010 Oct; 34(0 1):
doi:10.1038/ijo.2010.184 Adaptive thermogenesis in
humans Michael Rosenbaum and Rudolph L. Leibel
Weiss EC1, Galuska DA.

22. Am J Clin Nutr. 2014 Apr;99(4):779-91. doi:
10.3945/ajcn.113.071829. Epub 2014 Feb 5. Impact of
body composition during weight change on resting
energy expenditure and homeostasis model assessment
index in overweight nonsmoking adults. Pourhassan
M1, Bosy-Westphal A, Schautz B, Braun W, Glüer CC,
Müller MJ. Kettel Khan L, Gillespie C, Serdula MK.

25. Int J Obes (Lond). 2005 Sep;29(9):1130-6. Ghrelin
increases food intake in obese as well as lean subjects.
Druce MR, Wren AM, Park AJ, et al.

26. J Clin Endocrinol Metab. 2003 Nov;88(11):5478-83.
Neuroendocrine and metabolic effects of acute ghrelin
administration in human obesity. Tassone F, Broglio F,
Destefanis S, et al.

26. Physiol Behav. 2006 Aug 30;89(1):71-84. Epub 2006
Jul 21. Ghrelin and the short- and long-term regulation

of appetite and body weight. Cummings DE1.

26.   N Engl J Med. 2002 May 23;346(21):1623-30. Plasma
       ghrelin levels after diet-induced weight loss or gastric
       bypass surgery. Cummings, DE1, Weigle, DS, Frayo,
       RS, Breen, PA, Ma, MK, Dellinger, EP, Purnell, JQ.

27.   Int J Obes (Lond). 2015 May;39(5):727-33. doi:
       10.1038/ijo.2014.214. Epub 2014 Dec 26. Fasting for
       weight loss: an effective strategy or latest dieting trend?
       Johnstone A1.

28.   Am J Clin Nutr. 2005 Jan;81(1):69-73. Alternate-day
       fasting in nonobese subjects: effects on body weight,
       body composition, and energy metabolism. Heilbronn
       LK1, Smith SR, Martin CK, Anton SD, Ravussin E.

28.   Enhanced thermogenic response to epinephrine after
       48-h starvation in humans. Mansell, PI1, Fellows IW,
       Macdonald IA.

29.   In-Depth Review: Excess Adiposity and Disease
       Intermittent fasting vs daily calorie restriction for type
       2 diabetes prevention: a review of human findings
       Adrienne, R. Barnoskya, Kristin K., Hoddyb, Terry G.
       Untermana, Krista A. Varadyb.

29.   The Effects of Intermittent Energy Restriction on
       Indices of Cardiometabolic Health Rona Antoni, Kelly
       L. Johnston, Adam L. Collins and M. Denise Robertson
       (2014), "The Effects of Intermittent Energy Restriction
       on Indices of Cardiometabolic Health," Research in
       Endocrinology, Vol. 2014 (2014).

30.   Fasting: Molecular Mechanisms and Clinical
       Applications Valter D. Longo and Mark P. Mattson.

32.   Fasting enhances growth hormone secretion and
       amplifies the complex rhythms of growth hormone

secretion in man. K Y Ho, J D Veldhuis, M L Johnson, R Furlanetto, W S Evans, K G Alberti, and M O Thorner.

32.   Effects of human growth hormone in men over 60 years old. Rudman D, Feller AG, Nagraj HS, et al.

32.   Growth hormone and sex steroid administration in healthy aged women and men: a randomized controlled trial. Blackman MR, Sorkin JD, Münzer T, Bellantoni MF, et al.

32.   Augmented growth hormone (GH) secretory burst frequency and amplitude mediate enhanced GH secretion during a two-day fast in normal men. Hartman ML, Veldhuis JD, Johnson ML, et al.

32.   Alternate-day fasting in non-obese subjects: effects on body weight, body composition, and energy metabolism. Heilbronn LK1, Smith SR, Martin CK, Anton SD, Ravussin E.

32.   Short-term fasting induces profound neuronal autophagy. Mehrdad Alirezaei, #1 Christopher C. Kemball, Claudia T. Flynn, Malcolm R. Wood J. Lindsay Whitton, corresponding author and William B. Kiosses.

32.   Mitochondrial degradation by autophagy (mitophagy) in GFP-LC3 transgenic hepatocytes during nutrient deprivation. Kim I, Lemasters JJ.

32.   Caloric restriction and intermittent fasting: Two potential diets for successful brain aging. Bronwen Martin, Mark P. Mattson, and Stuart Maudsleya.

32.   Metabolic regulation of Sirtuins upon fasting and the implication for cancer. Zhu Y1, Yan Y, Gius DR, Vassilopoulos A.

33. 2015 Dietary Guidelines Advisory Committee. Scientific report of the 2015 Dietary Guidelines Advisory Committee. Office of Disease and Prevention and Health Promotion http://www.health.gov/dietaryguidelines/2015-scientific-report/. February 2015.

34. Fructose, insulin resistance, and metabolic dyslipidemia Heather Basciano, Lisa Federico and Khosrow Adeli Email author Nutrition & Metabolism 2005 2:5 DOI: 10.1186/1743-7075-2-5.

34. Consuming fructose-sweetened, not glucose-sweetened, beverages increases visceral adiposity and lipids and decreases insulin sensitivity in overweight/obese humans Kimber L. Stanhope, Jean Marc Schwarz, Nancy L. Keim, et al.

34. Am J Physiol Regul Integr Comp Physiol. 2008 Nov;295(5):R1370-5. doi: 10.1152/ajpregu.00195.2008. Epub 2008 Aug 13. Fructose-induced leptin resistance exacerbates weight gain in response to subsequent high-fat feeding. Shapiro A1, Mu W, Roncal C, Cheng KY, Johnson RJ, Scarpace PJ.

34. Allison DB. Liquid calories, energy compensation and weight: what we know and what we still need to learn. Br J Nutr. 2014 Feb 18;10 (2).

34. Quantitative effects on cardiovascular risk factors and coronary heart disease risk of replacing partially hydrogenated vegetable oils with other fats and oils. D Mozaffarian and R Clarke. Division of Cardiovascular Medicine, Brigham and Women's Hospital, Harvard Medical School, Boston, MA, USA Departments of Epidemiology and Nutrition, Harvard School of Public Health, Boston, MA, USA Clinical Trial Service Unit, University of Oxford, Oxford, England.

35.   Am J Epidemiol. 2005 Apr 1;161(7):672-9. Dietary fat intake and risk of coronary heart disease in women: 20 years of follow-up of the nurses' health study. Oh K1, Hu FB, Manson JE, Stampfer MJ, Willett WC.

35.   Chowdhury R, Warnakula S, Kunutsor S, et al. Association of dietary, circulating, and supplemental fatty acids with coronary risk: a systematic review and meta-analysis. Ann Intern Med. 2014 Mar 18;160 (6): 398-406.

36.   Nature. 2005 Sep 1;437(7055):45-6. Phytochemistry: ibuprofen-like activity in extra-virgin olive oil. Beauchamp, Keast, Morel, Lin, Pika, Han, Lee, Smith, Breslin.

36.   In vivo nutrigenomic effects of virgin olive oil polyphenols within the frame of the Mediterranean diet: a randomized controlled trial. FASEB J July 2010 24:2546-2557; published ahead of print February 23, 2010.

36.   Monounsaturated fatty acids, olive oil and health status: a systematic review and meta-analysis of cohort studies. Schwingshackl, Hoffmann G.

36.   Olive oil consumption, plasma oleic acid, and stroke incidence. The Three-City Study. C. Samieri, PhD, Féart, PhD, Proust-Lima, PhD, Peuchant, MD, PhD, Tzourio, MD, PhD, Stapf, MD, C. Berr, MD, PhD and P. Barberger-Gateau, MD, PhD.

37.   Neurology. 2004 Jan 27;62(2):275-80. Dietary intake of fatty acids and fish in relation to cognitive performance at middle age. Kalmijn, van Boxtel,Ocké, Verschuren, Kromhout, Launer.

37.   Am J Clin Nutr. 2006 Jul;84(1):5-17. n-3 Fatty acids

from fish or fish-oil supplements, but not alpha-linolenic acid, benefit cardiovascular disease outcomes in primary- and secondary-prevention studies: a systematic review. Wang, Harris, Chung, Lichtenstein, Balk, Kupelnick, Jordan, Lau.

38.   Eur Neuropsychopharmacol. 2003 Aug;13(4):267-71. Omega-3 fatty acids in major depressive disorder. A preliminary double-blind, placebo-controlled trial. Su, Huang, Chiu, Shen.

38.   BMJ. 2002 Oct 26;325(7370):932-3. Fish, meat, and risk of dementia: cohort study. Barberger-Gateau, Letenneur, Deschamps, Pérès, Dartigues, Renaud.

39.   Preliminary examination of contaminant loadings in farmed salmon, wild salmon and commercial salmon feed. M.D.L. Eastona, D. Luszniakb, E. Von der Geest.

39.   Quantitative Analysis of the Benefits and Risks of Consuming Farmed and Wild Salmon. Jeffery A. Foran, David H. Good, David O. Carpenter, M. Coreen Hamilton, Barbara A. Knuth, and Steven J. Schwager.

39.   The role of persistent organic pollutants in the worldwide epidemic of type 2 diabetes mellitus and the possible connection to Farmed Atlantic Salmon (Salmo salar). Crinnion WJ1.

39.   J Intern Med. 2014 Sep;276(3):248-59. doi: 10.1111/joim.12194. Epub 2014 Mar 17. Dietary exposure to polychlorinated biphenyls is associated with increased risk of stroke in women. Bergkvist, Kippler M, Larsson SC, Berglund M, Glynn A, Wolk A, Åkesson A.

39.   Risk-Based Consumption Advice for Farmed Atlantic and Wild Pacific Salmon Contaminated with Dioxins and Dioxin-like Compounds. Jeffery A. Foran, David O.

Carpenter, M. Coreen Hamilton, Barbara A. Knuth, and Steven J. Schwager.

39.   Science. 2004 Jan 9;303(5655):226-9. Global assessment of organic contaminants in farmed salmon. Hites RA1, Foran JA, Carpenter DO, Hamilton MC, Knuth BA, Schwager SJ.

40.   Curr Pharm Biotechnol. 2006 Dec;7(6):495-502. Mediterranean dietary traditions for the molecular treatment of human cancer: anti-oncogenic actions of the main olive oil's monounsaturated fatty acid oleic acid (18:1n-9). Menendez, Lupu R.

40.   J Epidemiol. 2007 May;17(3):86-92. Dietary intake of fatty acids and serum C-reactive protein in Japanese. Yoneyama S, Miura K, Sasaki S, Yoshita K, Morikawa Y, Ishizaki M, Kido T, Naruse Y, Nakagawa H.

40.   Ann Oncol. 2005 Mar;16(3):359-71. Epub 2005 Jan 10. Oleic acid, the main monounsaturated fatty acid of olive oil, suppresses Her-2/neu (erbB-2) expression and synergistically enhances the growth inhibitory effects of trastuzumab (Herceptin) in breast cancer cells with Her-2/neu oncogene amplification. Menendez, Vellon L, Colomer R, Lupu R.

40.   Arch Med Res. 1996 Winter;27(4):519-23. Monounsaturated fatty acid (avocado) rich diet for mild hypercholesterolemia. López Ledesma R1, Frati Munari AC, Hernández Domínguez BC, Cervantes Montalvo S, Hernández Luna MH, Juárez C, Morán Lira S.

40.   Diabetes Care. 1994 Apr;17(4):311-5. Effect of a high-monounsaturated fat diet enriched with avocado in NIDDM patients. Lerman-Garber, Ichazo-Cerro, Zamora-Gonzále, Cardoso-Saldaña, Posadas-Romero.

40.   Nutrition. 2005 Jan;21(1):67-75. Substitution of high

monounsaturated fatty acid avocado for mixed dietary fats during an energy-restricted diet: effects on weight loss, serum lipids, fibrinogen, and vascular function. Pieterse, Jerling , Oosthuizen, Kruger, Hanekom, Smuts, Schutte.

40. Arch Med Res. 1992 Winter;23(4):163-7. Effects of avocado as a source of monounsaturated fatty acids on plasma lipid levels. Alvizouri-Muñoz, Carranza-Madrigal, Herrera-Abarca, Chávez-Carbajal, Amezcua-Gastelum.

41. J Agric Food Chem. 2003 Dec 17;51(26):7698-702. Determination of sterol and fatty acid compositions, oxidative stability, and nutritional value of six walnut (Juglans regia L.) cultivars grown in Portugal. Amaral, Casal, Pereira, Seabra, Oliveira.

41. Jun 10;56(8):1231-41. doi: 10.1080/10408398.2012.760516. Walnuts (Juglans regia) Chemical Composition and Research in Human Health. Hayes D1, Angove MJ1, Tucci J1, Dennis C1.

41. Br J Nutr. 2005 Nov;94(5):859-64. Does regular walnut consumption lead to weight gain? Sabaté, Cordero-Macintyre Z, Siapco G, Torabian S, Haddad E.

41. Eur J Clin Nutr. 2003 Sep;57 Suppl 1:S8-11. Nut consumption, body weight and insulin resistance. García-Lorda, Megias Rangil, Salas-Salvadó J.

41. J Agric Food Chem. 2005 Jun 29;53(13):5467-72. Vitamin E composition of walnuts (Juglans regia L.): a 3-year comparative study of different cultivars. Amaral, Alves, Seabra, Oliveira.

42. Serum cholesterol response to changes in the diet: II. The effect of cholesterol in the diet. Ancel Keys, Ph.D.a, Joseph T. Anderson, Ph.D.b, Francisco Grande, M.D.C.

42.   Curr Opin Clin Nutr Metab Care. 2012 Mar;15(2):117-21. Rethinking dietary cholesterol. Fernandez.

42.   High-density lipoprotein cholesterol and cardiovascular disease. Four prospective American studies. D J Gordon, J L Probstfield, R J Garrison, J D Neaton, W P Castelli, J D Knoke, D R Jacobs, S Bangdiwala, H A Tyroler.

42.   High-density lipoprotein cholesterol as an independent risk factor in cardiovascular disease: assessing the data from Framingham to the Veterans Affairs High--Density Lipoprotein Intervention Trial. Boden WE. Division of Cardiology, Hartford Hospital, Connecticut 06102, USA. The American Journal of Cardiology [2000, 86(12A):19L-22L].

42.   Am J Cardiol. 2011 Apr 15;107(8):1173-7. doi: 10.1016/j.amjcard.2010.12.015. Epub 2011 Feb 4. Relation between high-density lipoprotein cholesterol and survival to age 85 years in men (from the VA normative aging study). Rahilly-Tierney, Spiro, Vokona, Gaziano.

42.   Low-Density Lipoprotein Subfractions and the Long-Term Risk of Ischemic Heart Disease in Men 13-Year Follow-Up Data From the Québec Cardiovascular Study. Annie C. St-Pierre, Bernard Cantin, Gilles R. Dagenais, Pascale Mauriège, Paul-Marie Bernard, Jean-Pierre Després, Benoît Lamarche.

42.   Small, Dense Low-Density Lipoprotein Particles as a Predictor of the Risk of Ischemic Heart Disease in Men Prospective Results From the Que´bec Cardiovascular Study. Benoiˆt Lamarche, Andre´ Tchernof, Sital Moorjani, Bernard Cantin, Gilles R. Dagenais, Paul J. Lupien, Jean-Pierre Despre´s.

42. Low density lipoprotein particle size and coronary artery disease. H Campos, J J Genest, E Blijlevens, J R McNamara, J L Jenner, J M Ordovas, P W Wilson, E J Schaefer. Arteriosclerosis, Thrombosis, and Vascular Biology. 1992;12:187-195. Originally published February 1, 1992.

42. September 18, 1996 Association of Small Low-Density Lipoprotein Particles with the Incidence of Coronary Artery Disease in Men and Women. Christopher D. Gardner, PhD; Stephen P. Fortmann, MD; Ronald M. Krauss, MD.

42. Arterioscler Thromb. 1992 Aug;12(8):911-9. Effect of dietary fatty acids on serum lipids and lipoproteins. A meta-analysis of 27 trials. Mensink, Katan.

42. Clinics. 2008 Aug; 63(4): 427–432. High Ratio of Triglycerides to HDL-Cholesterol Predicts Extensive Coronary Disease Protasio Lemos da Luz, Desiderio Favarato, Jose Rocha Faria-Neto Junior, Pedro Lemos and Antonio Carlos Palandri Chagas.

42. Curr Opin Clin Nutr Metab Care. 2006 Jan;9(1):8-12. Dietary cholesterol provided by eggs and plasma lipoproteins in healthy populations. Fernandez.

43. Metabolism. 2013 Mar;62(3):400-10. doi: 10.1016/j.metabol.2012.08.014. Epub 2012 Sep 27. Whole egg consumption improves lipoprotein profiles and insulin sensitivity to a greater extent than yolk-free egg substitute in individuals with metabolic syndrome. Blesso, Andersen, Barona, Volek, Fernandez.

43. Mol Nutr Food Res. 2009 Sep;53 Suppl 2:S330-75. doi: 10.1002 Phytate in foods and significance for humans: food sources, intake, processing, bioavailability, protective role and analysis. Schlemmer, Frølich, Prieto, Grases.

43.   Bacteriol Virusol Parazitol Epidemiol. 2010 Jan-
        Mar;55(1):19-24. [Aflatoxins--health risk factors].
        Miliţă, Mihăescu, Chifiriuc.

43.   Liver Cancer and Aflatoxin: New Information from the
        Kenyan Outbreak Julia R. Barrett.

46.   Foster GD, et al. A randomized trial of a low-
        carbohydrate diet for obesity. New England Journal of
        Medicine, 2003.

46.   Aude YW, et al. The national cholesterol education
        program diet vs a diet lower in carbohydrates and
        higher in protein and monounsaturated fat. Archives of
        Internal Medicine, 2004.

46.   Blundell et al., 1987 J. Blundell, P. Rogers, A. Hill
        Evaluating the satiating power of foods: implications
        for acceptance and consumption J. Colms, D.A. Booth,
        R.M. Pangborn, O. Raunhardt (Eds.), Food acceptance
        and nutrition (1987), pp. 205–219.

46.   JS Volek, et al. Comparison of energy-restricted very
        low-carbohydrate and low-fat diets on weight loss and
        body composition in overweight men and women.
        Nutrition & Metabolism (London), 2004.

48.   Blundell et al., 1994 J.E. Blundell, S. Green, V. Burley
        Carbohydrates and human appetite American Journal
        of Clinical Nutrition, 59 (3) (1994), pp. 728S–734S.

49.   J Med Food. 2014 Jul;17(7):733-41. doi:
        10.1089/jmf.2013.2818. Epub 2014 Jun 12. Sweet
        potato (Ipomoea batatas [L.] Lam)--a valuable
        medicinal food: a review. Mohanraj, Sivasankar S.

49.   Arch Latinoam Nutr. 1999 Sep;49(3 Suppl 1):26S-33S.
        The role of provitamin A carotenoids in the prevention

and control of vitamin A deficiency. Nestel P, Trumbo P.

50.   Arch Dermatol Res. 2008 Nov;300(10):569-74. doi: 10.1007/s00403-008-0858-x. Epub 2008 May 7. Avenanthramides, polyphenols from oats, exhibit anti-inflammatory and anti-itch activity. Sur, Nigam A, Grote D, Liebel F, Southall MD.

50.   Atherosclerosis. 2004 Jul;175(1):39-49. The antiatherogenic potential of oat phenolic compounds. Liu L1, Zubik L, Collins FW, Marko M, Meydani M.

50.   Arch Dermatol Res. 2008 Nov;300(10):569-74. doi: 10.1007/s00403-008-0858-x. Epub 2008 May 7. Avenanthramides, polyphenols from oats, exhibit anti-inflammatory and anti-itch activity. Sur, Nigam A, Grote D, Liebel F, Southall MD.

50.   Am J Clin Nutr. 2014 Dec;100(6):1413-21. doi: 10.3945/ajcn.114.086108. Epub 2014 Oct 15. Cholesterol-lowering effects of oat β-glucan: a meta-analysis of randomized controlled trials. Whitehead, Beck, Tosh, Wolever.

52.   BMJ. 1996 Feb 24;312(7029):478-81. Flavonoid intake and coronary mortality in Finland: a cohort study. Knekt, Jarvinen, Reunanen, Maatela.

52.   Ann Oncol. 2005 Nov;16(11):1841-4. Epub 2005 Aug 9. Does an apple a day keep the oncologist away? Gallus, Talamini, Giacosa, Montella, Ramazzotti, Franceschi, Negri, La Vecchia.

52.   DOI: 10.1002/jsfa.1264 Possible role for apple juice phenolic compounds in the acute modification of glucose tolerance and gastrointestinal hormone secretion in humans. Authors; Kelly L Johnston, Michael N Clifford, Linda M Morgan.

53.   J Sports Sci Med. 2004 Sep; 3(3): 118–130. Published online 2004 Sep 1. Jay R. Hoffman and Michael J. Falvo. Protein – Which is Best? International Society of Sports Nutrition Symposium, June 18-19, 2005, Las Vegas NV, USA - Symposium - Macronutrient Utilization During Exercise: Implications For Performance And Supplementation.

57.   Int J Vitam Nutr Res. 1993;63(3):229-33. Increased concentrations of omega-3 fatty acids in milk and platelet rich plasma of grass-fed cows. Hebeisen DF1, Hoeflin F, Reusch HP, Junker E, Lauterburg BH.

57.   J Dairy Sci. 1999 Oct;82(10):2146-56. Conjugated linoleic acid content of milk from cows fed different diets. Dhiman TR1, Anand GR, Satter LD, Pariza MW.

57.   Nutr Metab Cardiovasc Dis. 2009 Sep;19(7):504-10. doi: 10.1016/j.numecd.2008.10.004. Epub 2009 Jan 28. A high menaquinone intake reduces the incidence of coronary heart disease. Gast, de Roos, Sluijs, Bots, Beulens, Geleijnse, Witteman, Grobbee, Peeters, van der Schouw.

57.   Eur J Nutr. 2004 Dec; 43(6):325-35. Epub 2004 Feb 5. Beyond deficiency: potential benefits of increased intakes of vitamin K for bone and vascular health. Vermeer, Shearer, Zittermann, Bolton-Smith, Szulc, Hodges, Walter, Rambeck, Stöcklin, Weber.

59.   Am J Clin Nutr. 2008 Dec; 88(6): 1618–1625. Fish consumption and risk of major chronic disease in men Jyrki K. Virtanen, Dariush Mozaffarian, Stephanie E. Chiuve, and Eric B. Rimm.

CHAPTER THREE: MINDSET MASTERY

62.   Science. 2008 Oct 24; 322(5901): 606–607. doi: 10.1126/science.1162548 PMCID: PMC2737341 NIHMSID: NIHMS123203. Experiencing Physical Warmth Promotes Interpersonal Warmth Lawrence E. Williams and John A. Bargh.

CHAPTER FOUR: BODY REJUVENATION

77.   Archives of Toxicology July 2002, Volume 76, Issue 7, pp 430–436 | Cite as Assessment of DNA damage in workers occupationally exposed to pesticide mixtures by the alkaline comet assay.

77.   Pflugers Arch. 2010 Jan;459(2):277-89. Lanza IR, Nair KS. Mitochondrial function as a determinant of life span.

82.   Curr Aging Sci. 2009 Mar;2(1):12-27.Robb EL, Page MM, Stuart JA. Mitochondria, cellular stress resistance, somatic cell depletion, and life span.

82.   Clin Sci. 2004;107:355-364.Alexeyev MF, LeDoux SP, Wilson GL. Mitochondrial DNA and aging.

82.   Exp Gerontol. 2015;66:1-9. Pyrroloquinoline quinone (PQQ) producing Escherichia coli Nissle 1917 (EcN) alleviates age associated oxidative stress and hyperlipidemia, and improves mitochondrial function in ageing rats. Singh AK, Pandey SK, Saha G, et al.

82.   J Nutr Biochem. 2013;24 (12):2076-84. Dietary pyrroloquinoline quinone (PQQ) alters indicators of inflammation and mitochondrial-related metabolism in human subjects. Harris CB, Chowanadisai W, Mishchuk DO, et al.

86.   Endocr Rev. 1998 Dec;19(6):717-97. Pathophysiology of the neuroregulation of growth hormone secretion in experimental animals and the human.

87.   J Clin Invest. 1968 Sep; 47(9): 2079–2090. doi: 10.1172/JCI105893. Growth hormone secretion during sleep. Y. Takahashi, D. M. Kipnis, and W. H. Daughaday.

87.   J Clin Endocrinol Metab. 1969 Jan;29(1):20-9. Growth hormone secretion during nocturnal sleep in normal subjects. Honda Y, Takahashi K, Takahashi S, Azumi K, Irie M, Sakuma M, Tsushima T, Shizume K.

87.   J Gerontol A Biol Sci Med Sci. 1999 Aug;54(8):M395-9. Oral arginine does not stimulate basal or augment exercise-induced GH secretion in either young or old adults. Marcell, Taaffe, Hawkins, Tarpenning, Pyka G, Kohlmeier L, Wiswell RA, Marcus R.

87.   Int J Sport Nutr. 1997 Mar;7(1):48-60. Acute effect of amino acid ingestion and resistance exercise on plasma growth hormone concentration in young men. Suminski, Robertson, Goss, Arslanian, Kang, DaSilva, Utter, Metz.

87.   J Appl Physiol (1985). 2006 Sep;101(3):848-52. Epub 2006 Jun 1. Oral arginine attenuates the growth hormone response to resistance exercise. Collier SR1, Collins E, Kanaley JA.

88.   J Clin Endocrinol Metab. 1992 Apr;74(4):757-65. Augmented growth hormone (GH) secretory burst frequency and amplitude mediate enhanced GH secretion during a two-day fast in normal men. Hartman, Veldhuis, Johnson, Lee, Alberti, Samojlik, Thorner.

88.   J Clin Invest. 1988 Apr;81(4):968-75. Fasting enhances

growth hormone secretion and amplifies the complex rhythms of growth hormone secretion in man. Ho, Veldhuis, Johnson, Furlanetto, Evans, Alberti, Thorner.

88.   Eur J Appl Physiol. 2007 Jun;100(3):321-30. Epub 2007 Mar 15. The effect of exercise type on immunofunctional and traditional growth hormone. Consitt, Bloomer, Wideman.

88.   J Clin Endocrinol Metab. 1992 Jul;75(1):157-62. Effect of low and high intensity exercise on circulating growth hormone in men. Felsing, Brasel, Cooper.

88.   J Clin Endocrinol Metab. 1992 Jul;75(1):157-62. Effect of low and high intensity exercise on circulating growth hormone in men. Felsing, Brasel, Cooper.

88.   J Appl Physiol (1985). 1999 Aug;87(2):498-504. Impact of acute exercise intensity on pulsatile growth hormone release in men. Pritzlaff, Wideman, Weltman, Abbott, Gutgesell, Hartman, Veldhuis, Weltman.

89.   Metabolism. 1999 Sep;48(9):1152-6. Elevated insulin levels contribute to the reduced growth hormone (GH) response to GH-releasing hormone in obese subjects. Lanzi, Luzi, Caumo, Andreotti, Manzoni, Malighetti, Sereni, Pontiroli.

89.   J Clin Invest. 1966 Apr; 45(4): 429–436. doi: 10.1172/JCI105357. The plasma sugar, free fatty acid, cortisol, and growth hormone response to insulin. I. In control subjects. F C Greenwood, J Landon, and T C Stamp.

89.   Diabetologia. 1970 Feb;6(1):27-33. Diurnal patterns of blood glucose, serum free fatty acids, insulin, glucagon and growth hormone in normal and juvenile diabetics. Hansen, Johansen.

89.   Am J Clin Nutr. 1995 May;61(5):1058-61. Increased plasma bicarbonate and growth hormone after an oral glutamine load. Welbourne TC1.

89.   Exp Neurol. 1999 May;157(1):142-9. Creatine and cyclocreatine attenuate MPTP neurotoxicity. Matthews, Ferrante, Klivenyi, Yang, Klein, Mueller, Kaddurah-Daouk, Beal.

89.   J Sports Med Phys Fitness. 2000 Dec;40(4):336-42. Acute creatine loading enhances human growth hormone secretion. Schedel, Tanaka, Kiyonaga, Shindo, Schutz.

89.   Neurology. 1999 Mar 10;52(4):854-7. Creatine monohydrate increases strength in patients with neuromuscular disease. Tarnopolsky, Martin J.

90.   Int J Clin Pract. 2007 May;61(5):835-45. Epub 2007 Feb 13. Melatonin: therapeutic and clinical utilization. Altun, Ugur-Altun.

90.   Dev Med Child Neurol. 1999 Jul;41(7):491-500. Melatonin treatment of sleep-wake cycle disorders in children and adolescents. Jan, Freeman, Fast.

90.   Clin Endocrinol (Oxf). 1993 Aug;39(2):193-9. Melatonin stimulates growth hormone secretion through pathways other than the growth hormone-releasing hormone. Valcavi, Zini, Maestroni, Conti, Portioli.

90.   J Int Soc Sports Nutr. 2007; 4: 14. Published online 2007 Oct 23. doi: 10.1186/1550-2783-4-14 Effects of a single dose of N-Acetyl-5-methoxytryptamine (Melatonin) and resistance exercise on the growth hormone/IGF-1 axis in young males and females Erika Nassar, Chris Mulligan, Lem Taylor, Chad Kerksick, Melyn Galbreath, Mike Greenwood, Richard Kreider

and Darryn S Willoughby corresponding author.

97.   J Psychosom Res. 1999 Jun;46(6):591-8. Chronic
       burnout, somatic arousal and elevated salivary cortisol
       levels. Melamed, Ugarten, Shirom, Kahana, Lerman,
       Froom.

97.   Psychoneuroendocrinology. 2006 Apr;31(3):277-87.
       Cell aging in relation to stress arousal and
       cardiovascular disease risk factors. Epel, Lin, Wilhelm,
       Wolkowitz, Cawthon, Adler, Dolbier, Mendes,
       Blackburn.

97.   J Clin Endocrinol Metab. 1983 Sep;57(3):671-3. Acute
       suppression of circulating testosterone levels by cortisol
       in men. Cumming, Quigley, Yen.

97.   Obes Res. 1999 Jan;7(1):9-15. Stress-induced cortisol,
       mood, and fat distribution in men. Epel, Moyer,
       Martin, Macary, Cummings, Rodin, Rebuffe-Scrive.

98.   Nutrition. 2007 Nov-Dec;23(11-12):887-94. Epub 2007
       Sep 17. Relationship between stress, eating behavior,
       and obesity. Torres, Nowson.

98.   J Clin Endocrinol Metab. 1998 Jun;83(6):1853-9.
       Stress-related cortisol secretion in men: relationships
       with abdominal obesity and endocrine, metabolic and
       hemodynamic abnormalities. Rosmond, Dallman,
       Björntorp.

98.   Horm Metab Res. 2011 Mar;43(3):223-5. doi:
       10.1055/s-0030-1269854. Effect of vitamin D
       supplementation on testosterone levels in men. Pilz,
       Frisch, Koertke, Kuhn, Dreier, Obermayer-Pietsch,
       Wehr, Zittermann.

98.   Crit Care Med. 2011 Apr;39(4):671-7. doi:
       10.1097/CCM.0b013e318206ccdf. Association of low

serum 25-hydroxyvitamin D levels and mortality in the critically ill. Braun, Chang, Mahadevappa, Gibbons, Liu, Giovannucci, Christopher.

98.   Am J Clin Nutr. 2009 May;89(5):1321-7. doi: 10.3945/ajcn.2008.27004. Vitamin D supplementation enhances the beneficial effects of weight loss on cardiovascular disease risk markers. Zittermann, Frisch, Berthold, Götting, Kuhn, Kleesiek, Stehle, Koertke, Koerfer.

98.   Nutr Res. 2011 Jan;31(1):48-54. doi: 10.1016/j.nutres.2010.12.001. Prevalence and correlates of vitamin D deficiency in US adults. Forrest, Stuhldreher.

98.   Am J Clin Nutr. 2008 Apr;87(4):1080S-6S. Vitamin D deficiency: a worldwide problem with health consequences. Holick, Chen.

99.   Hum Reprod. 2010 Feb;25(2):519-27. doi: 10.1093/humrep/dep381. Occupational exposure to bisphenol-A (BPA) and the risk of self-reported male sexual dysfunction. Li, Zhou, Qing, He, Wu, Miao, Wang, Weng, Ferber, Herrinton, Zhu, Gao, Checkoway, Yuan.

99.   J Clin Endocrinol Metab. 2014 Nov;99(11):4346-52. doi: 10.1210/jc.2014-2555. Urinary phthalate metabolites are associated with decreased serum testosterone in men, women, and children from NHANES 2011-2012. Meeker, Ferguson.

99.   Reprod Toxicol. 2014 Aug; 47:70-6. doi: 10.1016/j.reprotox.2014.06.002. Prenatal and peripubertal phthalates and bisphenol A in relation to sex hormones and puberty in boys. Ferguson, Peterson, Lee, Mercado-García, Blank-Goldenberg, Téllez-Rojo, Meeker.

99.   Bioelectromagnetics. 2008 May;29(4):324-30. doi:
        10.1002/bem.20382. Non-thermal effects in the
        microwave induced unfolding of proteins observed by
        chaperone binding. George, Bilek, McKenzie.

99.   15 October 2003 https://doi.org/10.1002/jsfa.1585
        Phenolic compound contents in edible parts of broccoli
        inflorescences after domestic cooking. Vallejo, Tomás-
        Barberán, García-Viguera.

99.   Nutr Cancer. 2002;44(2):189-91. Food-borne radiolytic
        compounds (2-alkylcyclobutanones) may promote
        experimental colon carcinogenesis. Raul, Gosse,
        Delincee, Hartwig, Marchioni, Miesch, Werner,
        Burnouf.

99.   J Am Coll Cardiol. 2007 Sep 11;50(11):1009-14. Alcohol
        and cardiovascular health: the razor-sharp double-
        edged sword. O'Keefe, Bybee, Lavie.

99.   J Psychopharmacol. 2004 Dec;18(4):449-56. Alcohol,
        wine and mental health: focus on dementia and stroke.
        Pinder, Sandler.

99.   J Pharmacol Exp Ther. 1977 Sep;202(3):676-82. Effects
        of acute alcohol intake on pituitary-gonadal hormones
        in normal human males. Mendelson, Mello, Ellingboe.

99.   Alcohol. 2002 Mar-Apr;37(2):169-73. Effects of acute
        alcohol intoxication on pituitary-gonadal axis
        hormones, pituitary-adrenal axis hormones, beta-
        endorphin and prolactin in human adults of both sexes.
        Frias, Torres, Miranda, Ruiz, Ortega.

99.   Alcohol. 1984 Jan-Feb;1(1):89-93. Sex hormones and
        adrenocortical steroids in men acutely intoxicated with
        ethanol. Välimäki, Härkönen, Eriksson, Ylikahri.

100.   Heller, RF et al. Relationship of high-density lipoprotein cholesterol with total and free testosterone and sex hormone binding globulin. Acta Endocrinol (Copenh). 1983; 104(2): 253-6.

100.   Stanworth, RD et al. Testosterone levels correlate positively with HDL cholesterol levels in men with Type 2 diabetes. Endocrine Abstracts. 2007; 14: 628.

100.   Freedman, DS et al. Relation of serum testosterone levels to high density lipoprotein cholesterol and other characteristics in men. Arterioscler Thromb. 1991; 11(2): 307-15.

101.   Altern Med Rev. 2003 Feb;8(1):20-7. Therapeutic applications of fenugreek. Basch, Ulbricht, Kuo, Szapary, Smith.

101.   Int J Sport Nutr Exerc Metab. 2010 Dec;20(6):457-65. Effects of a purported aromatase and 5α-reductase inhibitor on hormone profiles in college-age men. Wilborn, Taylor, Poole, Foster, Willoughby, Kreider.

101.   Phytother Res. 2011 Sep;25(9):1294-300. doi: 10.1002/ptr.3360. Epub 2011 Feb 10. Physiological aspects of male libido enhanced by standardized Trigonella foenum-graecum extract and mineral formulation. Steels, Rao, Vitetta.

102.   Brain Res Rev. 2007 Feb;53(2):215-34. Epub 2006 Nov 21. D-Aspartic acid: an endogenous amino acid with an important neuroendocrine role. D'Aniello.

102.   D'Aniello, A., Giuditta, A. Identification of D-aspartic acid in the brain of Octopus vulgaris. J Neurochem. 1997;29:1053–1057.

102.   Reprod Biol Endocrinol. 2009 Oct 27;7:120. doi: 10.1186/1477-7827-7-120. The role and molecular

mechanism of D-aspartic acid in the release and synthesis of LH and testosterone in humans and rats. Topo, Soricelli, D'Aniello, Ronsini, D'Aniello.

103. Lancet. 2004 Oct 2-8;364(9441):1219-28. Antioxidant supplements for prevention of gastrointestinal cancers: a systematic review and meta-analysis. Bjelakovic, Nikolova, Simonetti, Gluud.

103. Am J Clin Nutr. 2004 Jun;79(6):1060-72. The 6-a-day study: effects of fruit and vegetables on markers of oxidative stress and antioxidative defense in healthy nonsmokers. Dragsted, Pedersen, Hermetter, Basu, Hansen, Haren, Kall, Breinholt, Castenmiller, Stagsted, Jakobsen, Skibsted, Rasmussen, Loft, Sandström.

104. Br J Nutr. 2014 Jan 14;111(1):1-11. doi: 10.1017/S000711451300278X. Epub 2013 Aug 16. Flavonoid intake and risk of CVD: a systematic review and meta-analysis of prospective cohort studies. Wang, Ouyang, Liu, Zhao.

104. Ann Intern Med. 2005 Jan 4;142(1):37-46. Epub 2004 Nov 10. Meta-analysis: high-dosage vitamin E supplementation may increase all-cause mortality. Miller, Pastor-Barriuso, Dalal, Riemersma, Appel, Guallar E.

106. Alcohol Alcohol. 2010 Mar-Apr;45(2):119-25. doi: 10.1093/alcalc/agp092. Epub 2010 Jan 18. Alcohol intake and systemic markers of inflammation--shape of the association according to sex and body mass index. Oliveira, Rodríguez-Artalejo, Lopes.

106. Diabetologia. 2010 Jan;53(1):10-20. doi: 10.1007/s00125-009-1573-7. Epub 2009 Nov 5. The global diabetes epidemic as a consequence of lifestyle-induced low-grade inflammation. Kolb, Mandrup-Poulsen.

106.   https://doi.org/10.1161/01.CIR.0000052939. 5909 345 Circulation.2003;107:499-511 Originally published January 28, 2003. Markers of Inflammation and Cardiovascular Disease Application to Clinical and Public Health Practice: A Statement for Healthcare Professionals From the Centers for Disease Control and Prevention and the American Heart Association. Thomas A. Pearson, George A. Mensah, R. Wayne Alexander, Jeffrey L. Anderson, Richard O. Cannon, Michael Criqui, Yazid Y. Fadl, Stephen P. Fortmann, Yuling Hong, Gary L. Myers, Nader Rifai, Sidney C. Smith, Kathryn Taubert, Russell P. Tracy, Frank Vinicor.

106.   Nature. 2002 Dec 19; 420(6917): 860–867. doi: 10.1038/nature01322. PMCID: PMC2803035. NIHMSID: NIHMS163568. Lisa M. Coussens, and Zena Werb.

106.   Lipids. 2016 Jan;51(1):49-59. doi: 10.1007/s11745-015-4091-z. Epub 2015 Nov 2. Low n-6/n-3 PUFA Ratio Improves Lipid Metabolism, Inflammation, Oxidative Stress and Endothelial Function in Rats Using Plant Oils as n-3 Fatty Acid Source. Yang, Song, Yin, Wang, Shu, Lu, Wang, Sun.

107.   Biochem Pharmacol. 2009 Mar 15;77(6):937-46. doi: 10.1016/j.bcp.2008.10.020. Epub 2008 Oct 28. Dietary n-6 and n-3 polyunsaturated fatty acids: from biochemistry to clinical implications in cardiovascular prevention. Russo.

107.   J Agric Food Chem. 2009 Nov 11;57(21):10408-13. doi:10.1021/jf901839h. California Hass avocado: profiling of carotenoids, tocopherol, fatty acid, and fat content during maturation and from different growing areas. Lu, Zhang, Wang, Wang, Lee, Gao, Byrns, Heber.

107.   Food Funct. 2013 Feb 26;4(3):384-91. doi:
        10.1039/c2fo30226h. Hass avocado modulates
        postprandial vascular reactivity and postprandial
        inflammatory responses to a hamburger meal in
        healthy volunteers. Li, Wong, Henning, Zhang, Jones,
        Zerlin, Thames, Bowerman, Tseng, Heber.

107.   J Agric Food Chem. 2014 May 7;62(18):3886-903. doi:
        10.1021/jf4044056. Epub 2014 Mar 17. Berries: anti-
        inflammatory effects in humans. Joseph, Edirisingh,
        Burton-Freeman.

107.   Int J Mol Sci. 2015 Oct 16;16(10):24673-706. doi:
        10.3390/ijms161024673. Bioactive Compounds and
        Antioxidant Activity in Different Types of Berries.
        Skrovankova, Sumczynski, Mlcek, Jurikova, Sochor.

107.   Cardiovasc Diabetol. 2015 Jun 10;14:75. doi:
        10.1186/s12933-015-0237-9. Protective role of oleic
        acid against cardiovascular insulin resistance and in the
        early and late cellular atherosclerotic process.
        Perdomo, Beneit, Otero, Escribano, Díaz-Castroverde,
        Gómez-Hernández, Benito.

107.   Br J Nutr. 2007 Aug;98(2):260-3. Minor compounds of
        olive oil have postprandial anti-inflammatory effects.
        Pacheco, Bemúdez, López, Abia, Villar, Muriana.

107.   FASEB J. 2010 Jul;24(7):2546-57. doi: 10.1096/fj.09-
        148452. Epub 2010 Feb 23. In vivo nutrigenomic
        effects of virgin olive oil polyphenols within the frame
        of the Mediterranean diet: a randomized controlled
        trial. Konstantinidou V1, Covas MI, Muñoz-Aguayo,
        Khymenets, de la Torre, Saez, Tormos Mdel, Toledo,
        Marti, Ruiz-Gutiérrez, Ruiz Mendez, Fito.

107.   Curr Pharm Des. 2011;17(8):754-68. Molecular
        mechanisms of inflammation. Anti-inflammatory

benefits of virgin olive oil and the phenolic compound oleocanthal. Lucas, Russell, Keast.

107. Nutr J. 2010 Jan 22;9:3. doi: 10.1186/1475-2891-9-3. The total antioxidant content of more than 3100 foods, beverages, spices, herbs and supplements used worldwide. Carlsen, Halvorsen, Holte, Bøhn, Dragland, Sampson, Willey, Senoo, Umezono, Sanada, Barikmo, Berhe, Willett, Phillips, Jacobs DR Jr, Blomhoff R.

108. Am J Hypertens. 2010 Jan;23(1):97-103. doi: 10.1038/ajh.2009.213. Epub 2009 Nov 12. Effect of cocoa products on blood pressure: systematic review and meta-analysis. Desch, Schmidt, Kobler, Sonnabend, Eitel, Sareban, Rahimi, Schuler, Thiele.

108. Nutrients. 2013 Aug; 5(8): 3299–3310. Published online 2013 Aug 19. doi: 10.3390/nu5083299 PMCID: PMC3775255 Docosahexaenoic Acid, Inflammation, and Bacterial Dysbiosis in Relation to Periodontal Disease, Inflammatory Bowel Disease, and the Metabolic Syndrome Maria Tabbaa, Mladen Golubic, Michael. Roizen, and Adam. Bernstein.

109. Calif Agric (Berkeley). 2011 Jul;65(3):106-111. Dietary omega-3 fatty acids aid in the modulation of inflammation and metabolic health. Zivkovic, Telis, German, Hammock.

109. Scand J Clin Lab Invest. 2011 Feb;71(1):68-73. doi: 10.3109/00365513.2010.542484. Epub 2010 Dec 8. Salmon diet in patients with active ulcerative colitis reduced the simple clinical colitis activity index and increased the anti-inflammatory fatty acid index--a pilot study. Grimstad, Berge, Bohov, Skorve, Gøransson, Omdal, Aasprong, Haugen, Meltzer, Hausken.

109. J Ethnopharmacol. 2018 Jan 10;210:296-310. doi:

10.1016/j.jep.2017.08.035. Epub 2017 Aug 31. Molecular understanding of Epigallocatechin gallate (EGCG) in cardiovascular and metabolic diseases. Eng, Thanikachalam, Ramamurthy.

109.   J Agric Food Chem. 2004 Jul 14;52(14):4472-6. Fluoride content in tea and its relationship with tea quality. Lu, Guo, Yang.

109.   Plant Foods Hum Nutr. 2015 Dec;70(4):441-53. doi: 10.1007/s11130-015-0503-8. Pharmacological Studies of Artichoke Leaf Extract and Their Health Benefits. Ben Salem, Affes, Ksouda, Dhouibi, Sahnoun, Hammami, Zeghal.

110.   Food Funct. 2015 Apr;6(4):1268-77. doi: 10.1039/c5fo00137d. Polyphenols from artichoke heads (Cynara cardunculus (L.) subsp. scolymus Hayek): in vitro bio-accessibility, intestinal uptake and bioavailability. D'Antuono, Garbetta, Linsalata, Minervini, Cardinali.

110.   Eur J Nutr. 2017 Oct;56(7):2215-2244. doi: 10.1007/s00394-017-1379-1. Epub 2017 Apr 8. The potential effects of chlorogenic acid, the main phenolic components in coffee, on health: a comprehensive review of the literature. Tajik, Tajik, Mack, Enck.

110.   J Agric Food Chem. 2008 Sep 24;56(18):8601-8. doi: 10.1021/jf800408w. Epub 2008 Aug 30. Effects of different cooking methods on antioxidant profile, antioxidant capacity, and physical characteristics of artichoke. Ferracane, Pellegrini, Visconti, Graziani, Chiavaro, Miglio, Fogliano.

110.   Biochem Biophys Res Commun. 2014 Jul 18;450(1):652-8. doi: 10.1016/j.bbrc.2014.06.029. Epub 2014 Jun 14. Anti-proliferative and pro-apoptotic activity of whole extract and isolated indicaxanthin

from Opuntia ficus-indica associated with re-activation of the onco-suppressor p16(INK4a) gene in human colorectal carcinoma (Caco-2) cells. Naselli, Tesoriere, Caradonna, Bellavia, Attanzio, Gentile, Livrea.

110.   Crit Rev Food Sci Nutr. 2016;56(6):937-45. doi: 10.1080/10408398.2012.740103. Biological Activities of Plant Pigments Betalains. Gandía-Herrero, Escribano, García-Carmona.

111.   Nutrients. 2015 Apr 14;7(4):2801-22. doi: 10.3390/nu7042801. The potential benefits of red beetroot supplementation in health and disease. Clifford, Howatson, West, Stevenson.

111.   Nutrients. 2013 Apr 9;5(4):1169-85. doi: 10.3390/nu5041169. Dietary sources of lutein and zeaxanthin carotenoids and their role in eye health. Abdel-Aal el, Akhtar, Zaheer, Ali.

111.   Nutrients. 2017 Feb 9;9(2). pii: E120. doi: 10.3390/nu9020120. Lutein and Zeaxanthin-Food Sources, Bioavailability and Dietary Variety in Age-Related Macular Degeneration Protection. Eisenhauer, Natoli, Liew, Flood.

111.   Annu Rev Food Sci Technol. 2010;1:163-87. doi: 10.1146/annurev.food.080708.100754. Anthocyanins: natural colorants with health-promoting properties. He, Giusti.

111.   Food Chem. 2016 Apr 1;196:1101-7. doi: 10.1016/j.foodchem.2015.10.037. Epub 2015 Oct 22. Cooking techniques improve the levels of bioactive compounds and antioxidant activity in kale and red cabbage. Murador, Mercadante, de Rosso.

112.   Planta Med. 2010 Jan;76(1):7-19. doi: 10.1055/s-0029-1186218. Epub 2009 Oct 20. Goji (Lycium barbarum

and L. chinense): Phytochemistry, pharmacology and safety in the perspective of traditional uses and recent popularity. Potterat.

112.   Optom Vis Sci. 2011 Feb;88(2):257-62. doi: 10.1097/OPX.0b013e318205a18f. Goji berry effects on macular characteristics and plasma antioxidant levels. Bucheli, Vidal, Shen, Gu, Zhang, Miller, Wang.

112.   Drug Des Devel Ther. 2014 Dec 17;9:33-78. doi: 10.2147/DDDT.S72892. eCollection 2015. An evidence-based update on the pharmacological activities and possible molecular targets of Lycium barbarum polysaccharides. Cheng J, Zhou ZW, Sheng HP et al.

CHAPTER FIVE: KEEPING THE FAT OFF

114.   Lewis SB, Wallin JD, Kane JP, Gerich JE. Effect of diet composition on metabolic adaptations to hypocaloric nutrition: comparison of high carbohydrate and high fat isocaloric diets. *AM J Clin Nutr*. 1977 Feb;30(2):160-70.

114.   DiNicolantonio JJ. The cardiometabolic consequences of replacing saturated fats with carbohydrates or polyunsaturated fats: do the dietary guidelines have it wrong? *Open Heart*. 2014 Feb 8;1(1):e000032.

114.   Teicholz N. *The Big Fat Surprise*. New York: Scribner; 2014.

114.   Food and Agriculture Organization of the United Nations. Fats and fatty acids in human nutrition: report of an expert consultation. 2010.

115.   Association of dietary, circulating, and supplement fatty acids with coronary risk: a systematic review and meta-analysis. R Chowdhury, S Warnakula, Kunutsor S, et al.

117.   Nutrition. 2012 Feb;28(2):118-23. doi: 10.1016/j.nut.2011.08.017. Saturated fat and cardiovascular disease: the discrepancy between the scientific literature and dietary advice. Hoenselaar R.

117.   Med Hypotheses. 2014 Feb;82(2):187-95. doi: 10.1016/j.mehy.2013.11.036. Saturated fat consumption may not be the main cause of increased blood lipid levels. Dias, Garg, Wood, Garg.

117.   Lipids. 2015 Apr;50(4):339-47. doi: 10.1007/s11745-015-4003-2. Postprandial lipid responses do not differ following consumption of butter or vegetable oil when

consumed with omega-3 polyunsaturated fatty acids. Dias, Phang, Wood, Garg.

118.   Lipids. 2010 Oct;45(10):947-62. doi: 10.1007/s11745-010-3467-3. Limited effect of dietary saturated fat on plasma saturated fat in the context of a low carbohydrate diet. Forsythe CE, Phinney SD, Feinman RD, et al.

118.   Biochim Biophys Acta. 1992 Jun 22;1126(2):199-205. Evidence for mechanisms of the hypotriglyceridemic effect of n-3 polyunsaturated fatty acids. Surette ME, Whelan J, Broughton KS, Kinsella JE.

118.   J Nutr. 2005 Sep;135(9):2075-8. Mechanisms by which dietary fatty acids modulate plasma lipids. Fernandez ML, West KL.

119.   Nutrients. 2014 Oct 28;6(11):4678-90. doi: 10.3390/nu6114678. Effects of dietary fat and saturated fat content on liver fat and markers of oxidative stress in overweight/obese men and women under weight-stable conditions. Marina A, von Frankenberg AD, Suvag S, et al.

119.   Plasma C-reactive protein concentration is not affected by isocaloric dietary fat reduction. *Nutrition* [2006] Apr;22(4): 444-48 Koren, M.S. Purnell, J.Q. Breen, P.A. Matthys, C.C. et al.

119.   J Pharmacol Exp Ther. 2001 Nov;299(2):638-44. Dietary saturated fatty acids reverse inflammatory and fibrotic changes in rat liver despite continued ethanol administration. Nanji AA, Jokelainen K, Tipoe GL, Rahemtulla A, Dannenberg AJ.

119.   J Pharmacol Exp Ther. 2001 Nov;299(2):638-44. Dietary saturated fatty acids reverse inflammatory and fibrotic changes in rat liver despite continued ethanol

administration. Nanji AA, Jokelainen K, Tipoe GL, Rahemtulla A, Dannenberg AJ.

119.   Am J Clin Nutr. 2010 Mar;91(3):502-9. doi: 10.3945/ajcn.2008.26285. Saturated fat, carbohydrate, and cardiovascular disease. Siri-Tarino PW, Sun Q, Hu FB, Krauss RM.

120.   Proc Nutr Soc. 2002 May;61(2):281-6. Changes in fat synthesis influenced by dietary macronutrient content. Parks EJ, Parks EJ.

120.   J Nutr. 2001 Feb;131(2):340S-3S. Atherogenic lipoprotein phenotype and diet-gene interactions. Krauss RM.

120.   J Lipid Res. 2000 Apr;41(4):595-604. Relationship between carbohydrate-induced hypertriglyceridemia and fatty acid synthesis in lean and obese subjects. Hudgins LC, Hellerstein MK, Seidman CE, Neese RA, Tremaroli JD, Hirsch J.

120.   Am J Clin Nutr. 2003 May;77(5):1146-55. Effects of dietary fatty acids and carbohydrates on the ratio of serum total to HDL cholesterol and on serum lipids and apolipoproteins: a meta-analysis of 60 controlled trials. Mensink RP, Zock PL, Kester AD, Katan MB.

121.   J Clin Lipidol. 2011 Sep-Oct;5(5):408-13. doi: 10.1016/j.jacl.2011.07.001. Epub 2011 Jul 18. Low-density lipoprotein particle number predicts coronary artery calcification in asymptomatic adults at intermediate risk of cardiovascular disease. Prado KB, Shugg S, Backstrand JR.

122.   J Clin Endocrinol Metab. 2015 Jun;100(6):2434-42. doi: 10.1210/jc.2014-3678. Effect of a High-Fructose Weight-Maintaining Diet on Lipogenesis and Liver Fat. Schwarz JM, Noworolski SM, Wen MJ, et al.

122.   Circulation. 2014 Jun 24;129(25 Suppl 2):S76-99. doi:
        10.1161/01.cir.0000437740.48606.d1. 2013 AHA/ACC
        guideline on lifestyle management to reduce
        cardiovascular risk: a report of the American College of
        Cardiology/American Heart Association Task Force on
        Practice Guidelines. Eckel RH, Jakicic JM, Ard JD, et
        al.

123.   Curr Opin Clin Nutr Metab Care. 2012 Mar;15(2):117-
        21. doi: 10.1097/MCO.0b013e32834d2259. Rethinking
        dietary cholesterol. Fernandez ML.

123.   N Engl J Med. 2005 Apr 21;352(16):1685-95.
        Inflammation, atherosclerosis, and coronary artery
        disease. Hansson GK.

125.   N Engl J Med. 2007 Sep 27;357(13):1301-10. HDL
        cholesterol, very low levels of LDL cholesterol, and
        cardiovascular events. Barter P, Gotto AM, LaRosa JC,
        et al. Treating to New Targets Investigators.

125.   Lancet. 2007 Jan 20;369(9557):168-9. Are lipid-
        lowering guidelines evidence-based? Abramson J,
        Wright JM.

126   N Engl J Med 2008; 358:1504-1507. April 3, 2008
        DOI: 10.1056/NEJMe0801608 Does ENHANCE
        Diminish Confidence in Lowering LDL or in Ezetimibe?
        B. Greg Brown, M.D., Ph.D., and Allen J. Taylor, M.D.

126.   Lancet. 2001 Aug 4;358(9279):351-5. Cholesterol and
        all-cause mortality in elderly people from the Honolulu
        Heart Program: a cohort study. Schatz IJ, Masaki K,
        Yano K, Chen R, Rodriguez BL, Curb JD.

128.   Am Heart J. 2014 Jul;168(1):6-15. doi:
        10.1016/j.ahj.2014.03.019. Epub 2014 Apr 12. A
        systematic review of statin-induced muscle problems in

clinical trials. Ganga HV, Slim HB, Thompson PD.

128.   CNS Drugs. 2014 May;28(5):411-9. doi: 10.1007/s40263-014-0147-5. Cognitive effects of statin medications. Kelley BJ, Glasser S.

129.   J Sex Med. 2015 Jan;12(1):158-67. doi: 10.1111/jsm.12745. Statins and male sexual health: a retrospective cohort analysis. Davis R, Reveles KR, Ali SK, Mortensen EM, Frei CR, Mansi I.

130.   Am J Cardiol. 2014 May 15;113(10):1765-71. doi: 10.1016/j.amjcard.2014.02.033. Statin intolerance. Ahmad Z.

130.   J Gen Intern Med. 2015 Nov;30(11):1599-610. doi: 10.1007/s11606-015-3335-1. Statins and New-Onset Diabetes Mellitus and Diabetic Complications: A Retrospective Cohort Study of US Healthy Adults. Mansi I, Frei CR, Wang CP, Mortensen EM.

130.   Am Heart J. 2009 Jan;157(1):111-117.e2. doi: 10.1016/j.ahj.2008.08.010. Lipid levels in patients hospitalized with coronary artery disease: an analysis of 136,905 hospitalizations in Get With The Guidelines. Sachdeva A, Cannon CP, Deedwania PC, et al.

130.   Eur Heart J. 2014 Aug 1;35(29):1917-24. doi: 10.1093/eurheartj/ehu208. Mendelian randomization studies in coronary artery disease. Jansen H, Samani NJ, Schunkert H.

130.   BMJ. 2013 Oct 22;347:f6123. doi: 10.1136/bmj.f6123. Should people at low risk of cardiovascular disease take a statin? Abramson JD, Rosenberg HG, Jewell N, Wright JM.

126.   Exp Biol Med (Maywood). 2008 Jun;233(6):674-88. doi: 10.3181/0711-MR-311. The importance of the

omega-6/omega-3 fatty acid ratio in cardiovascular disease and other chronic diseases. Simopoulos AP.

132.   Biomed Pharmacother. 2006 Nov;60(9):502-7. Evolutionary aspects of diet, the omega-6/omega-3 ratio and genetic variation: nutritional implications for chronic diseases. Simopoulos AP.

132.   Atheroscler Suppl. 2006 May;7(2):5-8. Trans fatty acids and cardiovascular disease-epidemiological data. Willett WC.

135.   Nutr Cancer. 2001;39(2):170-5. Trans-fatty acids and colon cancer. Slattery ML, Benson J, Ma KN, Schaffer D, Potter JD.

135.   August 2003. Updated Nov 08, 2017. US Food and Drug Administration. Guidance for Industry: Trans Fatty Acids in Nutrition Labeling, Nutrient Content Claims, Health Claims; Small Entity Compliance Guide. https://www.fda.gov/Food/GuidanceRegulation/Guida nceDocumentsRegulatoryInformation/LabelingNutriti on/ucm053479.htm August 2003. Updated Nov 08, 2017.

136.   Eur J Clin Nutr. 2002 Mar;56(3):181-91. Fatty acid analysis of wild ruminant tissues: evolutionary implications for reducing diet-related chronic disease. Cordain L, Watkins BA, Florant GL, Kelher M, Rogers L, Li Y.

137.   American Heart Association. Monounsaturated Fats, https://healthyforgood.heart.org/eat-smart/articles/monounsaturated-fats Last reviewed 2015. Last Updated: March 24, 2017

137.   Body Ecology. The 6 Benefits of Monounsaturated Fats (MUFAs)

https://bodyecology.com/articles/6_benefits_monosat urated_fats.php

138. MG Enig and SW Fallon. The Great Con-ola. Weston A. Price Foundation. July 28, 2002. https://www.westonaprice.org/health-topics/know-your-fats/the-great-con-ola/

139. Prostaglandins Leukot Essent Fatty Acids. 2012 Oct-Nov;87(4-5):135-41. doi: 10.1016/j.plefa.2012.08.004. Lowering dietary linoleic acid reduces bioactive oxidized linoleic acid metabolites in humans. Ramsden CE, Ringel A, Feldstein AE, et al.

141. Prostaglandins Leukot Essent Fatty Acids. 2009 Jan;80(1):77; author reply 77-8. doi: 10.1016/j.plefa.2008.12.002. Letter to the Editor re: Linoleic acid and coronary heart disease. Prostaglandins Leukot. Essent. Fatty Acids (2008), by W.S. Harris. Ramsden CE, Hibbeln JR, Lands WE.

142. Circulation. 1999 Feb 16;99(6):733-5. Dietary prevention of coronary heart disease: the Lyon Diet Heart Study. Leaf A.

143. LIFE EXTENSION UPDATE. Meta-analysis affirms association between EPA/DHA intake and lower heart disease risk http://www.lifeextension.com/Newsletter/2017/1/Met a-analysis-affirms-association-between-EPA-DHA-intake-and-lower-heart-disease-risk/Page-01

143. Nutrients. 2017 Aug; 9(8): 865. Published online 2017 Aug 11. doi: 10.3390/nu9080865 Omega-3 Fatty Acids and Cardiovascular Disease: Summary of the 2016 Agency of Healthcare Research and Quality Evidence Review. Ethan M. Balk and Alice H. Lichtenstein.

144. Omega-3 fatty acids. University of Maryland Medical

Center. June 13, 2015.
https://www.genetherapy.me/inflammation/omega-3-fatty-acids-university-of-maryland-medical-center.php

144.   CNS Neurosci Ther. 2009 Summer;15(2):128-33.
        Omega-3 fatty acids in depression: a review of three
        studies. Osher Y, Belmaker RH.

145.   Aust N Z J Psychiatry. 2008 Mar;42(3):192-8.
        Comparison of therapeutic effects of omega-3 fatty acid
        eicosapentaenoic acid and fluoxetine, separately and in
        combination, in major depressive disorder. Jazayeri S,
        Tehrani-Doost M, Keshavarz SA, et al.

CHAPTER 6: LONGEVITY SECRETS

152.   Cardiovascular diseases (CVDs) Fact sheet. March
        2013. WHO. World Health Organization.
        http://www.who.int/en/news-room/fact-sheets/detail/cardiovascular-diseases-(cvds) Retrieved
        20 September 2014.

153.   Harrison's Principles of Internal Medicine (18 ed.).
        McGraw-Hill Professional. p. 1811. Longo, Dan, Fauci,
        Anthony, et al. August 11, 2011.

153.   "Different heart diseases". World Heart Federation.
        12th March 2016.

153.   Harrison's Principles of Internal Medicine (18 ed.).
        McGraw-Hill Professional Longo, Dan, Fauci, Anthony,
        et al. August 11, 2011.

154.   Davidson's principles and practice of medicine (21st
        ed.). Edinburgh: Churchill Livingstone, Elsevier. Nicki
        R. Colledge, Brian R, et al. (2010).

154.   August 2016. ESC Guidelines for the diagnosis and
        treatment of acute and chronic heart failure: The Task

Force for the diagnosis and treatment of acute and chronic heart failure of the European Society of Cardiology (ESC). Developed with the special contribution of the Heart Failure Association (HFA) of the ESC. European Journal of Heart Failure. 18 (8): 891–975. doi:10.1002/ejhf.592 Ponikowski, Piotr, Voors, et al.

155.   Nov 2016. doi:10.1093/europace/euw295. ESC Guidelines for the management of atrial fibrillation developed in collaboration with EACTS. Europace: European Pacing, Arrhythmias, and Cardiac Electrophysiology: Journal of the Working Groups on Cardiac Pacing, Arrhythmias, and Cardiac Cellular Electrophysiology of the European Society of Cardiology. 18 (11): 1609–1678. Kirchhof, Paulus, Benussi, Stefano, et al.

155.   Nov 2013. doi:10.1161/01. ACC/AHA/ESC guidelines for the management of patients with supraventricular arrhythmias—executive summary: a report of the American College of Cardiology/American Heart Association Task Force on Practice Guidelines and the European Society of Cardiology Committee for Practice Guidelines (Writing Committee to Develop Guidelines for the Management of Patients With Supraventricular Arrhythmias). 108 (15): 1871–1909. Blomström-Lundqvist, Carina, Scheinman, et al. Circulation.

155.   Davidson's principles and practice of medicine (21st ed.). Edinburgh: Churchill Livingstone/Elsevier. Nicki R. Colledge, Brian R. Walker, Stuart H. Ralston, eds. (2010).

157.   Heart Attack Treatment Cost How Much Does Heart Attack Treatment Cost? http://health.costhelper.com/heart-attack-treatment-cost.html

158.   JAMA. 1998 Dec 16;280(23):2001-7. Intensive lifestyle changes for reversal of coronary heart disease. Ornish D, Scherwitz LW, Billings JH, et al.

160.   JAMA. 2007 Mar 7;297(9):969-77. Comparison of the Atkins, Zone, Ornish, and LEARN diets for change in weight and related risk factors among overweight premenopausal women: the A TO Z Weight Loss Study: a randomized trial. Gardner CD, Kiazand A, Alhassan S, et al.

168.   Potential Role of Carotenoids as Antioxidants in Human Health and Disease Joanna Fiedor and Květoslava Burda. Nutrients. 2014 Feb; 6(2): 466–488.

168.   Dietary Intake of Carotenoids and Their Antioxidant and Anti-Inflammatory Effects in Cardiovascular Care Marco Matteo Ciccone, Francesca Cortese, Michele Gesualdo, et al. Mediators Inflamm. 2013; 2013: 782137. Published online 2013 Dec 31.

168.   Linus Pauling Institute. Micronutrient Information Center - Garlic and Organosulfur Compounds. http://lpi.oregonstate.edu/mic/food-beverages/garlic Originally written in 2005 by Jane Higdon, Ph.D. Updated in September 2016 by Barbara Delage, Ph.D.

168.   Antioxid Redox Signal. 2011 Nov 15; 15(10): 2779–2811. doi: 10.1089/ars.2010.3697 Cocoa and Chocolate in Human Health and Disease David L. Katz, corresponding author Kim Doughty, and Ather Ali.

169.   Does chocolate reduce blood pressure? A meta-analysis Published online 2010 Jun 28. Thomas Sullivan, Peter Fakler, Oliver R, et al.

169.   Nutraceutical Properties of Olive Oil Polyphenols. An Itinerary from Cultured Cells through Animal Models to Humans. Int J Mol Sci. 2016 Jun; 17(6): 843.

Published online 2016 May 31. doi: 10.3390/ijms17060843 Stefania Rigacci and Massimo Stefani.

170. Comparison of antioxidant potentials of red wine, white wine, grape juice and alcohol. Curr Med Res Opin. 1999;15(4):316-20. Durak I, Avci A, Kaçmaz M, Büyükkoçak S, et al.

170. Fish Oil for the Treatment of Cardiovascular Disease Cardiol Rev. Author manuscript; available in PMC Nov 15. Daniel Weitz, MD, Howard Weintraub, MD, Edward Fisher, MD, and Arthur Z. Schwartzbard, MD.

171. Cardiovascular benefits of exercise Int J Gen Med. 2012; 5: 541–545. Published online 2012 Jun 22. doi: 10.2147/IJGM.S30113 Shashi K Agarwal 2011 .

172. Harvard Heart Letter. New guidelines refine aspirin prescription. Published: June, 2009 https://www.health.harvard.edu/heart-health/new-guidelines-refine-aspirin-prescription

172. Thromb J. 2015; Published online 2015 Dec 4. Aspirin for primary prevention of cardiovascular disease. Jobert Richie N. Nansseu, corresponding author and Jean Jacques N. Noubiap.

173. Neurology. 2007 Jun 12;68(24):2085-92. Chronic distress and incidence of mild cognitive impairment. Wilson RS, Schneider JA, Boyle PA, et al.

175. J Am Coll Cardiol. 2008 Apr 1; 51(13): 1237–1246. Psychological Stress and Cardiovascular Disease Joel E. Dimsdale, MD.

178. About Stem Cells https://www.cryo-cell.com/cord-blood/about-stem-cells

CHAPTER SEVEN: WHAT YOU NEED TO KNOW ABOUT DIETARY SUPPLEMENTS

184.   Articles| Volume 349, ISSUE 9067, P1715-1720, June 14, 1997 Randomised trial of α-tocopherol and β-carotene supplements on incidence of major coronary events in men with previous myocardial infarction. Dr Janne M Rapola, MD, Jarmo Virtamo, MD, Samuli Ripatti, MSc, et al.

184.   Health Care Reform. Oct 10, 2011 Dietary Supplements and Mortality Rate in Older Women. The Iowa Women's Health Study Jaakko Mursu, PhD; Kim Robien, PhD; Lisa J. Harnack, DrPH, MPH; et al

184.   17 December 2013 Vitamin and Mineral Supplements in the Primary Prevention of Cardiovascular Disease and Cancer: An Updated Systematic Evidence Review for the U.S. Preventive Services Task Force. Stephen P. Fortmann, MD; Brittany U. Burda, MPH; Caitlyn A. Senger, MPH; et al.

184.   Multivitamins in the Prevention of Cancer in Men. The Physicians' Health Study II Randomized Controlled Trial J. Michael Gaziano, MD, MPH; Howard D. Sesso, ScD, MPH; William G. Christen, ScD; et al

186.   Herbal Supplements Are Often Not What They Seem ANAHAD O'CONNORNOV. 3, 2013 https://www.nytimes.com/2013/11/05/science/herbal-supplements-are-often-not-what-they-seem.html

188.   Am J Clin Nutr. 2007 Jan;85(1):269S-276S. Multivitamin and multimineral dietary supplements: definitions, characterization, bioavailability, and drug interactions. Yetley.

189.   Am J Clin Nutr. 2003 Sep;78(3 Suppl):517S-520S. doi:10.1093/ajcn/78.3.517S. Health benefits of fruit

and vegetables are from additive and synergistic combinations of phytochemicals. Liu.

190. Am J Clin Nutr. 1998 Apr;67(4):669-84. Human plasma and tissue alpha-tocopherol concentrations in response to supplementation with deuterated natural and synthetic vitamin E. Burton, Traber MG, Acuff RV, Walters DN, Kayden H, Hughes L, Ingold KU.

193. Cancer Prev Res (Phila). 2014 Sep; 7(9): 886–895. Published online 2014 Jun 24. doi: 10.1158/1940-6207.CAPR-14-0058 PMCID: PMC4408535 Plasma Tocopherols and Risk of Prostate Cancer in the Selenium and Vitamin E Cancer Prevention Trial (SELECT) Demetrius Albanes, Cathee Till, Eric A. Klein, et al.

194. BMC Endocr Disord. 2017; 17: 12. Published online 2017 Feb 24. doi: 10.1186/s12902-017-0163-9. PMCID: PMC5324269 Differential effects of vitamin D2 and D3 supplements on 25-hydroxyvitamin D level are dose, sex, and time dependent: a randomized controlled trial Muhammad M. Hammami and Ahmed Yusuf.

195. Am J Clin Nutr. 2012 Jun;95(6):1357-64. doi: 10.3945/ajcn.111.031070. Comparison of vitamin D2 and vitamin D3 supplementation in raising serum 25-hydroxyvitamin D status: a systematic review and meta-analysis. Tripkovic L, Lambert H, Hart K, et al.

202. Eur J Clin Nutr. 2011 Feb;65(2):247-54. doi: 10.1038/ejcn.2010.239. Enhanced increase of omega-3 index in response to long-term n-3 fatty acid supplementation from triacylglycerides versus ethyl esters. Neubronner J, Schuchardt JP, Kressel G, et al.

202. Am J Clin Nutr. 1991 May;53(5):1185-90. Absorption of the n-3 eicosapentaenoic and docosahexaenoic acids as ethyl esters and triglycerides by humans. Nordøy A,

Barstad L, Connor WE, Hatcher L.

203.   Biochem Biophys Res Commun. 1988 Apr
        15;152(1):328-35. Human absorption of fish oil fatty
        acids as triacylglycerols, free acids, or ethyl esters.
        Lawson LD, Hughes BG.

203.   Arzneimittelforschung. 1990 Jun;40(6):700-4.
        Comparative bioavailability of eicosapentaenoic acid
        and docasahexaenoic acid from triglycerides, free fatty
        acids and ethyl esters in volunteers. [Article in German]
        Beckermann B, Beneke M, Seitz I.

203.   Prog Lipid Res. 2014 Oct;56:92-108. doi:
        10.1016/j.plipres.2014.09.001. Omega-3 long chain
        fatty acid "bioavailability": a review of evidence and
        methodological considerations. Ghasemifard S,
        Turchini GM, Sinclair AJ.

203.   J Lipid Res. 1990 Jan;31(1):137-47. Lipolysis of
        menhaden oil triacylglycerols and the corresponding
        fatty acid alkyl esters by pancreatic lipase in vitro: a
        reexamination. Yang LY, Kuksis A, Myher JJ.

203.   Journal of the American Oil Chemists' Society April
        2015, Volume 92, Issue 4, pp 561–569 Oxidation Rates
        of Triacylglycerol and Ethyl Ester Fish Oils Jenna C.
        Sullivan Ritter, Suzanne M. Budge, Fabiola Jovica,
        Anna-Jean M. Reid.

204.   Eur J Clin Nutr. 2011 Feb;65(2):247-54. doi:
        10.1038/ejcn.2010.239. Enhanced increase of omega-3
        index in response to long-term n-3 fatty acid
        supplementation from triacylglycerides versus ethyl
        esters. Neubronner J, Schuchardt JP, Kressel G, et al.

204.   Journal of the American Oil Chemists' Society
        November 1997, Volume 74, Issue 11, pp 1425–1429
        Preparation of highly purified concentrates of

eicosapentaenoic acid and docosahexaenoic acid
Harald Breivik, Gudmundur G. Haraldsson, Björn
Kristinsson.

204.   Nutr Rev. 2007 Feb;65(2):63-77. Krill for human
        consumption: nutritional value and potential health
        benefits. Tou JC, Jaczynski J, Chen YC.

204.   Lipids. 2011 Jan;46(1):25-36. doi: 10.1007/s11745-010-
        3472-6. Epub 2010 Sep 17. Elucidation of
        phosphatidylcholine composition in krill oil extracted
        from Euphausia superba. Winther B, Hoem N, Berge K,
        Reubsaet L.

204.   Lipids. 2011 Jan; 46(1): 37–46. Published online 2010
        Nov 2. doi: 10.1007/s11745-010-3490-4 Metabolic
        Effects of Krill Oil are Essentially Similar to Those of
        Fish Oil but at Lower Dose of EPA and DHA, in Healthy
        Volunteers Stine M. Ulven, Bente Kirkhus, Amandine
        Lamglait, et al.

204.   Vasc Health Risk Manag. 2015; 11: 511–524. Published
        online 2015 Aug 28. doi: 10.2147/VHRM.S85165
        PMCID: PMC4559234 Comparison of bioavailability of
        krill oil versus fish oil and health effect Stine M. Ulven
        and Kirsten B. Holven.

204.   Lipids Health Dis. 2011 Aug 22;10:145. doi:
        10.1186/1476-511X-10-145. Incorporation of EPA and
        DHA into plasma phospholipids in response to
        different omega-3 fatty acid formulations--a
        comparative bioavailability study of fish oil vs. krill oil.
        Schuchardt JP, Schneider I, Meyer H, et al.

204.   Food Chem. 2014 Aug 15;157:398-407. doi:
        10.1016/j.foodchem.2014.02.059. Epub 2014 Feb 22.
        Effect of temperature towards lipid oxidation and non-
        enzymatic browning reactions in krill oil upon storage.
        Lu FS, Bruheim I, Haugsgjerd BO, Jacobsen C.

205.   J Am Diet Assoc. 2008 Jul;108(7):1204-9. doi:
       10.1016/j.jada.2008.04.020. Algal-oil capsules and
       cooked salmon: nutritionally equivalent sources of
       docosahexaenoic acid. Arterburn LM, Oken HA, Bailey
       Hall, et al.

205.   Lipids. 2003 Apr;38(4):415-8. Dietary intake of fish vs.
       formulations leads to higher plasma concentrations of
       n-3 fatty acids. Visioli F, Risé P, Barassi MC, Marangoni
       F, Galli C.

205.   Biochem Biophys Res Commun. 1988 Oct
       31;156(2):960-3. Absorption of eicosapentaenoic acid
       and docosahexaenoic acid from fish oil triacylglycerols
       or fish oil ethyl esters co-ingested with a high-fat meal.
       Lawson LD, Hughes BG.

207.   Curry Compound Fights Cancer in the Clinic. Andrea
       Carter JNCI: Journal of the National Cancer Institute,
       Volume 100, Issue 9, 7 May 2008, Pages 616–617,
       https://doi.org/10.1093/jnci/djn141 Published: 07 May
       2008.

207.   AAPS J. 2009 Sep; 11(3): 495–510. Published online
       2009 Jul 10. doi: 10.1208/s12248-009-9128-x PMCID:
       PMC2758121 Curcumin and Cancer Cells: How Many
       Ways Can Curry Kill Tumor Cells Selectively? Jayaraj
       Ravindran, Sahdeo Prasad, and Bharat B. Aggarwal.

207.   World J Gastroenterol. 2014 Jul 28; 20(28): 9384–
       9391. Published online 2014 Jul 28. doi:
       10.3748/wjg.v20.i28.9384 PMCID: PMC4110570
       Therapeutic applications of curcumin for patients with
       pancreatic cancer.

208.   J Exerc Rehabil. 2017 Dec; 13(6): 684–692. Published
       online 2017 Dec 27 PMCID: PMC5747204 Short-term
       effects of Theracurmin dose and exercise type on pain,

walking ability, and muscle function in patients with knee osteoarthritis Yun-A Shin, Min-Hwa Suk, Hee-Seung Jang and Hye-Jung Choi.

209.   Med Sci Monit. 2003 Sep;9(9):BR325-30. Antioxidant and prooxidant properties of caffeine, theobromine and xanthine. Azam S, Hadi N, Khan NU, Hadi SM.

209.   The protective effects of guaraná extract (Paullinia cupana) on fibroblast NIH-3T3 cells exposed to sodium nitroprusside. March 2013.
https://doi.org/10.1016/j.fct.2012.11.041
LS.Bittencourt, D.C. Machadob, M.M.Machado.

209.   Medicines (Basel). 2017 Aug 15;4(3). pii: E61. doi: 10.3390/medicines4030061. Anti-Aging and Antioxidant Potential of Paullinia cupana var. sorbilis: Findings in Caenorhabditis elegans Indicate a New Utilization for Roasted Seeds of Guarana. Peixoto H, Roxo M, Röhrig T, et al.

209.   Appetite. 2008 Mar-May;50(2-3):506-13. Epub 2007 Oct 30. Improved cognitive performance and mental fatigue following a multi-vitamin and mineral supplement with added guaraná (Paullinia cupana). Kennedy DO, Haskell CF, Robertson B, et al.

209.   J Diet Suppl. 2013 Dec;10(4):325-34. doi: 10.3109/19390211.2013.830676. Purified dry extract of Paullinia cupana (guaraná) (PC-18) for chemotherapy-related fatigue in patients with solid tumors: an early discontinuation study. del Giglio AB, Cubero Dde I, Lerner TG, et al.

209.   J Altern Complement Med. 2011 Jun;17(6):505-12. doi: 10.1089/acm.2010.0571. Guarana (Paullinia cupana) improves fatigue in breast cancer patients undergoing systemic chemotherapy. de Oliveira Campos MP, Riechelmann R, Martins LC, et al.

209.   J Psychopharmacol. 2007 Jan;21(1):65-70. Epub 2006 Mar 13. A double-blind, placebo-controlled, multi-dose evaluation of the acute behavioral effects of guaraná in humans. Haskell CF, Kennedy DO, Wesnes KA, et al.

209.   Am J Clin Nutr. 1989 Jan;49(1):44-50. Normal caffeine consumption: influence on thermogenesis and daily energy expenditure in lean and postobese human volunteers. Dulloo AG, Geissler CA, Horton T, et al.

210.   Molecules. 2014 Oct 21;19(10):16909-24. doi: 10.3390/molecules191016909. Effects of yerba maté, a plant extract formulation ("YGD") and resveratrol in 3T3-L1 adipogenesis. Santos JC, Gotardo EM, Brianti MT.

210.   Nutrients. 2017 Jun 20;9(6). pii: E635. doi: 10.3390/nu9060635. Modulatory Effects of Guarana (Paullinia cupana) on Adipogenesis. Lima NDS, Numata EP, Mesquita LMS.

210.   Int J Vitam Nutr Res. 2008 Mar;78(2):96-101. doi: 10.1024/0300-9831.78.2.96. Studies on the nature of anti-platelet aggregatory factors in the seeds of the Amazonian Herb Guarana (Paullinia cupana).

210.   Lipids in Health and Disease https://doi.org/10.1186/1476-511X-12-12. February 8, 2013 Guaraná (Paullinia cupana Kunth) effects on LDL oxidation in elderly people: an in vitro and in vivo study. Rafael de Lima Portella, Rômulo Pillon Barcelos, Edovando José Flores da Rosa, et al.

210.   Chin Med. Published online 2010 Apr 6. doi: 10.1186/1749-8546-5-13 PMCID: PMC2855614 Beneficial effects of green tea: A literature review Sabu M Chacko, corresponding author Priya T Thambi, Ramadasan Kuttan and Ikuo Nishigaki1.

211.   J Ethnopharmacol. 2018 Jan 10. Epub 2017 Aug 31.
        Molecular understanding of Epigallocatechin gallate
        (EGCG) in cardiovascular and metabolic diseases. Eng
        QY, Thanikachalam PV, Ramamurthy S.

211.   The impact of caffeine on mood, cognitive function,
        performance and hydration: a review of benefits and
        risks. C. H. S. Ruxton February 13, 2008. Dr Carrie H.
        S. Ruxton, Freelance Dietitian, 6 Front Lebanon, Cupar
        KY.

211.   Asia Pac J Clin Nutr. 2008;17 Suppl 1:167-8. L-
        theanine, a natural constituent in tea, and its effect on
        mental state. Nobre AC, Rao A, Owen GN.

211.   J Herb Pharmacother. 2006;6(2):21-30. The
        neuropharmacology of L-theanine(N-ethyl-L-
        glutamine): a possible neuroprotective and cognitive
        enhancing agent. Nathan PJ, Lu K, Gray M.

211.   J Pharmacol Sci. 2007 Oct;105(2):211-4. Epub 2007
        Oct 6. Involvement of GABA(A) receptors in the
        neuroprotective effect of theanine on focal cerebral
        ischemia in mice. Egashira N, Hayakawa K, Osajima M

211.   Psychopharmacology (Berl). 2015 Jul;232(14):2563-76.
        Epub 2015 Mar 13. A double-blind, placebo-controlled
        study evaluating the effects of caffeine and L-theanine
        both alone and in combination on cerebral blood flow,
        cognition and mood. Dodd FL, Kennedy DO, Riby LM.

211.   J Nutr. 2008 Aug;138(8):1572S-1577S. L-theanine and
        caffeine in combination affect human cognition as
        evidenced by oscillatory alpha-band activity and
        attention task performance. Kelly SP, Gomez-Ramirez
        M, Montesi JL.

211.   Am J Clin Nutr. 2008 Mar;87(3):778-84. Green tea

extract ingestion, fat oxidation, and glucose tolerance in healthy humans. Venables MC, Hulston CJ, Cox HR, Jeukendrup AE.

212. Breast Cancer Res Treat. 2010 Jan;119(2):477-84. doi: 10.1007/s10549-009-0415-0. Green tea consumption and breast cancer risk or recurrence: a meta-analysis. Ogunleye AA1, Xue F, Michels KB.

212. Am J Epidemiol. 2008 Jan 1;167(1):71-7. Green tea consumption and prostate cancer risk in Japanese men: a prospective study. Kurahashi N, Sasazuki S, Iwasaki M, et al.

212. Oncotarget. 2017 Jun 6;8(23):37367-37376. doi: 10.18632/oncotarget.16959. An inverse association between tea consumption and colorectal cancer risk. Chen Y, Wu Y, Du M, et al.

212. Acta Pharmacol Sin. 2014;35(11):1402-10. Pyrroloquinoline quinone protects mouse brain endothelial cells from high glucose-induced damage in vitro. Wang Z, Chen GQ, Yu GP, et al.

212. J Nutr Biochem. 2013;24 (12):2076-84. Dietary pyrroloquinoline quinone (PQQ) alters indicators of inflammation and mitochondrial-related metabolism in human subjects. Harris CB, Chowanadisai W, Mishchuk DO, et al.

213. Aungst SL, Kabadi SV, Thompson SM, et al. Repeated mild traumatic brain injury causes chronic neuroinflammation, changes in hippocampal synaptic plasticity, and associated cognitive deficits. J Cereb Blood Flow Metab. 2014;34(7):1223-32.

213. Zhang L, Liu J, Cheng C, et al. The neuroprotective effect of pyrroloquinoline quinone on traumatic brain injury. J Neurotrauma. 2012;29(5):851-64.

214.   Clin Exp Metastasis. 1996 Mar;14(2):176-86. Acidic pH enhances the invasive behavior of human melanoma cells. Martínez-Zaguilán R, Seftor EA, Seftor RE, et al.

214.   Oncotarget. 2014 Dec; 5(23): 12070–12082. Published online 2014 Sep 25. doi: 10.18632/oncotarget.2514 Acidosis promotes invasiveness of breast cancer cells through ROS-AKT-NF-κB pathway Subash C. Gupta, Ramesh Singh, Radhika Pochampally.

215.   Acetic acid induces cell death: An in vitro study using normal rat gastric mucosal cell line and rat and human gastric cancer and mesothelioma cell lines. Susumu Okabe, Toshihiro Okamoto, Chun-Mei Zhao, Duan Chen, Hirofumi Matsui 18 December 2014 https://doi.org/10.1111/jgh.12775

215.   Asian Pac J Cancer Prev. 2003 Apr-Jun;4(2):119-24. Risk factors for oesophageal cancer in Linzhou, China: a case-control study. Xibib S, Meilan H, Moller H, et al.

215.   J Environ Public Health. 2012; 2012: 727630. Published online 2011 Oct 12. doi: 10.1155/2012/727630. PMCID: PMC3195546 The Alkaline Diet: Is There Evidence That an Alkaline pH Diet Benefits Health? Gerry K. Schwalfenberg.

216.   Letter to the Editor Nephron 1998;80:242–243. https://doi.org/10.1159/000045180 Hypokalemia, Hyperreninemia and Osteoporosis in a Patient Ingesting Large Amounts of Cider Vinegar Lhotta K. Höfle G. Gasser R. Finkenstedt G.

216.   Crit Rev Food Sci Nutr. 2016 Jul 29;56 Suppl 1:S171-5. doi: 10.1080/10408398.2015.1045966. Biological Function of Acetic Acid-Improvement in Obesity and

Glucose Tolerance by Acetic Acid in Type 2 Diabetic Rats. Yamashita H.

216.   Biosci Biotechnol Biochem. 2009 Aug;73(8):1837-43. Epub 2009 Aug 7. Vinegar intake reduces body weight, body fat mass, and serum triglyceride levels in obese Japanese subjects. Kondo T, Kishi M, Fushimi T, Ugajin S, Kaga T.

216.   Eur J Clin Nutr. 1995 Apr;49(4):242-7. Effect of neutralized and native vinegar on blood glucose and acetate responses to a mixed meal in healthy subjects. Brighenti F, Castellani G, Benini L, et al.

216.   Diabetes Care 2004 Jan; 27(1): 281-282. https://doi.org/10.2337/diacare.27.1.281 Vinegar Improves Insulin Sensitivity to a High-Carbohydrate Meal in Subjects With Insulin Resistance or Type 2 Diabetes Carol S. Johnston, PHD, Cindy M. Kim, MS and Amanda J. Buller, MS.

216.   Pak J Biol Sci. 2008 Dec 1;11(23):2634-8. Apple cider vinegar attenuates lipid profile in normal and diabetic rats. Shishehbor F, Mansoori A, Sarkaki AR, et al.

217.   Phytother Res. 2006 Jan;20(1):21-7. Effects of garlic oil on postmenopausal osteoporosis using ovariectomized rats: comparison with the effects of lovastatin and 17beta-estradiol. Mukherjee M, Das AS, Das D, et al.

217.   Phytother Res. 2004 May;18(5):389-94. Prevention of bone loss by oil extract of garlic (Allium sativum Linn.) in an ovariectomized rat model of osteoporosis. Mukherjee M, Das AS, Mitra S, Mitra C.

217.   J Diet Suppl. 2012 Dec;9(4):262-71. doi: 10.3109/19390211.2012.726703. Epub 2012 Oct 8. The effect of garlic tablet on pro-inflammatory cytokines in postmenopausal osteoporotic women: a randomized

controlled clinical trial. Mozaffari-Khosravi H, Hesabgar HA, Owlia MB, et al.

217. BMC Musculoskelet Disord. 2010 Dec 8;11:280. doi: 10.1186/1471-2474-11-280. Dietary garlic and hip osteoarthritis: evidence of a protective effect and putative mechanism of action. Williams FM, Skinner J, Spector TD, et al.

217. Basic Clin Pharmacol Toxicol. 2012 May;110(5):476-81. doi: 10.1111/j.1742-7843.2011.00841.x. Epub 2011 Dec 29. Comparison of therapeutic effects of garlic and d-Penicillamine in patients with chronic occupational lead poisoning. Kianoush S, Balali-Mood M, Mousavi SR, et al.

218. J Nutr. 2001 Mar;131(3s):951S-4S. doi: 10.1093/jn/131.3.951S. Historical perspective on the use of garlic. Rivlin RS.

218. Indian J Physiol Pharmacol. 2005 Jan;49(1):115-8. Effect of garlic (Allium sativum) oil on exercise tolerance in patients with coronary artery disease. Verma SK, Rajeevan V, Jain P.

218. Mol Nutr Food Res. 2007 Nov;51(11):1329-34. Garlic as an anti-fatigue agent. Morihara N, Nishihama T, Ushijima M, et al.

218. J Nutr. 2001 Mar;131(3s):955S-62S. doi: 10.1093/jn/131.3.955S. Intake of garlic and its bioactive components. Amagase H, Petesch BL, Matsuura H, et al.

218. Effects of garlic consumption on plasma and erythrocyte antioxidant parameters in elderly subjects. Gerontology. 2008;54(3):173-6. doi: 10.1159/000130426. Avci A, Atli T, Ergüder IB, et al.

218.   Clin Nutr. 2012 Jun;31(3):337-44. doi:
         10.1016/j.clnu.2011.11.019. Supplementation with aged
         garlic extract improves both NK and γδ-T cell function
         and reduces the severity of cold and flu symptoms: a
         randomized, double-blind, placebo-controlled nutrition
         intervention. Nantz MP, Rowe CA, Muller CE, et al.

219.   Mol Cell Biochem. 2005 Jul;275(1-2):85-94. Garlic
         supplementation prevents oxidative DNA damage in
         essential hypertension. Dhawan V, Jain S.

219.   J Nutr. 2006 Mar;136(3 Suppl):810S-812S. doi:
         10.1093/jn/136.3.810S. Garlic reduces dementia and
         heart-disease risk. Borek C.

219.   J Nutr. 2001 Mar;131(3s):1010S-5S. doi:
         10.1093/jn/131.3.1010S. Antioxidant health effects of
         aged garlic extract. Borek C.

219.   Molecules. 2014 Aug 19;19(8):12591-618. doi:
         10.3390/molecules190812591. Allicin: chemistry and
         biological properties. Borlinghaus J, Albrecht F,
         Gruhlke MC, et al.

219.   Eur J Pharmacol. 2017 Jan 15;795:13-21. doi:
         10.1016/j.ejphar.2016.11.051. Garlic active constituent
         s-allyl cysteine protects against lipopolysaccharide-
         induced cognitive deficits in the rat: Possible involved
         mechanisms. Zarezadeh M, Baluchnejadmojarad T,
         Kiasalari Z, et al.

219.   Adv Ther. 2001 Jul-Aug;18(4):189-93. Preventing the
         common cold with a garlic supplement: a double-blind,
         placebo-controlled survey. Josling P.

219.   Clin Nutr. 2012 Jun;31(3):337-44. doi:
         10.1016/j.clnu.2011.11.019. Supplementation with aged
         garlic extract improves both NK and γδ-T cell function
         and reduces the severity of cold and flu symptoms: a

randomized, double-blind, placebo-controlled nutrition intervention. Nantz MP, Rowe CA, Muller CE, et al.

219.   J R Coll Physicians Lond. 1994 Jan-Feb;28(1):39-45. Garlic as a lipid lowering agent--a meta-analysis. Silagy C, Neil A.

219.   Nutr Rev. 2013 May;71(5):282-99. doi: 10.1111/nure.12012. Effect of garlic on serum lipids: an updated meta-analysis. Ried K, Toben C, Fakler P.

219.   Ann Intern Med. 2000 Sep 19;133(6):420-9. Garlic for treating hypercholesterolemia. A meta-analysis of randomized clinical trials. Stevinson C, Pittler MH, Ernst E.

219.   Mol Cell Biochem. 2005 Jul;275(1-2):85-94. Garlic supplementation prevents oxidative DNA damage in essential hypertension. Dhawan V, Jain S.

219.   Mediators Inflamm. 2013;2013:285795. doi: 10.1155/2013/285795. Aged garlic extract improves adiponectin levels in subjects with metabolic syndrome: a double-blind, placebo-controlled, randomized, crossover study. Gómez-Arbeláez D, Lahera V, Oubiña P, et al.

219.   Lipids Health Dis. 2007 Mar 1;6:5. Effects of anethum graveolens and garlic on lipid profile in hyperlipidemic patients. Kojuri J, Vosoughi AR, Akrami M.

220.   PLoS One. 2016 Jan 22;11(1):e0147034. doi: 10.1371/journal.pone.0147034. eCollection 2016. Resveratrol Protects against TNF-α-Induced Injury in Human Umbilical Endothelial Cells through Promoting Sirtuin-1-Induced Repression of NF-KB and p38 MAPK. Pan W1, Yu H, Huang S, et al.

220.   Int J Food Sci Nutr. 2015;66(6):603-10. Resveratrol

and anti-atherogenic effects. Riccioni G, Gammone MA, Tettamanti G, et al.

220.   Int J Mol Sci. 2015 Nov 20;16(11):27757-69. doi: 10.3390/ijms161126061. Resveratrol Protects against Helicobacter pylori-Associated Gastritis by Combating Oxidative Stress. Zhang X, Jiang A2, Qi B, et al.

220.   Nutr Res. 2014 Oct;34(10):837-43. doi: 10.1016/j.nutres.2014.09.005. Resveratrol supplementation improves inflammatory biomarkers in patients with nonalcoholic fatty liver disease. Faghihzadeh F, Adibi P, Rafiei R.

220.   Cardiovasc Drugs Ther. 2013 Feb;27(1):37-48. doi: 10.1007/s10557-012-6427-8. Grape resveratrol increases serum adiponectin and downregulates inflammatory genes in peripheral blood mononuclear cells: a triple-blind, placebo-controlled, one-year clinical trial in patients with stable coronary artery disease. Tomé-Carneiro J, Gonzálvez M, Larrosa M, et al.

220.   Arch Med Res. 2015 May;46(4):280-5. doi: 10.1016/j.arcmed.2015.05.005. Anti-Inflammatory Effects of Resveratrol in Patients with Ulcerative Colitis: A Randomized, Double-Blind, Placebo-controlled Pilot Study. Samsami-Kor M, Daryani NE, Asl PR.

220.   Cell Metab. 2011 Nov 2;14(5):612-22. doi: 10.1016/j.cmet.2011.10.002. Calorie restriction-like effects of 30 days of resveratrol supplementation on energy metabolism and metabolic profile in obese humans. Timmers S,2, Konings E#2, Bilet L, et al.

220.   Characterization of Spirulina Biomass Y for CELSS Diet Potential
https://ntrs.nasa.gov/archive/nasa/casi.ntrs.nasa.gov/

19890016190.pdf Mahasin G. Tadros. Alabama AEM University, Normal, AI 35762

221. PLoS One. 2014 Apr 1;9(4):e93056. doi: 10.1371/journal.pone.0093056. C-phycocyanin confers protection against oxalate-mediated oxidative stress and mitochondrial dysfunctions in MDCK cells. Farooq SM, Boppana NB2, Devarajan A, et al.

221. Anesth Analg. 2009 Apr;108(4):1303-10. doi: 10.1213/ane.0b013e318193e919. Anti-inflammatory and antihyperalgesic activity of C-phycocyanin. Shih CM, Cheng SN, Wong CS, et al.

221. J Med Food. 2001 Winter;4(4):193-199. Role of Spirulina in the Control of Glycemia and Lipidemia in Type 2 Diabetes Mellitus. Parikh P, Mani U, Iyer U.

221. J Sci Food Agric. 2014 Feb;94(3):432-7. doi: 10.1002/jsfa.6261. The hypolipidaemic effects of Spirulina (Arthrospira platensis) supplementation in a Cretan population: a prospective study. Mazokopakis EE, Starakis IK, Papadomanolaki MG, et al.

222. Lipids Health Dis. 2007; 6: 33. Published online 2007 Nov 26. doi: 10.1186/1476-511X-6-33 Antihyperlipemic and antihypertensive effects of Spirulina maxima in an open sample of Mexican population: a preliminary report Patricia V Torres-Duran, Aldo Ferreira-Hermosillo, and Marco A Juarez-Oropeza corresponding author.

222. Ann Nutr Metab. 2008;52(4):322-8. doi: 10.1159/000151486. A randomized double-blind, placebo-controlled study to establish the effects of spirulina in elderly Koreans. Park HJ, Lee YJ, Ryu HK, et al.

222. Nutr Cancer. 1995;24(2):197-202. Evaluation of

chemoprevention of oral cancer with Spirulina fusiformis. Mathew B, Sankaranarayanan R, Nair PP, et al.

222. J Clin Diagn Res. 2013 Dec; 7(12): 3048–3050. Published online 2013 Dec 15. doi: 10.7860/JCDR/2013/7085.3849 PMCID: PMC3919363 Spirulina and Pentoxyfilline – A Novel Approach for Treatment of Oral Submucous Fibrosis Bhavana Sujana Mulk, Prasannasrinivas Deshpande, Nagalakshmi Velpula.

222. J Med Food. 2009 Feb;12(1):15-20. doi: 10.1089/jmf.2007.0713. Effects of dietary Spirulina on vascular reactivity. Juárez-Oropeza MA, Mascher D, Torres-Durán PV, et al.

222. Med Sci Sports Exerc. 2010 Jan;42(1):142-51. Ergogenic and antioxidant effects of spirulina supplementation in humans. Kalafati M, Jamurtas AZ, Nikolaidis MG, et al.

222. Eur J Appl Physiol. 2006 Sep;98(2):220-6. Epub 2006 Aug 30. Preventive effects of Spirulina platensis on skeletal muscle damage under exercise-induced oxidative stress. Lu HK, Hsieh CC, Hsu JJ, et al.

227. Crit Rev Food Sci Nutr. 2016;56(4):614-34. doi: 10.1080/10408398.2014.972498. Consumption of Red/Processed Meat and Colorectal Carcinoma: Possible Mechanisms Underlying the Significant Association. Hammerling, Bergman Laurila, Grafström, Ilbäck.

227. J Nutr. 2009 Jun; 139(6): 1236S–1241S. doi: 10.3945/jn.109.106641 Fructose Consumption: Considerations for Future Research on Its Effects on Adipose Distribution, Lipid Metabolism, and Insulin Sensitivity in Humans1,2. Kimber, Stanhope and Peter

J. Havel.

228.   Am J Clin Nutr. 2004 Apr;79(4):537-43. Consumption of high-fructose corn syrup in beverages may play a role in the epidemic of obesity. Bray, Nielsen, Popkin.

Made in USA - North Chelmsford, MA
1293589_9780578760377
12.02.2021 1606